Multicultural Literature and Literacies

SUNY Series, Literacy, Culture, and Learning:
Theory and Practice

Alan C. Purves, Editor

Multicultural Literature and Literacies

Making Space for Difference

Edited by
Suzanne M. Miller
and Barbara McCaskill

State University of New York Press

Published by
State University of New York Press, Albany

© 1993 State University of New York

For information, address State University of New York Press,
State University Plaza, Albany, N.Y. 12246

Production by M.R. Mulholland
Marketing by Bernadette LaManna

Library of Congress Cataloging-in-Publication Data

Multicultural literature and literacies : making space for difference
 / Suzanne M. Miller, Barbara McCaskill, co-editors.
    p.   cm. — (SUNY series, literacy, culture, and learning)
    Includes bibliographical references and index.
    ISBN 0-7914-1645-3. — ISBN 0-7914-1646-1 (pbk.)
    1. Literature—Study and teaching—United States.   2. Pluralism
(Social sciences) in literature—Study and teaching—United States.
3. Literature—Minority authors—Study and teaching—United States.
4. Minorities in literature—Study and teaching—United States.
5. Critical pedagogy—United States.   I. Miller, Suzanne M.
II. McCaskill, Barbara.   III. Series.
LB1575.5.U5M85   1993
808—dc20   92-39543
                                                      CIP
                                                      Rcv.

10 9 8 7 6 5 4 3 2 1

Contents

Contents

Acknowledgments

We are gratefully indebted to numerous individuals, groups, and institutions for providing the encouragement, intellectual stimulation, material sustenance, and labor so crucial for completing this project. This book would not have been initiated without the inspiration and imagination generated in Spring 1991 by the participants of the 4th Gutenberg Conference on Literacy and Literature in a Multicultural Society, cosponsored by the University at Albany's Center for Writing and Literacy and its National Research Center for Literature Teaching and Learning. We thank all of the writers, teachers, administrators, and students who participated in the discussions of those two days. Your visions for an inclusive national culture, your strategies for resisting the backlash against this cultural inclusion, and your insights on issues of global literacy and curricular change have guided us in advising our contributors and generating a framework for this book. The themes and papers of the Conference have influenced the interdisciplinary connections that the essays published here undertake.

We wish to extend a special appreciation to the National Research Center for Literature Teaching and Learning—Director Arthur Applebee and Codirectors Alan Purves and Judith Langer—for providing services and technology during the two and one-half years of manuscript preparation and production. It was Alan, Editor of the SUNY Series on Literacy, Culture, and Learning, who began all this by approaching us to co-chair a conference, and who continued to support us through his inquiries and suggestions. Additionally, Linda Papa and Kathleen Sims of the Center eased the pressures of editing with their calm during deadline rushes, creative solutions to difficulties, hard work, and assiduous attention to detail. Both have been essential in this project's progress toward completion, and both of us co-editors are beholden to them for their assistance.

Priscilla Ross, our editor and reality checker at SUNY Press, has never been stationed more than a telephone call away for advice, answers, alternatives, reassurances, and requests. We have valued her expertise in the business and the experience and foresight that she has supplied.

Personal expressions of thanks go out from both of us to family and friends.

From S.M.: I am grateful to the many teachers who allowed me into their classrooms and made time for extended conversations. Special thanks to Noreen Benton, Mariana Lawlor, Sharon Legge, Eleanor Lindberg, Diane Longe, Cheryl Parshall, Kate Vrtiak, Nedra Stimpfle, and Lillian Turner. I have learned from all of them the artful inquiry dialogic teaching requires.

Whatever I learned about the power of classroom discussion began in Tony Petrosky's pedagogy seminars; his wise questions prompted conversations that transformed my ideas about teaching and learning. I owe a debt to colleagues who have found time to continue such sustaining conversation, particularly Lil Brannon, Jim Collins, Steve Koziol, Cy Knoblauch, Michael Moore, Marie Nelson, Alan Purves, and Bill Smith. I am especially grateful to Vladimir Ageyev, whose cross-cultural perspectives and multicultural experiences have enriched my understanding. Our talks have caused me to focus anew on what is important in classrooms and in life.

I am grateful to many students—both the diverse high-school students who so eloquently described their ways of seeing and being in classrooms and my graduate students who have worked with me in classrooms to understand those ways. In particular, I want to thank Steve DeMaio, Beatrice Hall, Jamie Mandel, Natalie Mathis, Carol Morris, Jennifer Nix, Catherine Parsons, Lisa Scafidi, and Kathleen Trott. All of them have been generous and thoughtful; they have taught me well.

I owe deep thanks to Casey Hart Miller and Bernard Miller, who with understanding and good humor often carried on without me. And, finally, I want to thank my father, Ernest Dominic Miale, for telling me stories of good teachers. When I was growing up I pondered how it was for him starting first grade in Pittsburgh speaking only Italian and how it was for those few teachers who made space for his difference. Throughout my career, these stories have stood for me as the proper spirit of teaching in a multicultural society.

From B. M. thanks are extended to the undergraduates of my 1988–92 African American literature courses, my first real undergraduates ever, who escalated my understanding of this literary tradition and motivated me to write about reading and teaching it. May you gather the determination and grit to make your own "space for difference." My energies on this project have been fueled by and are dedicated especially to these graduate students and alumni/ae of SUNY from the US, Africa, Asia, the UK, and the Caribbean: Thanks to

Suzette Bishop, Wendy Brown, Esperanza Cintrón, Stacey Dawes, Yvonne Felarca, Elizabeth Ginexi, Douglas Holt-Holiday, Ioney James, Carlton Jordan, Ronald Longmire, Jacynth Mair, Ardella McClarty, Paul Parris, TaMárah Philpot, Joel Pierre-Louis, Cecilia Rodríguez Milanés, Elizabeth Santiago, Tania Shilliam, Norene Walden, Derek Westbrook, Shawn Williams, Theresa Williams, Cassaundra Worrell, and Weihua Zhang. Two soul sisters at SUNY, Deborah Curry of University Libraries and Marcia Sutherland of Africana Studies/Psychology, kept me talking about my work until I did it. And not least, thanks go to Dad and Mom, Col. John L. and Inez Owens McCaskill, to my sister Sandra and family, brother David and family, to Ed, and to the extensive Whittlesey tribe for inspiration and tolerance. Mom, I am happy to inform you that this book is done.

S.M. and B.M.

Introduction
Multicultural Literature and Literacies: Making Space for Difference

Suzanne M. Miller
Barbara McCaskill

Like baseball, Main Street, mainframes, and fireworks on the Fourth of July, the little red schoolhouse has embodied both the accomplishments and the dreams, both the past and the future, of our American culture. One bell summoned: then, up the little red schoolhouse stairs—or so the story goes—marched eager-eyed students from the world's four corners, up the stairs through one large room to identical aisles of desks and chairs. Visions merged on one lone instructor, one Bible, one pendant flag. Voices rose in unison from matching primers and practice books. Once the students surrendered to their teacher's enchanting mien, handwriting abandoned idiosyncracy and loops and strokes became uniform and unvarying. With another wave of the chalk-ensconced wand, one literature and one language of the literate—written English—reigned supreme.

This story might have varied from region to region and throughout time zones and space: from loggers' shacks in the 1880s Adirondacks to tenements in a midwestern railroad town, from a boarding school for Christianizing the "savages" out West to an A&M college founded down South for uplifting the African race. In so many of these "little red schoolhouses," the sentiment prevailed that success would be achieved when pupils vied for similar accomplishments and dreams. A seeming agreement arose that students' investments in America's dream relied upon their pledging allegiance to a disapproval and a united distrust of difference. Never mind that only a faction of the few had determined that democracy's face was singular and white. Setting aside one's difference was a central and loyal gesture of the "little red schoolhouse" education.

And this kind of education, as recounted with particular horror in the personal narratives of Native Americans, has meant more than merely a slap on the wrist of difference. "Civilize Them with a Stick" is the title by which Sioux activist Mary Crow Dog (1990) recalls her boarding school education in 1960s America. Beaten and starved when they sought to keep alive their tribal languages and literacies, Mary and her classmates represent a long procession of so-called heathen children pressured to transform themselves from divergent Indian "problems" to conformist, cartoonish, assembly-line whites:

> The kids were taken away from their villages and pueblos, in their blankets and moccasins, kept completely isolated from their families—sometimes for as long as ten years—suddenly coming back, their short hair slick with pomade, their necks raw from stiff, high collars, their thick jackets always short in the sleeves and pinching under the arms, their tight patent leather shoes giving them corns, the girls in starched white blouses and clumsy, high-buttoned boots—caricatures of white people. (p. 30)

In Crow Dog's example, the children's rigid school clothes are clothes of uniformity and sameness, of one culture, white and American, to be shared. Yet the clothes constrict, attempt to inhibit the children's native culture, and in the classroom, narrow the space available for difference. From head to feet, literally, these children are encaged in the clothing of an alien culture, and their skin is rubbed sore and mutilated in order to present them as identical results of a single kind of education. In such children's classrooms, or so it appears, no spaces are allowed for difference.

This twofold process that Crow Dog's description implies— disguising difference in order to eventually dispose of it altogether— also can assume a gentler, well-intended guise in the classroom. In her memoirs *The Woman Warrior*, Maxine Hong Kingston (1976, p. 167) remembers the Chinese girls like her in grammar school who were excluded from activities, shouted at, ridiculed, or punished, for their "too soft," "nonexistent," non-American voices. Even one Asian teacher, "lovely and Hawaiian," overlooked the cultural distinctions and Asian-ness accounting for the Chinese girls' silences, and she abandoned them to an empty room while the rest of their classmates practiced for the second-graders' play. These memories that Kingston recalls underscore that when schools in the United States seek the goals of nationalizing, acculturating, and making citizens of their children, all too often these goals are contingent on the process of eliminating space for difference. Ignored, mocked, or "left...behind" when they did not behave like "Americans," Kingston and her classmates learned that at the core of American schools functions an either/or proposition: either students must discard their indigenous cultures, or they will be excluded.

Kingston and Crow Dog remember classrooms that camouflage difference, ultimately to obliterate it, because in those rooms operated the following assumption: that the fundamental function of an American school is to educate its pupils toward a singular, convergent literature and literacy. This assumption still sustains a mighty influence; its adherents suggest that such a push toward cultural convergence would prompt unity in our increasingly disunited times.

For instance, E. D. Hirsch, Jr. (1988, pp. xi–xii) advises that in issues of literacy American education should carry the torch of what he calls "cultural conservatism." In the Preface to the Vintage Edition of his *Cultural Literacy: What Every American Needs to Know,* Hirsch underscores the necessity for this conservatism to endure. Prerequisite for students' success, and for the stability and harmony of the nation, Hirsch argues, has been the ability of American schools to transmit "traditional reference points of literate culture," a broad array of facts and vocabulary, traditions and civic principles. These "reference points," Hirsch explains, make for the effective exchange of ideas among the classes, ethnic and racial groups, religious alliances, political organizations, regional divisions, and so on, that make up the diversity that is called the United States. The advantage of cultural conservatism, he writes, is its potential to nourish, stimulate, flower, and maintain the "national communication" so essential for America's prosperity:

> If each local school system imparts the traditional reference points of literate culture, then everybody will be able to communicate with strangers. In the modern age, effective communication with strangers is altogether essential to promote the general welfare and insure domestic tranquility. The inherent conservatism of literacy leads to a subtle but unavoidable paradox: the goals of political liberalism require educational conservatism. We make social and economic progress only by teaching myths and facts that are predominantly traditional. (p. xii)

It is only by "accident of history" (p. 106), Hirsch is mindful to point out, that a predominance of these "reference points" of traditional "names, phrases, dates, and concepts" derive from a male, Anglo-

Saxon, Anglophile legacy; "women and minorities and [those] of non-Western cultures" are "right" to press for educational reform. However, key to national progress, and central to the mission of the little red schools, has been and must continue to be the transmission of the mutual "reference points." Out of these schools must continue to emerge communities of "common readers" who can be assumed to know "What Every American Needs to Know."

At least, so goes the story. For another look at America's schools, in the past and in this "modern age," exposes this paradox: the goals of educational conservatism—national communication, transmission of civic principles, improvement of one's condition in a pluralistic and changing society—all have been been imparted simultaneously with the practice of multicultural literature and literacies.

Hirsch himself acknowledges this simultaneity. He praises as "life-enhancing" this "contranational element" of heterogenous traditions and disparate readerships, only to conclude that "the brute fact of history in every modern nation has been the increasing dominance of the national culture over local and ethnic cultures" (pp. 96–97). Using the example of class—that contemporary Americans have tended to locate themselves along lines of class rather than culture—he argues for a kind of natural selection that favors and demands increasing cultural homogeneity.

His example builds upon two erroneous assumptions. One is that class ascension—economic stability, savings, flexible purchasing power, good credit—results in an instant equalizing among individuals in this society. The other assumes that how an American identifies herself or himself translates directly into how she or he is perceived, and treated, by members of other hyphenated American groups. Both assumptions are rooted in the American ideals of justice, open-mindedness, and success gained through persistence and hard work. The truth is that in America race itself can be a *determinant* of economic advancement, and that advancement works both ways: for example, black people have "passed" into whiteness for access to better jobs and lives; or, on the other hand, communities such as New Jersey's Ramapoughs have petitioned to be officially recognized as Native Americans for entitlement to government benefits and casino franchises.

The meaning of "the second side of the American hyphen," what Hirsch uses to refer to the American collective (pp. 95, 99), must encompass our country's agonies of class *and* race struggle as much as it does our aspirations toward tolerance, collaboration, and economic success. Both in his "Appendix: What Every Literate American Knows" and in passages throughout his book, *Hirsch himself* cites, in alphabetical order, Muhammad Ali, John Brown, Chicanos, Crazy Horse, Thomas Jefferson (recall his life's contradiction: owner of slaves and founding father of freedom), Eleanor Roosevelt (recall her resignation from the Daughters of the American Revolution), Sojourner Truth, and other examples of this heritage of agitation revolving around issues of racial difference. Ours is not a pristine, spontaneously generated ethos that originated and continues to be shaped free and independent of the factor of race. Attesting to this dynamic is the ongoing proliferation, on or near the doorsteps of our little red schools, of multicultural literature and literacies (and white ones are included!) that borrow from and signify on and navigate the unhyphenated mainstream.

As well intended and accommodating as the effort may seem, ranking literature and literacies into some cultural Great Chain of Being is a process that, as with the mythic red schools and the schoolrooms of Kingston and Crow Dog, leads to exclusion rather than accommodation. At the bottom of the Chain crouch the unstable, secondary multicultural literatures and literacies, soon destined to devolve into nothingness. On the top looms an *ens perfectissimum* of one literature and literacy: ominpotent and omnipresent. All too often this ranking is an effort that masks insidious implications. At best, what is accomplished is that the different forms at the bottom, like atoms, no longer can be seen. A Chain or continuum or scale or series, whatever it is called, is another method of minimizing difference, eventually to expunge it altogether from the scene.

Hirsch's "cultural conservatism" can too easily bend toward civic harmony yet blind us to difference. His suggestion that "to be conservative in the means of communication is the road to effectiveness in modern life" implies one direction of effective communication. His argument obscures the many directions that effective communication has taken in American life. For example, beginning with enslavement, African Americans have had to struggle for access to the pen and book and so have used spoken language as a means toward progress and liberation. The street corner speech, the radio rap, the sermon, the song, the slogan, the ritual of the protest march and rally—all these oral forms and spoken or sung words have been used by African Americans as means of effective communication.

When Hirsch applauds the "conservative" passages of the Black Panthers' newspaper alluding to the Declaration of Independence and the Bible, he ignores the fact that this written discourse assumed its fullest meaning when coupled with the intonations and nuances of African American speakers! Seeking the support and aiming for the uplift of impoverished, undereducated African American youth, the

Panthers shrewdly calculated that their radical ideas must be rapped and heard as well as written and read. Though appearing to allow for disparate ideologies, Hirsch's praise of the "conservative," implies that any such different discourse is uncivil and divisive. Geneva Smitherman (1988, p. 148), in her "Discriminatory Discourse on Afro-American Speech," argues that these different means of communication have been treated not as "African *differentness* but African derived *deficiency.''* This "deviant model," she says (p. 149), "views black speech (and black culture, generally) as deficient and pathological."

Across class lines, an enduring cultural legacy of many cultural communities has been the centrality, artistry, and galvanizing force of *oral* as well as written forms of expression. But the important oral literacies in the histories of many American cultural groups in America have all suffered. As Gayl Jones argues,

> Oral stories, seen merely as the "first stories" of a pre-literate culture, are often dismissed as crude rather than appreciated as the continuing, complex, inventive heritage of African, African American, Native American, and other Third World literatures. Many of the writers within these traditions draw upon their oral heritage for the power and diversity of its narrative forms and storytelling techniques. (1991, p. 1)

Jones and many other cultural critics contend that the very existence of these oral discourses provides evidence that multicultural literature and literacies are and always have been critical, essential, to the process of creating a multidimensional picture of how Americans communicate between and within groups.

The "brute fact," as the histories of individual Americans show, is not so much a hegemony of one national literature and literacy, but an interplay and transmutation and polymorphization of many literatures and literacies within and without the official borders of the schoolroom. Simultaneously with the vision of national "reference points" and mutually literate "common readers" have existed a vision and a practice that demonstrate how making space for difference, paying attention to many literatures and many literacies, need not impede national progress, curb meaningful communication, or foment backwardness and division. Making space for difference need not mean disintegrating national identity, heritage, and culture.

We can return to Kingston's childhood for an example. During her girlhood, in contrast to the individual activity stressed in American school, pupils in the afternoon Chinese school "chanted together, voices rising and falling, loud and soft, some boys shouting, everybody reading together, reciting together and not alone with one voice" (p. 167). In the decades before court-ordered integration of America's public schools, teachers of segregated African American classes took a polyrhythmic approach to the three R's that mixed McGuffy's Readers and recitations of Whitman and Poe with their own distinctive spin on the ritual of Morning Assembly. With a program that might begin with a prayer and the singing of "Columbia, The Gem of the Ocean," continue with announcements and readings from the poetry of Phillis Wheatley and Langston Hughes, and end with the singing of James Weldon Johnson's "Lift Every Voice and Sing," the Morning Assembly at an all-Black school at once acquiesced to Hirsch's unhyphenated American culture and made space for students to keep their distinctive cultural legacies alive.[1]

We need only glance at last year's calendar of events from Any School, U.S.A., to gather an additional indication that the mythic schoolhouse is enlarging for those literatures and literacies of all of us Americans. Along with the Presidents' birthdays, Columbus Day, and similar events, receiving attention are Women's History Weeks, Black History Month, Cinqo de Mayo, and The Holocaust. Although the extent of their inclusion, the weight of their importance, and the degree to which they are taken seriously can leave much to be desired, their presence attests to the dynamism of our multicultural society. They are continuing evidence that space can be made in our classrooms for difference.

This volume articulates the means of making space for cultural difference in classrooms and communities. We confront the process of teaching multicultural literature and literacies, yet in doing so we engage more than teachers. In fact, the writers of this volume converge on the issue of multicultural literature and literacies from three respective positions: writing literature, writing policy, and teaching.

We use the term *writer* with a generous meaning that applies to every contributor in the book. *Writer* conveys a meaning that accounts for both creative and critical writers, those discussing literature and those discussing teaching; it conveys a meaning that does not oppose the roles of teacher and artist, but sees them as continuous; and, finally, *writer* suggests a meaning that resists the assumption that a particular kind of writing, or that writing about a particular kind of subject, is more scholarly and authoritative than another point of view. In fact, as most of the contributors speak, they occupy such multiple roles as teacher/literary critic/creative writer and teacher/theorist/policymaker, among other combinations. With essays on literature, policymaking, and education, the groups of writers discuss pedagogical strategies, program philosophies, aesthetics and poetics, and research agendas that have arisen from the debates on multicultural literature and literacies.

Our volume emerged from dialogues which began at the Fourth Gutenberg Conference on Literature and Literacy in a Multicultural Society, University at Albany, March 1–2, 1991. The conference was organized more along the lines of a graduate seminar than the typical model that calls for three presenters to read, the audience (and quickly!) to respond, with no one ever getting to see the papers. Prior to the conference itself, all of the participants received the working papers of the featured writers so that they could read and reflect upon them at a leisurely pace. Once the conference actually convened, all the participants, including the featured writers, divided into randomly selected groups to discuss the papers. After discussion within these smaller groups, the writers received an additional opportunity to share their reactions with and invite suggestions from the entire conference body. Out of the conference has come this book.

Because the writers discussed their topics face to face and honed their ideas through actual conversation with each other,[2] the essays in this volume gained power from the apparent interplay of ideas. The writers' creative and critical interests at times overlap; their meanings of *multicultural society* at times diverge. They all agree, however, that making space for difference means managing three important tasks: (1) making room for the voices of the "different" ones themselves; (2) prompting discussion and debate, a give-and-take among these voices, and between these voices and the mainstream; and (3) holding fast against the shouts that wish to drown out all conversation and dictate difference on their terms.

Making space thus hinges on stimulating dialogue. Accordingly, the separate essays in this volume reflect the dialogues that refined them; they are interwoven in their themes and references. The writers build upon issues raised in preceding sections, and they extend or challenge the discussion of issues raised by other essays. In the first section, for example, Reggie Young and Valerie Babb call attention to each other with the similar themes of literacy as liberation and empowerment. Alan C. Purves and Alpana Sharma Knippling reconnoiter in their critiques of the *Heath Anthology of American Literature.* Occasionally the writers comment directly upon each other's ideas, as when Purves taps back to Ron Welburn to explain how using Welburn's essay in this book transformed his "Reading Poetry" course. And the editors of this volume have replied to Violet J. Harris's call for identification of resources on multicultural literature and literacy. Included in this volume is a guide to selected resources, to institutes, conferences, organizations, libraries, museums, clearinghouses, and publishers.

Defining *literature* in different ways and for different purposes, the writers relocate the multicultural class from dreaming and reflection to action and reality. These writers possess distinct ideologies—they offer many interpretations of how multicultural literature can be incorporated into communities, schools, and individual classrooms.

One of the topics that the writers explore is how texts have been constructed in many communities to ensure identity, spiritual power, history, freedom, and social survival as much as to promote educational achievement. Babb offers her own course on "White Male Writers" as an example of this strategic reconsideration of texts. Similarly, the policymakers herein reflect upon the roles that literature has played in privileging American economic and political orders. They posit making room for multicultural literatures as forging the path for national transformation and parity. For the educators represented in this book, some who occupy simultaneous roles as artists and policymakers, *literature* refers to many kinds of texts, such as the slave's narratives, that might be classified as artifact or document in a traditional literature classroom. Harris critiques the latter distinction as part of a conservative, additive philosophy easy to enact and difficult to erode.

In their dialogue on multicultural literacy, the writers in this volume present a variety of definitions: ones that center on ethnic and racial identities, ones that accent writing and reading processes, some that call attention to communities created by shared stories and mutual beliefs, others that emphasize communities revolving on polyphony or heteroglossia—the voices of multiple groups interacting at once and seeking audience and mutual understanding instead of ascendancy. Welburn writes of coming to literacy in such a polyphonic world: "This combination," he recalls, "of Native and African, . . . [of] rural and small-town birth and urban upbringing, have all profoundly affected my listening and seeing as a poet and writer." And Young describes his own creation of a shared story for his West Chicago home, a novel, *Crimes in Bluesville*, that will define the West Side and express its residents' pride with its themes of education, identity, and individual and social change. By writing a culture into being, his novel can provide a kind of "spiritual healing" for those cut off from a sense of their own humanity.

Writing and reading from a cultural perspective is presented in these chapters as a promising means of celebrating difference. Teachers preserve culture, as does Hasna Muhammad when she has her seventh-grader tell his family stories. She says he told them "like a true griot," and she adds, "I told him that." To this end of empowerment, Gonzales mounts an argument for "reading against the grain" in California's secondary schools, for reading so that politics, culture, and status become part of studying texts. As students read and write multicultural literatures in the schools, the further promise of creating a new consciousness is held. Suzanne K. Sutherland works toward students' changes from qualities of intolerance and alienation to a "bonding with the school" concurrent with improved academic achievement. Muhammad works toward qualities of "acceptance, tolerance, and coexistence." All of these qualities Miller finds to be components of a "dialogic consciousness," a reasoning that relies upon difference to empower individuals and contribute to social justice.

A *multicultural society,* many of our writers argue, means a society committed to resurrect—rather than merely accommodate, or to absorb only then to silence—the neglected literary contributions of America's peoples of color. "The shortest month of the year," as Muhammad chides, "is not the only time to pull African American history from the shelves." Who it is that names an institution or nation a "multicultural society," and the hierarchies that "*multi*cultural" might disguise, are "questions of pedagogy" that press Sharma Knippling as much as those of choosing texts, foregrounding readings, or revising curricula. What the teacher does, she argues, is largely constrained by the status of literatures and multiple cultures within the university as well as within the society. Investigating these constructions of culture inside and outside the university's walls are necessary and productive pedagogical strategies.

All herein would seem to agree that refining the meaning of *multicultural society* and making space for difference involve reconsidering social histories and institutional hierarchies and reevaluating the exclusive attention in classrooms on teacher-student(s)-text(s). As Purves warns, "What may have worked for an age of insular nationalism without electronic media does not suffice in a global village where all inhabitants claim equal status." The "little red schoolhouse" story may not quite have disappeared; but with this volume the scaffolds have been raised and the overhaul begun. With this volume several wings and stories are attached, the criteria for its blueprints reevaluated, and more than one dominant cultural perspective permitted inside. Walking on scaffolds, however, requires great will not to fall: it requires communication, coassistance, concentration, and care. Collaborating for change, these writers sooner or later confront—head-on—forces seeking to undermine or destroy it.

In addition to their problems with defining literature and literacy, the writers in these sections admit the many impediments to teaching and reading multicultural literatures. The tension of whether to approach multicultural literature to emphasize similarities or diversities is one recurring question among the groups. All argue for emphasis on both connections and differences, but in varied ways. Sharma Knippling sums up this Hobson's choice that teachers invariably face when she describes one student's astonished response to the reading list—"only Indian literatures in English"—for her course in multicultural literature. "Why *should* a course in Indian literatures in English," she reflects, "be considered multicultural? Then again, why shouldn't it be. . .?" An additional dilemma—she, and Purves all concur—involves how to respond to students who read ethnic literatures only from one dominant cultural perspective.

Other problems of creating change by introducing multicultural literatures into schools include the politics of canon formation. In the history of Anglo-American academic life, literature has sometimes taken on the cast of sacred text, and interpreting "the great books" has become, or so it seems, the job of priests and priestesses who extract truth and wisdom about universal human nature from the mysteries of aesthetic scripture (Scholes, 1985). But in the past twenty years many have lost faith in this naive vision of human nature as always the same. If we each are constituted by our time and place and languages—by our cultures—then literary texts, too, are products of culture, constituted by the cultural vision of an author and values of her or his time, a partial vision, not universal truth.

Some have been unable to put aside the historical pretense to a secular scripture, however, and still work at justifying the process of canonization of great books. In this volume, Alan C. Purves and Catharine R. Stimpson provide a historical and political context for the caprice of this canon formation, and the partial vision of culture that it has privileged. Both problematize notions of texts as "instruments of inclusion" or "agents of acculturation." Both suggest how canon civil wars and canon cease-fires reflect the changing purposes for literature and, to quote Stimpson, "the consequence[s] of turbulent, impure historical dramas." Expanding the canon to include multicultural literatures is a conscious political act in a long history of literary politics, brought to us, Stimpson shows, not by divine inspiration but by some version of "Great Books, Inc." And both caution that these canon quarrels not blind us to the more important goals of changing how we teach and of changing, as Purves considers, our assumptions behind what we teach, or "what it is we are about when we teach."

As much as they discuss issues of canonicity, the writers evaluate limits to change that inevitably arise from these reasons: the pragmatic and inviolable demands of the academic calendar, ignorance of culturally specific learning styles, ignorance of the literatures themselves, the availability or purchasability of texts, and nativistic backlash. Classroom sizes, competing agenda, and the accessibility—or lack thereof—of resources for teacher training and scholarly research also pose difficulties in integrating multicultural texts into the syllabus. Even how various groups define "resource," Harris's essay suggests, must be critiqued. "Resources exist," she assures! They include not single chapters on multiculturalism at the end of mainstream texts but "summer institutes, conferences, organizations, librarians, scholars, texts, and teachers [themselves] who specialize in or possess knowledge about multicultural literacy and literature."

Such commonsense solutions stitch a common thread through the essays of Gregory A. Morris, Phillip C. Gonzales, and Suzanne K. Sutherland on curricular change within public school districts; and linking one group to another—teachers to resources, writers to teachers, distributors to presses, academia to communities—is a theme that binds all thirteen essays in one multicultural quilt. They engage in a mutual effort to challenge traditions that deny the richness of our cultures and the voices of diversity. They elaborate a multicultural aesthetic and exhibit this aesthetic in their individual essays.

Social interaction as the basis for change may be the most prominent collective theme in this volume. In and out of schools, individuals serve as literacy bridges, moving a silent student or group to voice identities, articulate beliefs, and assume a new awareness of culture, self, and difference. From in and out of classrooms, the writers in this volume act to transform communities, huge school districts, individual schools or classrooms, and themselves. They gather forces of change, not naively conceived, but optimistic in the face of knotty problems, tensions, questions. Spurred at first by changing demographics, desegregation, racial achievement gaps, alienation, bias, inhumanity, they work as bridges toward change in the "house of culture" (Stimpson, this volume). All of them in some way echo literacy bridge and teacher Paolo Freire (1970): that our cultures, our institutions and communities, ourselves, "are not built in silence, but in word, in work, in action-reflection."

Welburn begins the first section, "Defining Difference: Perspectives on Writing Literature," with an account of the instructive legacy of tales and music that has enriched his listening and seeing as an African American/Native American writer and poet. Turning to examples from written traditions, from the slave narratives to modern American novels, Babb connects reading and writing historically to issues of cultural inclusion and exclusion, of access and denial, of political identity and social equity. The historical importance of literacy within Black communities and its relationship to liberation is a similar focus in Young's chapter. In his story of barriers to full literacy, Young argues for the healing and humanizing benefits to specific African American communities—such as his own West Side ("wrong side") home in Chicago—that possess their own texts written from an insider's perspective. And McCaskill connects these themes of liberation and literacy to her syncretism of a variety of literacies—visual and aural, written and read, public and personal—in the classroom. All attempt to define literature and literacy in the context of cultural identities within a multicultural society.

In "Making Space: Perspectives on Writing Policy," the five writers draw from recent events in multicultural education in order to examine school policy. Purves and Stimpson analyze both theoretical problems of canon formation and such practical issues as censorship and ambiguities of purpose. Sutherland offers one approach to canons in her essay on the NEH-sponsored summer institutes with the University of Houston and the Houston Independent School District. As national models for school-university collaborations, these institutes enabled teachers to read and select multicultural literatures, to reassess their views, and then, returning as group leaders in their own schools, to revise their classroom practices. Morris describes how the creation of a multicultural education task force in the Pittsburgh Public School district catalyzed the middle school curriculum with the cultures of five American groups. He traces the rationale for this multiracial, multi-ethnic, and multicultural (Triple M) project; and like Sutherland, he describes the importance of collaborating with teachers to select texts, create curricula, and develop new pedagogies. Connecting to these on the West Coast is the California Literature Project for training and retraining teachers who work with large populations of Latino/Latina students: Gonzales portrays the subtle attitudes that ethnic literatures may shape and analyzes how learning to teach students to take a critical stance toward all texts, a "reading against the cultural grain," can empower teachers and students.

Harris begins the final section, "Making Space for Difference: Perspectives on Teaching," with an overview of the components which enable teachers to implement multicultural curricula. After defining the underlying philosophic approaches to literacy in the schools, she emphasizes the need for curricula that provide diverse learning contexts for diverse learners. Sharma Knippling contributes to this list of productive pedagogical strategies by suggesting that teachers scrutinize definitions of literary artifacts and cultural identity, and she suggests that university teachers must investigate constraints on the status of literatures and cultures within the university's own institutional structure. At any educational level, Muhammad's essay warns, an additive approach to multicultural literatures is inadequate and ossified. Also, she cautions that a multicultural environment in itself may not promote multicultural literacy: through reading and writing, listening and talking, students must study how culture affects their own lives. Junko Yokota explores important considerations in selecting and teaching Asian American literatures if teachers and librarians want their students to understand Asian American cultures and feel pride in their heritage. These transformational principles put forth here by Muhammad, Sharma Knippling, Yokota, and Harris are confirmed in Miller's account of a "dialogic pedagogy." She derives a very similar set of principles for creating change by synthesizing results from ethnographic studies of successful literature discussion in multicultural classroom contexts.

It is not a coincidence that our entire volume is framed with essays (Welburn, Young—Muhammad, Sharma Knippling) that discuss the centrality of personal narrative to multicultural literacy and literature projects. As Muhammad has observed among her adolescent students, personal examinations of culture become an essential prelude to engaging cultures in the literature:

Memoirs, autobiographies, and other forms of personal narratives serve as guiding lights in the students' personal writing endeavors. From journal entries to autobiographical short stories, the various forms of personal narratives lend themselves to the maturation that occurs during adolescent and teen years. They provide a close, safe place for students to discover and to react to the culturally diverse world around them.

Writing and speaking words and images in their own personal narratives has enabled Muhammad's students, and many more, to retrieve the term "multicultural society" from an impalpable, twilight place and to consider its connections to their own felt, daily lives. Inspiriting actions such as these explode the roof off the consecrated old red school!

This connection of the personal examination of culture to examinations of literature and literacies was also established by the philosopher and social scientist W. E. B. Du Bois. In his *Souls of Black Folk* (1903), Du Bois recounted his own experience as a freshly minted Fisk graduate teaching in a one-room, segregated Tennessee schoolhouse. His assignment was to teach the black sons and daughters of sharecroppers under a single roof. The terrain which these children inhabited—craggy, mountainous, wooded—seemed to vivify the steep battle they faced to overcome the poverty, racism, ignorance, and disease that militated against any possibility of their successfully becoming educated, mature adults.

At first, however, this challenge did not loom as much as other, more cosmetic, considerations. "I was haunted," Du Bois recalled (p. 99), "by a New England vision of neat little desks and chairs, but, alas! the reality was rough plank benches without backs, at times without legs." To further erode his "neat" presuppositions about what and what not a schoolhouse should be, Du Bois' own desk was not pedestaled auspiciously in the manner of the day. Instead, his privileged perch was modestly composed "of three boards, reinforced at critical points." His chair, "borrowed from the landlady, had to be returned every night." The school itself, a mere "log hut," had formerly been used to store grain.

Yet the young Du Bois remained unperturbed by this contradiction between reality and expectation, and he initiated encounters among the children there that reveal how our assumptions about culture and being cultured can belie what stands before our own eyes. In spite of the hardships and obstacles that his pupils often endured—ceaseless crop rotations, sudden disease and death, harassment by not-so-neighborly whites—Du Bois became both inspired and invigorated by the eagerness, industry, and potential in the class. Straight out of one of the most esteemed institutions for black youth, straining with lessons he thought he had mastered, Du Bois became a student to the lessons of his students. When a pupil had been kept too long away from studies to tend to younger siblings or assist parents in the fields, he would march upon the home and "put Cicero 'Pro Archia Poeta' into the simplest English with local applications" (p. 100) and convince the family of the importance of that student's return. Whether the studies of the day were "simplest" or complex, Du Bois learned to consider the "local applications" of literature and literacies to his students' own felt daily lives.

What kept this realization at the fore of all of Du Bois' scholarly achievements was the "longing to know" that "hovered like a star" (p. 99) in the eyes of his students during those Tennessee mountain days. As he wrote these words in *Souls of Black Folk,* Du Bois must have meant to remind his American readers of the North Star. This star only decades before had guided the slaves, the grands and great-grands of his students, to freedom and fulfillment of the "longing to know." Upon emancipation, the challenge to Americans, black and white, had been to shape a system of education offering the star's most salutary, transformative benefits. In a similar spirit, this volume is offered as an additional guiding light, toward a society that grants its children not one cramped pew, but circulation and scores of rooms.

Notes

1. Barbara is grateful to her mother, Mrs. Inez Owens McCaskill, for reminding her to be mindful of this fact. Her mother's experiences growing up in the 1940s and 1950s at Manley Taylor School and Spencer High School in segregated Columbus, Georgia, have contributed to this description of Assembly.

2. Exceptions to this are Phillip C. Gonzales and Junko Yokota, who were engaged after the conference had ended in order to contribute their essays on Latino/Latina and Asian/Asian American literature and literacies. Nevertheless, they share themes and references similar to those of the remaining writers.

References

Crow Dog, M. (1990). *Lakota woman.* New York: HarperCollins.

Du Bois, W. E. B. (1903). *The souls of Black folk.* New York: New American Library.

Franklin, J. H. (1990). A life of learning. In H. L. Gates, Jr. (Ed.), *Bearing witness: Selections from African-American autobiography in the twentieth century* (pp. 350–368). New York: Pantheon. (Reprinted from *Race and history: Selected essays 1938–1988,* 1989, pp. 277–291).

Freire, P. (1970). *Pedagogy of the oppressed* (M. Bergman Ramos, Trans.). New York: Seabury.

Hirsch, E. D., Jr. (1988). *Cultural literacy: What every American needs to know.* New York: Vintage.

Jones, G. (1991). *Liberating voices: Oral tradition in African American literature.* Cambridge, MA: Harvard University Press.

Kingston, M. H. (1976). *The woman warrior: Memoirs of a girlhood among ghosts.* New York: Vintage International.

Scholes, R. (1985). *Textual power.* New Haven: Yale University Press.

Smitherman, G. (1988). *Discriminatory discourse on Afro-American speech.* In her and Teun A. van Dyk (Eds.), *Discourse and discrimination* (pp. 144–175). Detroit: Wayne State University Press.

Part 1

Defining Difference:
Perspectives on Writing Literature

1

Seeing and Listening: A Poet's Literacies

Ron Welburn

Stories and Styles from Home

My father enjoyed telling a story about how you were supposed to bury money with the blood of a bull or a vicious animal. I always found this tale to be fascinating yet certainly implausible. Years ago, he said, a person buried a stash of money or valuables like that. And when anyone or a group of men went to dig up this cache, the odor of the bull's blood would become overpowering. Sometimes men quit digging. If you intended to continue the digging, however, you weren't supposed to say anything or complain before getting the money out of the ground else you would lose it all. One time this happened. A group of men were digging for money and the deeper they dug the stronger became the scent of the bull's blood. Finally, they struck a box and the smell threatened to sicken them. Then one of the men became so aggravated that he said aloud, "Get that damn bull outta here!" The money then divided within the ground and could be heard jingling as it moved off in many directions. It was never recovered. So the story goes.

My father's mother never believed this story. But it's a good tale and I enjoy it. I like the fact that it's weird and unbelievable and that it involves money, something that we tend to be avaricious about in ways that can bring us no good in the end. This is one of the many stories I heard as a child in my hometown of Berwyn, Pennsylvania, and as I was growing up in Philadelphia and visiting relatives back in Chester County. The stories that particularly fascinated me were those of ghostly and inexplicable occurrences set in Chester County from Devon through Berwyn to West Chester on down to Kennett Square and Avondale; and you could include parts of Lancaster County and eastward along the Lancaster Highway to Wayne and Radnor. I love these tales and stories because my family enjoyed them as part factual and part lies that make up the essence of a good story. These stories were as real to me as for any young reader hearing or reading Washington Irving's "Legend of Sleepy Hollow." In fact, there used to be a headless horseman who rode around Devon Hill. Or so the story goes. And there would be automobile accidents in Radnor as people claimed they were trying to avoid hitting an old woman crossing Lancaster Pike in her nightgown at a section called Marth Brown's Woods.

This was part of the orality and oral tradition that I inherited from my family. How and why I became a writer and poet in light of all this I cannot explain. What I understand of literacy and my own experience stems from these local legends, from my family's cultural heritage and Native American/African American mix on both sides, and as I prefer to believe, from my appreciation of their collective narrative styles. My father's manner, for example, was dry and matter-of-fact, but he appreciated humor and loved to tease. His mother's recitations were concentrated and musical and as reverent as another of her son's, my uncle Charlie's, were irreverent. My mother's family by contrast has a style based in the wonder of fact and supposition. I learned a lot from my mother about the ghostly stuff, and how her grandmother, who was born a slave in Delaware, took in her son and his six children after his wife, a Cherokee woman, died. One of my uncles tells stories with this tone of wonder, and another could hold us spellbound by emphasizing the kind of details that begged plausibility. As much as I read and was encouraged to read as a youngster, all these family members were and still are special to me as my first real storytellers. Their stories instructed me in style, technique, and theme. I appreciated their individuality of style. They helped develop my ears.

I developed writing skills by another means. I did quite well with four years of high school Latin. In ninth grade I engaged in a perverse little enterprise when a few of my classmates offered me a nickel each if I wrote out their translation assignment. I was reading ahead, you see, because I wanted to keep pace with a close buddy who attended another school. A few Latin teachers were at first suspicious about my ability to translate so well, but at that time in my youth I enjoyed languages. I tried a little Russian and bits of the Lenni Lenape language, which I felt was important for me to know. The Latin of Caesar and Cicero is not "oral," but I was attracted to its lofty cadences and rhetorical elements, especially those of Cicero.

I think that those years of reading and translating the periodic sentences and extended clauses of Caesar's Gallic Wars, Cicero's orations, and Vergil's *Aeneid* affected my syntax irrevocably; but this experience seemed to give me some facility for reading stylists like Faulkner and some modernist poets. In these days of discussions about cultural literacy I believe that the combination of what I listened to at home and what I read in and out of school enriches me constantly, because I remember, and because I never felt my Chester County legacy of stories was any less significant to my identity than Cicero's brillant exposé of Cataline. School never formally encouraged or reenforced my oral tradition; but readings from the Bible in the mornings, especially by a good reader who knew how to emphasize the cadences of the Psalms and Ecclesiastes, also left their influence on my senses. And so my favorite poets and fictionists blend a learned sophistication with the ironies of traditional storytelling: in no particular order I have a deep respect for Faulkner, Ellison, some Fitzgerald, Borges, Toni Morrison, García Márquez, Wallace Stevens, Leslie Silko, Scott Momaday, Felix Tchicaya U'Tamsi, Jay Wright, and Anaïs Nin.

I am a Pennsylvanian, descended from the original inhabitants of the Delmarva Peninsula, the Chesapeake region, and the Great Smokies. And I'm descended from peoples brought here forcibly from Africa. This combination of Native and African, at one time in my life the African American holding emphasis, this rural and small-town birth and urban upbringing, have all profoundly affected my listening and seeing as a poet and writer. I don't know if my poems and stories or their personae sound Pennsylvanian. Wallace Stevens is eastern Pennsylvania's best-known poet and I've come rather late to a real appreciation of his work. We enjoy apparently the colors and birds and the sky, and we know something of love and disappointment that we express in special ways. Like Stevens, I love music; I doubt that we sound the same, though. When I heard a tape of Stevens speaking, or reading his poems, although I realize that one's reading voice may differ from one's casual speech, I listened and didn't hear the kinds of patterns I grew up with.

Wherever I've lived, even in Philadelphia, or Arizona, upstate or downstate New York, and now New England, besides asking me what race or ethnic group I'm of, people ask where I'm from and a few can pick out the Pennsylvanian. Our speech manner is distinct. Geographically, a band of similar speech sound stretches from South Jersey and Delaware along the Mason-Dixon line at least to York and up to Harrisburg. It's countrified and urbane; it's neither southern nor drawled, though it mixes long syllables with sharp ones. Philadelphians are noted for having a distinct way of pronouncing *couch* and *coach*, but in Chester County the old-timers had their own way of rolling the vowels around. My grandparents were on close terms with Quakers and Mennonites and took on some of their diction and at times their syntax. And they butchered it, too, to keep everybody honest. We often use *your* in place of the definite article, and it comes out "yir." And Pennsylvania speech is conscious of endings to words: if you dropped anything out of a word it was from the middle, not the end or the beginning. Vowels underwent change, so that *Maryland* and *Delaware* sound "Merleland" and "Delawere." We youngsters had to be careful lest we sounded too southern. We were not encouraged to adopt Black urban speech or other forms of "Blackeze"; in fact, I was barely conscious of those patterns when I was growing up. My mother was five when she lost her mother, a Cherokee woman of the West family born near Richmond, Virginia; so much of my mother's speech came from her father and his mother, an ex-slave from Delaware whose reproduced humor sounds very distinctly articulated to me. My father's mother was a Lenape, Piscataway, or Nanticoke mixed with a tribal group that had secluded themselves in the mountains of upstate Pennsylvania. Considering these speech mannerisms and attitudes, I've come to appreciate a certain aloftness they have. Part of their ease about things lay in knowing who they were and are, just enough not to want to be bothered with nonsense. They are independent and proud but not arrogant.

That's another long legacy. It's their stories that mean so much for now. I can't separate their content from the inflections of the way they were told in that pure rural southern Pennsylvania speech where parts of words are swallowed, where *e*'s sound like *i*'s and a *fire* is a *fahr*. With these mannerisms, I listened to the stories of people being sealed up in walls of old houses, of my great-grandmother struggling with her horse to drive past a scene of roadside death, or an old woman who fed the bodies of the dead to the crows. It was my inheritance, and at age twenty-three I made a conscious decision to be a writer. It was the best way I knew to preserve some of that legacy and extend it.

Listening with the Eyes; Seeing with the Heart.

My grandmother taught me how to listen just by pointing out what she was listening to; and from my father I guess I learned the importance of seeing what I was trying to look at. My mother introduced me to subtle irony. How my responses and perceptions, how the sum total of my imagination and my understanding, are the result of whatever parts of my Native American ancestry or African American ancestry I don't fully know. A love of sky and the land, of birds, a belief that this Turtle Continent and not someplace else is my motherland, have always been in me. And yet I respond to field hollers and blues, to jazz and orchestrations, and to the romantic spirit in academic music. So many Native Americans throughout the eastern United States have lived in the African American world, thus constituting a unique color line, responding to all sorts of seemingly contradictory symbols and impulses, but holding on to something that is Native. This might be in the preference for a certain type of shoe or an innate ability to put certain kinds of things together and ensure survival in hard times. I've learned to see many sides of an emotion and an issue, even when I disagree. I appreciate and see relationships and shapes, ideas and designs, peripheries and vortices—my first published poetry collection was entitled *Peripheries* (1972). It seems that I can understand the edge of things because that's where I've been: looking in, almost good enough, watching, measuring, and absorbing, listening. I find great poetry in a flock of birds rising to the air and changing shape; and there is something of absolute poetry in certain recorded jazz solos like John Coltrane's on "Autumn Serenade" sung by Johnny Hartman, and George Adams for his "Flowers for a Lady" on *Mingus Moves*.

My alma mater, Lincoln University in Pennsylvania, invited me in 1981 to participate in a Langston Hughes festival. I spent the nights at the home of emeritus psychology professor Henry Cornwell and his wife, Sophie, a librarian and Spanish teacher, and my campus "mother." The day of the festival, as the professor and I set out eastward across the track field which when I was in school was a field of thistle and grasses, two red-tailed hawks flew above, intersecting our path, performing, as it seemed, some kind of playful yet celebratory ritual. I stopped and watched them swoop and glide and soar and speed upward in the air drafts heading north over the rolling hills that characterize Chester County. They were not eagles, but they reminded me of Scott Momaday's description of two eagles in *House Made of Dawn* (1968). They made spirals and arabesques and I saw their presence and their flight as special and just as holy as Momaday's eagles. I felt blessed and was honored to be alive that day. Those red-tails may have been there to celebrate the award I did not then realize I would receive that evening. But at that moment they confirmed for me the beauty and freedom of the imagination and reaffirmed my connection to the land, that I was a part of this very old land. I saw their flight to be as wonderfully mysterious as birth and love and dying. I have never written about that morning until now; obviously, I will never forget it.

Poets and writers I think tend to see with the heart. The hawks and I were in the same place for a reason. I suppose I attach significance to these kinds of events, and I cannot separate them from academic questions and concerns about cultural literacy. That moment with the red-tailed hawks and my self was a spiritual moment, just as the making of a poem or a story is a spiritual act or event. I believe in cycles and the strength of circles. With this my poems and stories are attempts to articulate my emotions and perceptions, and I employ concrete or abstract and even elliptical diction as the occasion within the poem demands. Seeing and listening interact, and sometimes the function and capabilities of one suit the other.

One poem in my latest collection, *Council Decisions* (1991), is called "A Theory of Art," and even I am amazed at its regenerative qualities as a statement of values personal and cultural about art and literacy. Here is the poem:

Birds of prey and hawkweed
out of my mouth, I consider
the valley of theories; then
laying aside my mantle
I climb through the wordy slopes
of definition to my place
of stone and thistle on the hill.
Around this perimeter
I hesitate responsibility,
cannot burden and imbue my songs
with nooses to dangle artifice.
Maker of images,
I am irreverent now, for
when in good heart vision
I can raise my songs like birds
hundreds at a time that
spin oblong circles
changing character
to resettle on the lake or field
in a glorious rush.
This art, a holy action of minds
and feathers jelled as one.

The title, "A Theory of Art," is certainly commonplace; yet I had in mind the title of a jazz composition by trumpet player Bill Hardman, recorded by a 1957 edition of drummer Art Blakey's Jazz Messengers for the Vik label: *A Night in Tunisia*. The opening meaning of this phrase always intrigued me. Here it meant the art of Art Blakey and his tutelage of young musicians who become masters. On the other hand, the phrase concerns aesthetics and theoretical formulations.

I set out in this poem to comment about how critical theory can stifle the very expression it seeks to scrutinize. Thus, I consider "the valley of theories" to be in conflict with the natural expression and order of life forms which themselves are forms of art that adhere to their own aesthetics. We all engage in some degree of theoretical formulation, but for some people it becomes an identifiable trait. Taking an image maker's position, I reverse the location of this valley of the theoretical with a personal lofty position as "I climb through the wordy slopes / of definition" to my special rugged vantage point. I shed my "mantle," academic vestments if you will, and find refuge in "my place / of stone and thistle on the hill." I enjoy the rough natural beauty there as I am tied to these characteristics of the land. I hesitate, resorting to categorical *isms* to define even my most clever expressions; I cherish an appropriate irreverence; and I am willing to wait, in the face of impositions on my imagery and style, to best capture the world around me "like birds / . . .that / spin oblong circles," capable of changing shape and identity. To me this is what the poet or word imager does, and is what I do best.[1]

Art created for our well-being is holy. The poet who writes honestly of the interaction of life forms' subtleties writes of the sacred. Having "good heart vision" enables a poet to see with the heart, the inner eye, and the soul. I have never not seen a flock of birds changing shape in flight as a poetic presence resulting from what Native people refer to as the Great Mystery. In "A Theory of Art" the birds, as artists and art form, demonstrate and reaffirm the spirit of my connection to the land. Perhaps "A Theory of Art" is an ethnic poem or statement; perhaps it embodies my reaction to critical excesses in poetics and is a posture toward ethnopoetics and deconstruction and ethnic-centered semiotics. This is a difficult poem for me to say more about; but I can add that in the poem I am being ironical in my irreverence, knowing how a good story elicits a chuckle from the teller. This sense of humor comes from how one sees, what one listens to in people and in life's events.

Seeing and Hearing the Other Artist

Statement I hear in poetry and prose; and in music. A jazz solo is a narrative act. During my early twenties, I wrote poetry, journalism, and tales; and I played cornet and saxophones, and drums, too, in a jazz band whose style pushed some of the limitations of conventional melody and harmony. I composed and arranged for this band without ever having studied music formally, and years later I learned that my harmonic structures were accurate. The respective narratives of all these artistic and expressive media collectively kept me in balance.

Writer-in-residence at Lincoln University during 1966–1968 was playwright Ronald Milner (*Whose Got His Own; What the Winesellers Buy*). Unable to participate in his creative writing workshops, I took satisfaction in our chance meetings on campus between classes. One of his remarks I'll never forget: "William Faulkner is the funkiest writer in the English language." "Now he's from Mississippi," Milner reminded me, "and if there was to be another Civil War he and I would probably be on opposite sides of the gun—if he was still alive. But he can swing! He's like a Charlie Parker or a Gene Ammons."

This idea about Faulkner's prose style had led Ron Milner to something inevitable. Before the disdain among academics in 1990 over cultural studies, before the earnest ascent of critical theorists, Milner in 1966, like many practicing artists, had known the profound connections between the arts as expressive cultural and social forms. He had learned, as I would come to understand, that the expressive forms like painting and music, poetry and dance, all possess vocabularies rooted in the imaginative dimension. An observer-critic may employ the language of literature such as the term *narrative* to describe a painting. But Milner had expressed what the *isms* makers were too busy to comprehend: that each artist could discover in the medium of another artist something that he or she wanted to say.

A writer would tell a musician, as Milner told me, "Man, what you are saying is exactly what I'm trying to say in this poem or story." Seeing the world around me as a painting to be narrated; articulating the dancing at grand entry during pow wow, or people dancing to Motown or James Brown or El DeBarge; offering a substance to the pungent trombones of salsa, or to the various moods of jazz—these sometimes are what motivate a poem in me. I tell inexperienced poets to listen and look. Advising and guiding them puts me in a chain of tradition. Some may sooner or later be able to articulate what they experience, and some won't. As alumnus poet Melvin B. Tolson (*The Harlem Gallery*) told a group of us cocky young poets in 1966: "Some people never see anything."

Tolson is but one of many artist-thinkers and intellectuals of color I have admired over the years, and I've probably gotten more from their deliberations than from their Anglo counterparts. Ralph Ellison, Albert

Murray, Scott Momaday, Audrey Shenandoah, Wilmer Lucas, Alex Seowtewa, and Max Salazar, among others, have expansive intellects and imaginations. To know them or to hear them speak is to know history and the interrelatedness of cultural expression; they are people who know who they are. When alumnus Hildres Poindexter, a renowned specialist in tropical diseases, spoke to a student assembly at Lincoln, we were overwhelmed by his command of history, science, philosophy, languages, and culture—all of which he related to contemporary issues. I doubt that many of us had ever heard anyone speak like him, of whatever race. Profound reasoning, erudition, faith in the intuition, and an intellectual range made sense to me as tools that I could employ when the occasion demanded.

George Russell's musical concept of tonal gravity, Ornette Coleman's theory of harmolodics, Paula Gunn Allen's ideas about gynocentrism in literary and cultural studies, and Vine Deloria's perceptions of holistic metaphysics represent examples of how we can utilize our senses. They help us to see what we are supposed to know and to understand what we are thinking about. Such ideas feed me. I can look at the world around me and, relying on my own judgment and imagination, I can know my world more intimately.

Cultural Illiteracy Is Relative

Creative-expressive people give society a reflection of itself and where it is going. Musician-composers and painters lead with their work, followed by writers and poets who in turn propel forward at moments of crisis. It has been said that poets are dangerous people. In times of social upheaval, the average Joe who thinks that poets are pansies comes to fear they might instead be revolutionaries out for the violent overthrow of the government. Everyone has some definition of the poet: unacknowledged legislator; word sorcerer; you name it.

Because we make images derived from our cultural and multi-cultural experiences, the Anglo culture writes off us poets of color as exotic or alien. Whose idea of literacy is at question here? In the 1970s, editors of little magazines would reject poems by people of color and claim that they didn't understand the cultural backgrounds of our work. Consider the sources of Jay Wright's poetry in Dogon mysticism and Aztec culture, or Scott Momaday's Kiowa ethos. To the average undergraduate today (or thirty years ago) isn't Ezra Pound comparably just as obscure? Can even the most casual reader of Pound tune in to all his metaphors of Greco-Roman or ancient Chinese cultures, to London or Italy as he saw them, or to Mauberley's angst? Is there an intellectual problem here, and whose is it and under what condition? Is what Jay Wright sees of his New Mexico beginnings as an African American less valid than Pound's distress? When Momaday identifies with and assimilates the elements in his physical and spiritual landscape on the plains, why is there such hesitation to treat his work other than something exotic? When T. S. Eliot provides a glossary from *The Waste Land* (1922), scholars appreciate his intellect; but those same scholars will treat as disdainfully alienating the thought of having to investigate terminology in poems taken from the Kiowa or the Dogon. A high-class literary gerrymandering indeed!

Our collective experience as Americans is one of the central issues in the topic and reality of cultural diversity. American poets of color face having to legitimize ourselves and what we do. All this is of course microcosmic in relation to the larger world. We're still cautious about being in those special issues of literary periodicals that might otherwise not want our writings. Some poems that I sent to a periodical were rejected by editors who essentially claimed that they had recently absolved their editorial conscience in their "special ethnic issue." I think that these editors had at least a cultural literacy problem. And sometimes our own work against us, perhaps unwittingly. A magazine published one of my poems but changed my word *starling* to the word *startling*, the word the copyeditor must have thought I mistyped. If I then footnote a word like *starling*, a species of bird introduced into this country in 1890 from England, readers will mock me as pedantic as T. S. Eliot (my ironic association of an imported bird species from England with Eliot is purely coincidental).

In the 1960s I didn't write a lot of poetry with heavy Black revolutionary overtones, and that bothered some people I knew who must have figured me terribly restrained. I think independently; I'm individualistic about how I perceive what I'm dealing with. I don't like my imagination fenced in and pigeonholed. I try to meet the audience halfway. Beyond some brief, descriptive, introductory explanation, I encourage them to seek what they don't already know. I was taken aback, but not discouraged, when in 1972 a Black woman told me that a poem I'd read was "irrelevant" to her because she didn't know who Sonny Rollins was. You have to keep going in the face of that, name-dropping if necessary, so that a listener or reader may be led to find out that Rollins has been indisputably proclaimed the greatest living tenor saxophone player—in terms of his technique—for the twentieth century.

Cultural literacy is relative, and its relativity was proven two decades ago when ethnic studies programs were young. My heritage of stories about Devon Hill may share elements with Poe and Hawthorne, but they are not in imitation of that tradition. The people who expressed this oral tradition may not care a lick for American Romanticism. I am in a unique position of knowing both traditions, and if my students or audience know nothing about my—or their own!—oral traditions, I sabotage their learning by using oral traditions as examples.

Mark Twain, one of my favorite authors, once said that "truth is precious and should be used sparingly." Isn't it peculiar how fact and fiction about an event may be treated differently by a community on the one hand and by "scholars" on the other? Everyone deserves to know family history and community, ethnic and racial histories, and everyone ought to know why the chips fell as they did. The collective experiential legacy of Americans belongs inescapably to Americans, whether we came here last year or forty thousand years ago. If ten people out of a dozen know nothing of the Wounded Knee massacre of 1890, or of Manzanar where Japanese Americans were interned during World War II, of Coleman Hawkins or of what the Young Lords were all about, the remaining two have a job on their hands; and the ten should listen.

People never really forget, though they try awfully hard. Someone will always remember the historical information about people and events and how things were accomplished. It is more polite to say, then, that memory is selective. The real problem with cultural illiteracy in America is that Americans have been taught very well to distrust the significance of their unique historical and cultural inheritance. Americans still waste lots of intellectual and academic energy trying to prove themselves to an ideal of European expectations. Americans have never understood that the British and the Europeans cut us off long ago just as we Americans wanted to go it alone, and that Europeans are actually more interested in how hip we are today. Europe and the rest of the world "have taken our blues and gone," as Langston Hughes once said of Euro-Americans. Kids in North Africa wear tee-shirts bearing logos of American universities; the Germans—and the Russians too, we hear—have Native American hobbyist organizations; the late jazz critic Harry Lim edited a jazz magazine in his native Indonesia (then the Dutch East Indies) in 1937; the average pedestrian in Denmark, from what musicians performing there have related, knows more about jazz figures living and dead than the average student and faculty in an American college. The onus of such cultural illiteracy is something

Americans prefer to deny. Outside of Eurocentrism, the world is perceived and understood in holistic and intuitive terms, a sort of both/and approach that values inconclusiveness, not exclusivity. We are products of many things and we are related and connected to the simplest forms of life.

It is no wonder that a greater percentage of writers of color engage in more than one form than do Euro-descended writers. A poem by itself may not be the only venue to relate my story or my feeling. The traditional Euro-descended academic does not know how to deal with something unless it is either fish or fowl. What has always humored me about the apples and oranges routine is that they are both fruit. Oversimplification, perhaps, but I realize the distinction is important in context; yet these two are edible fruits! Many traditional academics persist in distrusting interdisciplinary and holistic study and methodology and therefore are confused about how to categorize people who write poems *and* fiction. The worthy examples of Thomas Hardy, Stephen Crane, and Edgar Allan Poe escape them, and it is easy to proclaim such writers as better by far at one form than another. Academics prefer to know what we are *primarily*, whether we are either/or kinds of writers instead of those disconcerting both/and types.

If, as Frederick Mayer said in 1988, culture in the life of a civilization "should be regarded as a direct source of inspiration for development," then perhaps we as Americans have been careless and narrow about what we perceive to be important to our literacy. Even in terms of a national cultural identity that I believe does exist, but I know we disagree about, great art and immature but stylized expression have coexisted. Well through mid-century, the generalized, opposite natures of the great and the immature remained intimate, yet whatever our preferences we have recognized the differences. Americans have been the best in the world at marketing bad art because the culture that Americans take pride in is not music or letters or painting but business and finance. No wonder we are in our current state, where our spiritual existence is vulnerable and decried. "You can't pray a lie." I think Mark Twain said that. Bad literature and bad music, to invoke Ezra Pound again, of all people, are inexcusable. The nature of our excesses results from, in part, our protection of a European ideal of culture while disclaiming the worth of what is indigenous. We don't want to accept jazz as a classical music; how can we come to terms with such writers as a Leslie Silko who so beautifully orchestrates the fusion of traditional Western literary forms?

Mediocrity survives, and it allows us to invoke the principles of free speech when the issues may be aesthetic taste and even morality.

Our puerile cultural rebellion and ensuing debate in recent years only demonstrate how comic certain rights issues and censorship charades have become. I am not underestimating the function of a charade because a charade can raise havoc. But definitions can still be relative. I accept categories, too. Erotica may be lovely and aesthetically enriching while pornography may be exploitative and a self-indulgent auto-stimulant even for the person who produces it. The term *indecent* is occasionally open-ended. I'm leading here to the Mapplethorpe controversy. Perhaps I'm a conservative (who still enjoys the jazz avant–garde from the sixties), but I fail to understand what I or the public at large is supposed to gain from photographs of individuals engaged in bodily functions customarily carried out in private by oneself. Should the audience for this be a "public" one, or a specialized one? A writer can make decent (hah!) money writing pornography; but if you use public funds to do so and then admit it, you're dumber than Balaam's billy goat! As it is, the girlie magazines pay quite a bit for one story, from what I've been told by an academic who placed a few stories during difficult financial times; and some porno novel publishing houses have writers on salary. But because we promote mediocrity in our arts and market it to mediocre minds, we have rather effectively jettisoned any real understanding of aesthetic values in what we do. I suspect that the Mapplethorpe controversy reflects, from artist to spectator to legislator, this century's fin de siècle hysteria compounded by tensions about the environment and the dissolution of the Iron Curtain. Nuclear holocaust is still the real obscenity, and this is all a condition ripe for proclaiming perversion as art.

Charlotte Moorman, where are you now?[2]

What Still Matters about Literacy and Culture?

There are probably fewer arguments about E. D. Hirsch's book on cultural literacy than about the content and origins of his list. The list includes "what literate Americans know"; but do they? And how much do they know about these items and with what degree of accuracy? The list is presumptuous, and Hirsch's omissions tend to subvert the idea of the list being a set of potential source elements. Hirsch is illiterate about foods: tortillas; Indian fry bread; borscht—none are on his list. And while he mentions Tecumseh and Geronimo, he neglects Powhatan and Samoset, people who figured prominently and so dynamically with the survival of the earliest British colonists, and who are probably known to grade school youngsters in connection with Captain John Smith and the Puritans respectively.

Now, if I write a poem mentioning or describing Powhatan or fry bread, what does that make me? Am I back in the box as I was two decades ago over the Sonny Rollins "relevancy"? Must I await Hirsch's updated list to verify and legitimize my existence, my culture, my way of life? Must all of us stand in line or along the sidelines waiting for Hirsch to anoint us? I think we've been there before. . . . If the information about the American world of color is so specialized, will that specialization place us outside the realm of Hirsch's brand of cultural literacy?

Persons of color in America have *lived* a cultural literacy and diversity and know more than one vocabulary. We've had to legitimize ourselves to the dominant intellectual powers by learning Anglo ways; but in a much less formal manner we learned our own traditions. I have both inherited and made great discoveries of my Native American traditions since childhood, and of African-diasporic traditions gained mostly during my twenties. And I have shared ideas about traditions with Hispanic and Asian American artists, among others, teaching their poems and stories and broadening the canon every chance I got. How many of my white colleagues and poets are as comfortable with all these literary cultures? And who is culturally deficient, anyway? The notion of "Great Books" and protecting the canon-as-is from invasion by hoards and rebels is simply sheltering one narrow cultural hegemony in the face of a cultural and social reality that was always there. In some English departments the disdain for American writing is so strong that students are lucky to find more than three courses on the subject. The one thing worse than lying about history is pretending or believing that a history didn't exist. People who practice that are promoting a fatal illiteracy. Americanists and cultural pluralists must continue to effect changes leading to more holistic and inclusive formulations about literature, culture, and literacy.

I could continue some of these issues and wax polemical. My poems get around and I uphold a modest reputation. My poems are no more dense than Ezra Pound's, nor more factually detailed than the oddities Marianne Moore's poems contain. I have heard the sounds of the land, have always heard and watched birds and people and found something inspiring enough to re–create. I have nothing to prove to the editors of prestigious magazines or to grant-funding jurists. I am primarily concerned with writing well and having the time to write and the "headroom" and the "dreamtime" to work out my stories and poems. I have been most lucky. I've read my poems from New York to Arizona, from Wisconsin to Louisiana, and at least one utter stranger has expressed thanks for what I showed, and some have discovered I'm the guy who wrote a particular poem they enjoyed. I've managed to reach some people, and these people, of all races, are not cultural illiterates. They can feel emotions and they can see images that make them happy or proud, or that compel them to think or remember or simply ask questions.

My story is my literacy. My literacy is what my family taught me about themselves; what I learned in school, from experience, from self-motivation; and I also learned from things I was not told about while growing up. As a poet, a word and image maker, I offer ways of seeing and listening. If only one person gains something from the poem, that is important. That is what matters most of all.

Notes

1. And others have found something relevant in this poem. At this writing "A Theory of Art" has been selected to grace the brochure for a Columbus Quincentenary lecture series produced by the American Indian Archaeological Institute in Washington, Connecticut; I will lead the "Music from Turtle Island" portion.

2. During the early 1960s cellist Charlotte Moorman staged several "happenings" in New York City that occasionally featured her performing nude or wrapped in cellophane. She was summarily arrested for such "indiscretions."

Bibliography

Allen, P. G. (1986). *The sacred hoop: Recovering the feminine in American Indian traditions*. Boston: Beacon.

Blangger, T. (December 1990/January 1991). George Russell. *Coda Magazine*, pp. 11–13.

Deloria, V. (1979). *The metaphysics of modern existence*. New York: Harper & Row.

Ellison, R. (1965). *Shadow and act*. New York: Random House.

Ellison, R. (1986). *Going to the territory*. New York: Random House.

Hirsch, E. D. (1988). *The dictionary of cultural literacy: What every American needs to know*. New York: Random House.

Momaday, N. S. (1968). *House made of dawn*. New York: Random House.

Murray, A. (1970). *The Omni-Americans: New perspectives on black experiences and the American culture*. New York: Outerbridge & Dienstfrey.

Murray, A. (1973). *The hero and the blues*. Columbia: University of Missouri Press.

Welburn, R. (1991). *Council decisions: Poems*. American Native Press Archives.

Wright, J. (1976). *Dimensions of history*. Austin: University of Texas Press.

2

Liberation Literacy: Literacy and Empowerment in Marginalized American Texts

Valerie Babb

In much contemporary academic discourse, gender, race, ethnicity, class, and sexuality are increasingly acknowledged as shaping influences in the creation and teaching of literature. One result of the new interest paid to these cultural constructs are pedagogical approaches that seek to integrate works by traditionally marginalized writers into what is commonly referred to as "the canon." Certainly attempts to produce curricula that reflect the richness of multicultural societies are necessary and admirable, but care has to be taken that *multiculturalism* is not defined superficially, and that heretofore neglected works are not accorded the status of "enrichers," texts that add depth, another dimension, or variety to an established canon. Any curricular or pedagogical reform should avoid allotting works by socially marginalized writers to a ghettoized status in which they are tokens within an otherwise immutable canon. To do otherwise would relegate these works to a position of voicelessness, a position which marginalized writers have fought since the inception of American literature.

For curricular reform to be truly successful, to produce courses that give students both equal access to literacy and a full sense of a pluralistic society, a reconsideration of canonical texts must complement any inclusion of new texts. During the spring semester of 1991, I offered a course entitled "White Male Writers." The course was designed as an approach to redefining the American literary canon, not necessarily by combining canonical texts with traditionally marginalized texts but by rethinking canonical texts in light of constructions of race, class, gender, ethnicity, sexuality, and access to literacy and social power. Ultimately, the course came to discuss how authorial voices were established or muted within the American literary canon; how belonging to the dominant race-gender group and having access to literacy privileged writers such as James Fenimore Cooper, Herman Melville, Nathaniel Hawthorne, and William Faulkner, whose works came to define the American canon.

Response to the course was overwhelming and provided a context in which to view the nature of the relationship between the academy and society, between literacy and social access. Within the university the course was frequently a topic for discussion; without, it received considerable attention in the popular media. Various publications, such as the *New York Times* and the *Washington Post*, ran articles on it or mentioned it in pieces covering the debate over curricular reform on university campuses. The publicity the course received is telling, for it indicates the ethnocentrism and "gender centrism" that have made canon and curriculum reform necessary. What distinguished this course from other courses whose titles incorporate labels of race and gender— Black Women Writers, for instance (a course I have taught for years without notoriety)—is that it redefines white males not as the traditional literary "majority" but as a "minority" who because of their special access to literacy and political enfranchisement were subsequently able to move past contributing to and on to dominating the larger canon of American literature.

The impact caused by the course makes clear that we cannot divorce considerations of literary production from considerations of other forms of social power. The ability to read and write, the ability to produce literature, have long been linked to equal social and political participation. In *Tristes Tropiques* (1973), for example, Claude Levi-Strauss eloquently describes the relationship between writing and social hierarchies in the following manner:

> The only phenomenon with which writing has always been concomitant is the creation of cities and empires, that is the integration of large numbers of individuals into a political system, and their grading into castes or classes.... [I]t seems to have favored the exploitation of human beings rather than their enlightenment.... My hypothesis, if correct, would oblige us to recognize the fact that the primary function of written communication is to facilitate slavery. (Levi Strauss, 1973, p. 239)

Levi-Strauss's linking of writing and slavery is a significant one, for it reveals the potential use of literacy to preserve and value one culture while destroying and devaluing another. By associating writing with subjugation, Levi-Strauss provides a useful context for understanding why the acquisition of literacy comes to be a dominant literary motif in the works of many socially marginalized peoples and how this motif can help us understand the need for a recognized voice, and as such is a fitting representation of the recognition sought through pedagogies that focus on multiculturalism. Historically, American authors from marginalized groups have fought for the right to read and write and thereby to have a voice, and currently, it falls to educators to ensure that this voice is not lost in the teaching of literature.

The body of American literature is full of examples which illuminate the connection between literacy and social liberation, from early texts such as slave autobiographies to modern novels such as Alice Walker's *The Color Purple* (1982). In most, literacy is both an act—that of being able to read and write—and a symbolic device exploring issues of cultural inclusion or exclusion. A brief overview of the varying manifestations of literacy in this second sense is instructive to understanding how literacy validates the experience of one race or culture while making that of another all but invisible and why pedagogical revision is needed if we are to meet the needs of a student body that comes from a multicultural society.

There are, no doubt, as many treatments of literacy in texts as there are texts, but one of the most lucid illustrations of the connection between access to literacy and social participation occurs in an early form of African American literature, the slave narrative. The centrality of reading and writing to the physical and psychic survival of slaves and their descendants is repeated in virtually all narratives, and the roots of this motif can be traced directly to the forbidden literacy so much a part of slavery's maintenance. During slavery, African Americans were denied access to the written word by law. It was a crime to teach a slave to read or write, and the denial of literacy assisted in perpetuating a strict racial, and subsequently sexual, hierarchy. Illiteracy was vital to the imposed impotency that was the mainstay of "the peculiar institution," for literacy accorded social power. With literacy, escaping slaves were able to read reward notices; with literacy, slaves were able to forge passes allowing them to leave plantations and begin journeys to freedom; and with literacy, former slaves were able to write and distribute eloquent abolitionist documents calling for an end to human bondage and the beginning of political enfranchisement. In many slave narratives the ability to read and write becomes the forerunner of freedom. In a culture dominated by literacy, the creation of literature by a slave forbidden to read and write or by a free Black writer marginalized because of his or her color made textual production itself a political act asserting equality.

Olaudah Equiano, an ex-slave with experiences as varied as accompanying Constantine Phipps to the North Pole in 1772 and participating in the Seven Years War, penned his autobiography in 1789, entitling it *The Interesting Narrative of the Life of Olaudah Equiano, or Gustavus Vassa, the African. Written by Himself*. Though Equiano ultimately became an English citizen, he spent a significant portion of time in the Americas, and his narrative foreshadowed thematic uses of literacy in later American texts. That he included the phrase "written by himself" in his title, suggests the value Equiano placed on the acquisition of literacy to confer authorship of the self as human rather than chattel.

Of learning to read and write Equiano reflects, "I had often seen my master. . .employed in reading; and I had a great curiosity to talk to the books. . . .I have often taken up a book, and have talked to it, and then put my ears to it, when alone, in hopes it would answer me; and I have been very much concerned when I found it remained silent" (Equiano, 1789, pp. 106–107). According to Paul Edwards, Equiano borrowed the metaphor of the "talking book" from Ukawsaw Gronniosaw.[1] By borrowing Gronniosaw's analogy, what Equiano ultimately compares is the differing methods of communication indigenous to different cultures. He approaches a book, and hence literacy, with the premise of his oral culture that the book will talk to him, and is disappointed when it does not. The metaphor discloses the alienation he feels upon trying to achieve self-definition in what is essentially the tradition of the Other. The talking book is Equiano's way of juxtaposing self-creation and communication as manifested in two distinct cultures, and it represents his rite of passage as he moves from an oral culture into a written one.

For Equiano, literacy is at first a barrier, but ultimately it becomes a bridge leading him into another worldview. As he becomes more familiar with an alien culture, he experiences a greater desire to learn its mode of expression and communication. Upon arriving in England he recalls,

> I could now speak English tolerably well and I perfectly under-
> stood everything that was said. I now not only felt myself quite
> easy with these new countrymen but relished their society and
> manners. I no longer looked upon them as spirits, but as men
> superior to us, and therefore I had the stronger desire to resemble
> them, to imbibe their spirit and imitate their manners; I therefore
> embraced every occasion of improvement, and every new thing
> that I observed I treasured up in my memory. I had long wished

to be able to read and write, and for this purpose I took every opportunity to gain instruction. (Equiano, 1789, pp. 43–44)

The link Equiano makes between cultural superiority and literacy is a significant one. His main motivation for learning to read and write is his desire to belong, to become a member of a "superior" culture. The superiority of this culture has been most clearly manifested through its ability to enslave Equiano and to restrict his movements, and on a more subtle level, it has influenced his perceptions of himself and his culture by awing him with particular aspects. Though we get no explicit details of Equiano's psychological transition that allows him to conclude this to be a superior culture, we are told of his fascination with things as varied as framed pictures, instruments used for navigation, and the speed of tall ships. His enchantment with this new civilization is transformed into a desire for literacy, for he feels it will accord him social acceptance. This conception of literacy is at the root of a pragmatic figuration in which an author who was formerly a slave writes himself into society by using literacy to assist him in communicating with a new audience unaware of his world and its traditions. In putting pen to his life, Equiano produces a marketable text which he sells while lecturing for the cause of abolition. He thereby garners modest economic independence along with a social recognition denied most Blacks at the time. His narrative thus reveals literacy's power to effect enfranchisement.

As much as being an account of the injustice and brutality of slavery, Equiano's narrative is a picaresque adventure tale detailing his passage from one culture to another. The early portions provide a utopic vision of his society and also describe the oral traditions that perpetuate it:

We are almost a nation of dancers, musicians, and poets. Thus every great event such as a triumphant return from battle or other cause of public rejoicing is celebrated in public dances, which are accompanied with songs and music suited to the occasion....Our land is uncommonly rich and fruitful, and produces all kinds of vegetables in great abundance. We have plenty of Indian corn, and vast quantities of cotton and tobacco. Pineapples grow without culture....We have also spices of different kinds, particularly pepper, and a variety of delicious fruits which I have never seen in Europe....All our industry is exerted to improve those blessings of nature. (Equiano, 1789, pp. 3–8)

When Equiano is kidnapped from this idyll, not only is he severed from familial and cultural ties, but he is also severed from his traditions of orality. He notes the growing distance enslavement places between him and his language: "From the time I left my own nation I always found somebody that understood me till I came to the sea coast. The languages of different nations did not totally differ, nor were they so copious as those of the Europeans, particularly the English" (Equiano, 1789, p. 20). Once he is removed from the west coast of Africa, the distance becomes unbridgeable, and his kidnapping also constitutes a silencing, a loss of voice. On a slaver, he makes many references to having no one to talk to, save the few fellow slaves of his own nation whose presence "in a small degree gave ease" (Equiano, 1789, p. 27). With no audience, Equiano's oral tradition is truncated, and his attempt to regain freedom is simultaneously an attempt to replace a lost tradition with a new one.

For Equiano, literacy replaces his lost orality, and eventually he comes to believe it will also confer social equality. Although he succeeds in adopting a new tradition, the equality he desires is limited and continually complicated by his race. He receives his manumission paper, a written document confirming an oral agreement between him and his master, but he is still liable to be abducted and placed back into slavery at any moment. Without full social enfranchisement, Equiano's literacy affords little social power. As such, his narrative ultimately shows the complex relationship between literacy, race, and social acceptance. His narrative can be read as symbolic of the first step many marginalized peoples take toward full social participation, the gaining of a society's literacy. Whether it is through formal education or through naturalization exams, acquiring the literacy of a culture is the prerequisite to citizenship.

Equiano's experience is instructive in another vein, however, as a reminder that citizenship requires more than literacy; it also requires political empowerment. Again, literature is useful for illustrating the more complicated transition from literacy acquisition to political empowerment. To return to the example of the slave narrative, texts after Equiano's would exhibit a less pragmatic and increasingly politicized figure of literacy. In *The Narrative of the Life of Frederick Douglass* (1845), for instance, Frederick Douglass elaborates upon Equiano's conception of literacy by linking it directly to social empowerment. That equality and justice are central concerns in Douglass's narrative is evident as early as his choice of subtitle, "An American Slave," which constitutes an act of naming that juxtaposes the American ideal of liberty to the American practice of enslavement.

Douglass expands on Equiano's notion of "the talking book," or literacy as a means of gaining acceptance by adopting the tradition of the Other, when he argues that as an *American* slave, literacy is his tradition, one he is denied access to by law and one he must illegally seize. The distinct endings of the two works underscore the difference in the way the figure of literacy is used. Whereas Equiano closes his narrative with a standard apologia, "I am far from the vanity of thinking there is any merit in this narrative," and hopes the reader will learn "to do justly, to love mercy, and to walk humbly before God" (Equiano, 1789, pp. 158–159), Douglass closes his with an appendix that shows his work's primary aim to be an indictment of slavery: "Sincerely and earnestly hoping that this little book may do something toward throwing light on the American slave system, and hastening the glad day of deliverance to the millions of my brethren in bonds...I subscribe myself, Frederick Douglass" (Douglass, 1845, p. 127). His narrative is more than the adventurous incidents of his life in which literacy represents the transition from one culture into another; his is an allegorical narrative in which each event in his life becomes a consciously crafted representation critiquing slavery's inhumanity. A crucial element in that allegory is the image of literacy.

In the sixth chapter of his narrative, Douglass describes his first encounter with the power of literacy. He details a scene in which his master, Mr. Auld, discovers his wife, Mrs. Auld, teaching Douglass to read, and he relates Auld's response in the following manner: "If you teach that nigger (speaking of myself) how to read, there would be no keeping him. It would forever unfit him to be a slave" (Douglass, 1845, p. 47). Auld's words engender a new cognizance in Douglass, who concludes, "I now understood what had been to me a most perplexing difficulty—to wit, the white man's power to enslave the black man.... From that moment, I understood the pathway from slavery to freedom" (Douglass, 1845, p. 47). The parenthetical addition, "speaking of myself," reveals Douglass's conception of his identity being distinct from that of a "nigger." His discovery of literacy's omnipotence actualizes this conception and assists him in crafting a social self in keeping with his personal vision. Realizing that the ability to express rational thoughts through reading and writing is denied slaves by masters wishing to dehumanize them, Douglass casts literacy as a subversion designed to undermine a morally corrupt social system. He learns to read surreptitiously, by bribing white boys into teaching him, and learns to write in an equally subversive manner by falsely boasting of his capacity to do so. In each scene where he describes the process of acquiring literacy, he makes clear his sense of appropriation, of secretly stealing something that belongs to the foe but by all rights should also be his.

Douglass's new capacity to read and write affords him access to abolitionist texts which give him the inspiration to author a new self. In a telling scene relating his discovery of *The Columbian Orator* and the antislavery sentiments within it, he reveals the manner in which writing can confer identity:

> Every opportunity I got, I used to read this book. Among much of other interesting matter, I found in it a dialogue between a master and his slave. The slave was *represented* as having run away from his master three times. The dialogue *represented* the conversation which took place between them, when the slave was retaken the third time. . . .The slave *was made to say* some very smart as well as impressive things in reply to his master—things which had the desired though unexpected effect. . .the voluntary emancipation of the slave on the part of the master. (Douglass, 1845, p. 52)

I have italicized Douglass's verb choices, "represented" and "was made to say," to show his awareness of literacy crafting a particular identity, in this case that of an enslaved cognitive human capable of arguing against slavery, not a nonthinking brute deserving of chattel status. This scene might serve as a mini-allegory for Douglass's conception of literacy, enabling the authorship of a new African American self existing outside of slavery.

As he proceeds in his narrative Douglass continues to signify his psychic state through allusions to literacy: "As I read and contemplated the subject, behold! that very discontentment which Master Hugh had predicted would follow my learning to read had already come, to torment and sting my soul to unutterable anguish. As I writhed under it, I would at times feel that learning to read had been a curse rather than a blessing" (Douglass, 1845, p. 53). This statement is a remarkable illustration of the many double meanings Douglass hides in a narrative written to what he knows is at best a sympathetic abolitionist audience, or at worst an impassible slaveholding audience. It is not the intent of this statement to describe the professed pain fostered by a literacy-engendered knowledge, but rather the danger posed by literacy's power to create the discontent that leads to subversive practices. Douglass is not bemoaning his fate; he is describing the frustration that will serve as an impetus to move him from the acquisition of literacy to its use. His narrative later depicts his forging a pass in an attempt to secure escape for himself and other slaves; his establishing a Sabbath school which subversively spreads the dangerous knowledge of literacy to other slaves; and though we are not told of this in the 1845 edition, his creating *The North Star,* a newspaper "devoted to the cause of Liberty, Humanity and Progress."

In Douglass's narrative, access to literacy becomes a symbol of freedom and equality and a means of attaining both. Reading and writing allow him to counter the denial of his humanity, to actualize his plight by reading of it in other literatures, and to evaluate critically the meaning of texts such as the Bible, a text for the most part used to encourage submission among slaves. In another vein, literacy also allows Douglass to *write down* his history, and thus become part of a literacy-centric culture. Douglass's experience illustrates the importance of literary production to authors who are marginalized within their own society. By gaining access to the written word, he and they gain a permanent place in American society by producing documents that subsequently become part of the American canon. Thus their works are both acts of creation and acts of enfranchisement.

As we think of the many ways the impact of literacy is represented in literature, we must also consider that not all manifestations are as overtly political as Douglass's. A more intimate motif of literacy can be found in slave narratives written by women who revise this figure to address female experience. The narrative of Harriet Jacobs is an example. Just as Douglass uses the figure of literacy to explore issues of social justice, so too does Jacobs; but her explorations are more gender-specific. The very act of producing an autobiography is different for Jacobs than for Douglass or Equiano precisely because she is a woman. Engaged as a nurse and housekeeper during the day, she can write only at night, and in a letter to Amy Post voices the difficulty in balancing her duties with her desire to write: "Patience. Perhaps it will not be always thus. I have kept Louisa [her daughter] here this winter so that I might have my evenings to write, but poor Hatty [Harriet] name is [*sic*] so much in demand that I cannot accomplish much. If I could steal away and have two quiet months to myself I would work night and day" (Jacobs, 1854, p. 80). Jacobs's identity as both a slave and a woman influences the figure of literacy in her text, *Incidents in the Life of a Slave Girl* (1861). The aim of her narrative is to feminize the experience of slavery, and her treatment of literacy within this context is feminized as well.

Jacobs brings the figure of literacy into the cult of domesticity so prevalent in nineteenth-century literature. In her study of women's novels, Nina Baym thoroughly outlines the conventions of what she terms "woman's fiction," and that most all are present in Jacobs's narrative—among them the pairing of antagonistic heroines, abuses of power, the abandonment of the heroine, and most importantly, the hope of secure "domesticity" (1980, pp. 11–50). Incorporating these conventions into her own life story, Jacobs exalts the security of the family and critiques the powerlessness of slaves to enjoy such security. Within this framework she frequently represents literacy as a device able to maintain secure and loving family ties and to eradicate the commodification of women. It is this representation that distinguishes her work from that of her male counterparts, Equiano and Douglass. Where Equiano's literacy motif emphasized the transition from one culture to another, and where Douglass's emphasized the transition from political impotency to empowerment, Jacobs's stresses the empowerment that comes from a secure family and domestic situation.

Writing under the pseudonym Linda Brent, Jacobs recounts a history of sexual exploitation at the hands of her master, Dr. Flint.[2] It is while Flint's property that she first learns to write, describing the scene in the following manner:

> One day he caught me teaching myself to write. He frowned, as if he were not well pleased; but I suppose he came to the conclusion that such an accomplishment might help to advance his favorite scheme. Before long, notes were often slipped into my hand. I would return them, saying, "can't read them, sir." "Can't you?" he replied; "then I must read them to you." (Jacobs, 1861, p. 30)

Jacobs's joining of literacy to sexual exploitation is an effective means of allowing literacy to condemn not only slavery but also sexist oppression. In *Incidents*, however, literacy is cast most frequently as a device to maintain familial unity.

Jacobs's narrative chronicles the passing of love letters and their interception by malevolent masters; it recounts the passing of letters that keeps family members abreast of the movements of others as they are bought, sold, or escape into freedom; and it describes the constant vigil of reading the Northern newspapers for notices of arrivals that might signal the advent of a master coming to retrieve a fugitive slave. In each instance the power of literacy to sustain family bonds and provide access to freedom is evident. Ultimately, the strategic passage of letters assists in Jacobs's escape and the reunification of her family. Though Jacobs also details the importance of literacy to psychic liberty, saying "There are thousands, who. . .are thirsting for the water of life;

but the law forbids it, and the churches withhold it" (Jacobs, 1861, p. 75), for the most part her images of literacy involve intimate portrayals of its importance to familial continuity.

The feminized literacy found in *Incidents* repeats itself in modern fictional texts which address the importance of literacy to female self-determination, as is movingly illustrated in Alice Walker's *The Color Purple* (1982). The epistolary form of this novel itself calls attention to the act of writing by using letters to construct a tale, and here, as if drawing on a female African American literary legacy, Walker repeats *Incidents*'s treatment of literacy as a figure empowered to maintain severed family links while giving voice to women's subjugation. For both Celie and Nettie, the sisters whose exchange of letters makes up the novel, literacy equals familial survival and spiritual freedom. They are separated early in the novel, and their parting words contain a reference to literacy:

> She say, What?
> I say, Write.
> She say, Nothin but death can keep me from it.
> (Walker, 1982, p. 26)

Their vow to write constitutes the only link joining them, but their letters are intercepted by the malice of Celie's husband, Albert. It is only with her friend and lover Shug's help that Celie discovers Nettie's letters detailing their family history, and through that discovery finds the conviction that ultimately liberates her from the tyranny of Albert.

Both sisters believe that neither receives the other's letters; as a result, both transform literacy into a vehicle for personal autonomy. Early in the novel the liberating image of literacy is evident as Celie writes of herself and her sister, "Us both be hitting Nettie's schoolbooks pretty hard, cause us know we got to be smart to git away" (Walker, 1982, p. 19); later she adds, "All day she read, she study, she practice her handwriting, and try to get us to think" (p. 25). These two statements are illustrative of the equation Walker makes between literacy and intellectual freedom and for Nettie, at least, actual freedom from an oppressive environment where men subject women to physical, sexual, and psychological abuse.

The image of literacy as a catalyst for freedom is paralleled by its image as a mode of articulating female suffering. For Celie, the ability to read and write constitutes the creation of a voice that counters the muting imposed upon her. By writing her pain she frees herself of it.

In an analogous sense Nettie effects a spiritual articulation through literacy. In one of her early letters she writes, "I remember one time you said your life made you feel so ashamed you couldn't even talk about it to God, you had to write it....Well, now I know what you meant...when I don't write to you I feel as bad as I do when I don't pray" (Walker, 1982, p. 122). In these and other instances, literacy is more than a means of communication; it is a key to the emotional survival of women within a society that discounts their value.

Walker also uses the figure of literacy to render the imposition of one culture on another that has been effected through the manipulation of written records. In one of her letters to Celie, Nettie describes the use of the Bible to distort cultural history: "All the Ethiopians in the bible were colored. It had never occurred to me, though when you read the bible it is perfectly plain if you pay attention only to the words. It is the pictures in the bible that fool you....All of the people are white and so you just think all the people from the bible were white, too" (Walker, 1982, p. 125). This theme of distortion is complemented by passages portraying the capacity of writing to preserve culture. In a subsequent letter relating the oral traditions joining Africans and African Americans, Nettie depicts the necessity of oral cultures utilizing literacy for their own self-preservation in an increasingly literacy-centric world:

> Sometimes Tashi comes over and tells stories that are popular among the Olinka children. I am encouraging her and Olivia to write them down in Olinka and English....Olivia feels that, compared to Tashi, she has no good stories to tell. One day she started in on an "Uncle Remus" tale only to discover Tashi had the original version of it! Her little face just fell. But then we got into a discussion of how Tashi's people's stories got to America, which fascinated Tashi. She cried when Olivia told of how her grandmother had been treated as a slave. (Walker, 1982, p. 152)

As well as illustrating the cultural links between the tales produced in Africa and Black America, the above quotation also shows the passing on of family history through the experience of Olivia's grandmother. The implication here is, that as societies become increasingly literate, familial as well as cultural elements are lost unless placed in a written record.

The ultimate fate of the Olinkas, the passing of their culture, so poignantly detailed in Nettie's correspondence, is one shared by many oral cultures as they face extinction or face being encased in what becomes a shrine of literacy. A text which approaches this question from the experience of another marginalized American group is Leslie Marmon Silko's *Storyteller* (1981). Perhaps *Storyteller* can best be described as a collage of prose, poems, photos, and reminiscences that give written form to the oral tales that inspire it; however, while the collection uses writing to glorify the oral tradition of Native Americans, it tellingly reveals the role of literacy in endangering this culture. *Storyteller* opens with an untitled prelude that reveals the tenuous balance between literacy and orality that must be achieved by any oral culture seeking to survive within a society dominated by writing. By depicting the "european intrusion" (Silko, 1981, p. 6) that takes Laguna children away from their storytellers and places them in Indian schools, Silko's opening sets the stage for subsequent segments which explore a variety of cultural losses, some which use literacy as a metaphor representing the domination of one people by another.

The tale "Lullaby" tells of Ayah who, confused by the bureaucratic language of an official and unable to read the papers she is requested to sign, relinquishes rights to her ill children who are taken to a boarding school run by the Bureau of Indian Affairs.[3] Her confusion and anguish are described in terms laced with references to literacy:

> They were wearing khaki uniforms and they waved papers at her and a black ballpoint pen, trying to make her understand their English words. She was frightened by the way they looked at the children, like the lizard watches the fly.... Ayah could see they wanted her to sign her name. It was something she was proud of. She only wanted them to go, and to take their eyes away from her children.
>
> She took the pen from the man without looking at his face and she signed the papers in three different places he pointed to. (Silko, 1981, p. 45)

Ayah is proud of her ability to sign her name because it represents her facility to navigate, however minimally, within another culture. But when her children are removed from her world, no longer speak her language, and no longer recognize her as their mother, she, impotent to lay blame elsewhere, blames her husband for teaching her to write: "She hated Chato, not because he let the policemen and doctors put the screaming children in the government car, but because he had taught her to sign her name. Because it was like the old ones always told her about learning their language or any of their ways: it endangered you" (Silko, 1981, p. 47). What Silko's figure of literacy suggests is that limited literacy, imposed literacy, or literacy accorded without accompanying social equality becomes a malevolent literacy, useful only for disintegrating cultures that are not literacy-centric.

In contrast to Silko, who uses literacy to explore one culture's treatment of another, Maxine Hong Kingston uses reading and writing to explore the intimate construction of the self as it straddles two cultures. Unlike the writers discussed previously, Kingston does not contrast literacy to orality, and there is no transition from orality to literacy. She comes from a literacy-centric world, and for her literacy is the norm. Her work portrays how a lack of voice can be perpetuated even when literacy has been acquired. The total absence of representative elements of her culture in the dominant culture imposes a status of invisibility on her in spite of her being literate. In her memoirs *The Woman Warrior* (1975), references to reading and writing are casually filtered through many of her recollections, as is the case in her recalling the details of her mother's medical schooling: "At the dormitory the school official assigned her to a room with five other women, who were unpacking when she came in. . . . [S]he took out her pens and inkbox, an atlas of the world, a tea set and a tea canister, sewing box, her ruler with the real gold markings, writing paper, envelopes with the thick red stripe to signify no bad news, her bowl and silver chopsticks" (Kingston, 1975, p. 62). In this description, the tools of literacy—pens, inks, and papers—are placed equally with other items of day-to-day living and learning and are not given any special reverence. Kingston continues,

> The women who had arrived early did not offer to help unpack, not wanting to interfere with the pleasure and the privacy of it. Not many women got to live out the daydream of women— to have a room, even a section of a room, that only gets messed up when she messes it up herself. The book would stay open at the very page she had pressed flat with her hand. . . .
>
> To shut the door at the end of the workday, which does not spill over into evening. To throw away books after reading them so they don't have to be dusted. (Kingston, 1975, p. 62)

The final image of throwing away books is a compelling one. Within this literate world, books become an encumbrance for women. After providing their knowledge they remain as domestic objects reinforcing women's roles as housekeepers and little else. This is certainly a different vision from the liberating literacy found in Jacobs's *Incidents* or Walker's *The Color Purple*. What Kingston does share with these two authors, however, is an appreciation of the luxury that exercising literacy becomes in woman's experience, as is shown through this community of women respecting the right of another woman to unpack and move into her private space, her "room of her own."

Another significant representation of literacy emerges in *The Woman Warrior*, and that is literacy as a clash of letters and characters indicative of the larger clashes in cultural identification throughout the text. Recalling her experiences at school, Kingston makes the following reference to literacy:

> It was when I found out I had to talk that school became a misery, that the silence became a misery. . . .
>
> Reading aloud was easier than speaking because we did not have to make up what to say, but I stopped often, and the teacher would think I'd gone quiet again. I could not understand "I." The Chinese "I" has seven strokes, intricacies. How could the American "I," assuredly wearing a hat like the Chinese, have only three strokes, the middle so straight? Was it out of politeness that this writer left off strokes the way a Chinese has to write her own name small and crooked? (Kingston, 1975, pp. 166–167)

By juxtaposing two forms of literacy, writing and ideographs, Kingston clearly shows the relationship between literacy and cultural dominance. The American *I* is imposing; it accords itself uppercase status while according lowercase to the *you* that is different from it. The American *here* is a region of flatness Kingston finds difficult to traverse after becoming acclimated to the inclines of the same idea in characters. Ultimately, it is not the inability to read and write that endangers her conception of self and makes finding place in American society difficult, but the inability to see the self, to see its place in the symbols of literacy that belong to dominant culture. Again we see that literacy without social acceptance amounts to a cultural erasure, and in Kingston's work it represents an experience of isolation, a loss of the self shown through an inability to understand the *I* and *here* in English as in Chinese.

From Equiano to Kingston, the figures of literacy present in these works are all examples of how the act of reading and writing can be transformed into a metaphor for social voice and place. Moreover, these treatments remind us how important the notion of inclusion is to an author writing within a society and to students learning within it. That literacy is so central to the works of authors from traditionally marginalized groups attests to the power of reading and writing within a literacy-centric culture that increasingly uses the term *literacy* in a variety of contexts, from cultural literacy to mathematical literacy, connoting a variety of concepts from erudition to privilege. In each context, however, what emerges as a subtext of meaning is the assumption of access and denial. What, for example, is meant by *cultural literacy*, and how can it be defined in an increasingly diverse American community? How does a literate society view cultures rooted in traditions of orality? How does literacy preserve or eradicate elements of race and ethnicity?

Ultimately, values defining what constitutes literacy in its many forms cannot be determined without considering how traditions outside the group that define a particular literacy have been valued at different points in American history. As we teach certain texts while allowing others to remain on the margins, we perpetuate the silencing that many American authors have employed literacy to lift. The experience presented in the foregoing texts reminds us that there is a fundamental equation of literacy to the conception of a liberated self and, by extension, a fundamental equation of an inclusive approach to literature to a responsible vision of a multicultural community. The silencing imposed on these authors is a silencing repeated in the larger society and fostered by any curriculum that does not accurately represent the mosaic of American culture. The adoption of multicultural pedagogies, then, does not mean integrating "minority" texts into the "majority" canon, but rather underscoring the equal and integral relationships shared by all works produced in a pluralistic society.

Notes

1. In *The Signifying Monkey* (New York: Oxford, 1989) Henry Louis Gates, Jr., gives an interesting exploration of the intertextual links created by this symbol.

2. In *Reconstructing Womanhood* (New York: Oxford, 1987) Hazel Carby provides an illuminating analysis of the tenuous position of a nineteenth-century Black woman writer and relates this to Jacobs's need to adopt a pseudonym.

3. In describing the effects of boarding schools on Native American cultures, Leonard Dinnerstein et. al. conclude the following:

Beginning in 1970, the government earmarked funds specifically for Indian education, and reservation and boarding schools competed for money and the chance to "civilize" their charges. From the late 1890s to the 1930s thousands of Indian children were legally kidnaped and forced to attend school far from home. When their parents could not pay for their transportation home during vacations, the youngsters remained at school. The government curriculum, designed to eradicate all signs of Indianness, made no concession to the children's cultures. As a general policy the school's staff cut off the boys' long hair, punished children for speaking their native languages, and replaced their clothes with ill-fitting hand-me-downs (to prohibit the children from holding tribal dances or ceremonies). Bureau of Indian Affairs' employees cooperated with zealous Christian missionaries to prohibit [what] they considered pagan rites that had to be abolished (*Natives and Strangers: Blacks, Indians, and Immigrants in America* [New York: Oxford University Press, 1990], p. 232).

References

Baym, N. (1980). *Woman's fiction: A guide to novels by and about women in America, 1820–1970.* Ithaca, NY: Cornell University Press.

Douglass, F. (1845). *The narrative of the life of Frederick Douglass, an American slave.* New York: Modern Library, 1984.

Equiano, O. (1789). *The interesting narrative of the life of Olaudah Equiano, or Gustavus Vassa, the African. Written by himself.* London: Dawsons of Pall Mall, 1969.

Jacobs, H. (1854). Letter to Amy Post, 11 January 1854. Quoted in Dorothy Sterling (Ed.), *We are your sisters* (New York: Norton, 1984), p. 80.

Jacobs, H. (1861). *Incidents in the life of a slave girl.* New York: Harcourt, Brace, 1973.

Kingston, M. (1975). *The woman warrior: Memoirs of a girlhood among ghosts.* New York: Vintage.

Levi-Strauss, C. (1973). *Tristes tropiques.* (John and Doreen Weightman, Trans.). New York: Atheneum.

Silko, L. M. (1981). *Storyteller.* New York: Arcade-Little, Brown.

Walker, A. (1982). *The color purple.* New York: Washington Square Press.

3

Literacy, Literature, and the Liberation of the American Bluesvilles: (On Writing Our World into Being)

Reggie Young

I am invisible...simply because people refuse to see me.

—Ralph Ellison, *Invisible Man*

I have not written about being a Negro at such length because I expected that to be my only subject, but only because it was the gate I had to unlock before I could hope to write about anything else.

—James Baldwin, *Notes of a Native Son*

You ain't nobody unless somebody's done written your name down somewhere.

—Great Aunt Nannie Watkins

After typing parts of the novel I wrote for my dissertation, Dorothy, a secretary employed by another department at the university who offered to help me out, expressed her interest concerning the nature of the work. She said that she did not have much experience reading literature, except for what she had to read as a student in high school. She admitted that she was not sure she really understood much of what she had encountered in my manuscript. She smiled, however, as she handed me a pile of pages she had just typed onto a disk and said, "After reading your book, people will at least know we exist."

The novel I wrote, *Crimes in Bluesville* (1990), is set in the Chicago West Side community where I grew up and where Dorothy used to

live. Since she knew that the finished dissertation would be available
to the public through the library, for Dorothy the completion of the
thesis and its approval by the university was as significant as if the book
were about to be published by a major publishing house. It was one
of the few times she had read about the West Side anywhere, except
for the depressing stories about the area's crime and poverty which often
were run in the local media, and it was the first time she had ever heard
of stories and poems about that part of Chicago (the novel contains
a volume of poems from the perspective of the protagonist). Her
enthusiasm stemmed from her belief that my novel would help put the
West Side on the map, which might stop others—especially those from
Chicago's South Side—from having such condescending attitudes
toward the people who live in that part of the city. She also stressed
how it would greatly encourage the young people growing up there
to have an appreciation for books since "they'll have something to read
from their own world for once, seeing how difficult it is to understand
everyone else's when you don't have a basis for understanding your
own."

A few years ago, after reading Dempsey Travis's *An Autobiography
of Black Chicago* (1981), a book which, for the most part, excluded my
particular part of *black* Chicago (as most works on the African American
experience in Chicago have done), I felt a need—a calling to be more
precise—to write about the *other* African American community in
Chicago. Because of the historical value of literacy within the African
American community, one that has traditionally equated social status
with culture—as in *being cultured* (Frazier, 1957)—I realized that it was
of extreme importance for African Americans to have their stories told
in the printed word, and that even the mention of their names in print
is of tremendous significance. But Chicago's West Side, the place where
I grew up and which claims me as one of its own, had seldom found
its name in print, and, at that point, had never had its own text (in
the Western sense of the *printed* text). That was the nature of my calling,
one which led me into the graduate program in creative writing in the
English Department at the University of Illinois at Chicago (UIC).

After several years of studying the important writers of the Western
world, which, according to the department's curriculum, included less
than a handful of writers of color, and after completing all of the
required classes in my specialization of creative writing, I began to read
as many works by African American writers as I could find the time
to do (the English faculty had no African American professors, and
offered no courses in African American literature until after I left, except
for one I taught myself). Influenced by some of these works, as well

as by the works I had read for my classes, the novel I eventually wrote for my thesis turned out to be a quasi-slave narrative, of all things, set in the urban North of the 1960s.

One of my committee members, a scholar of romanticism who was also the person in the department most deeply involved with the literature of American minorities, recognized what I had done before I did and called it to my attention. At first, I interpreted her comments to mean that she was not pleased with what I had written, but she assured me that wasn't the case at all. After all, she reminded me, she was the one who insisted I read Frederick Douglass's narratives, something I hadn't done since high school, more than a decade before; she also encouraged me to read as many other slave narratives as I could. What I discovered in my readings over and over again was the relationship between literacy and liberation in the African American experience, and, while writing the novel, I realized that it is a relationship that is as important for African Americans today as it was before emancipation. My research led me to see that from the beginning of the slave trade the theology of liberation for the African American has been a struggle for literacy.

The relationship *Crimes in Bluesville* shares with the slave narratives is its exploration of the conditions of a people in bondage through the narrative of one who escapes to give voice to their story in the outside world. J. P. Bailey (June Bug), the novel's protagonist, like many of his peers, finds himself in bondage through an addiction to alcohol (virtually all of the youths in his community are addicted to alcohol or drugs). But it is not the booze and drugs which keep J. P. and his peers enslaved; their addictions only serve to disguise the true conditions of their slavery, and to blind them from seeing their only true means of escape. Bailey does, eventually, overcome his bondage; in doing so, he creates the text of his escape. Like most fugitive slave writers, he is the author of his own story, and he uses his literary skills to write his own pass to the outside world—a letter of admission to a university.

The inhabitants of Chicago's Bluesville are families who migrated to cities in the North after World War II, over a quarter of a century after the "great migration" of African Americans who left the South and moved to northern cities such as Chicago. By World War II, the communities made up of these earlier migrants had fully acculturated themselves to the ways of the North, and their inhabitants, for the most part, had become northern people; at least they considered themselves as such. The African Americans who left the South after World War II, however, found themselves merely moving "up south," to borrow a term from a poem by Don L. Lee (now known as Haki Madhubuti; 1970), because the cities of the North, especially their already established black communities, were reluctant to open their arms to their newest inhabitants to help aid them in their process of adjusting to urban life (it is important to note, however, that there are pockets of bluesville-type communities on Chicago's South Side). This is not to say, however, that the African American migrants of the earlier periods had it any better; it merely means that they have had several decades to acclimate themselves to life in the North. As a result, the new northern urban black communities turned into southern rural communities in northern urban settings. They soon became enclosed, isolated, self-containing settlements because virtually no one bothered coming into them from the outside, and few from within had access to the world beyond their physical and cultural boundaries.

Many of the families who moved "up south" after World War II and settled into what I call the "bluesvilles" of the North were headed by the sons and daughters of sharecroppers: they were men and women whose grandparents were born into slavery. But even after the Emancipation Proclamation ended the practice of legal slavery in the South, it did little to eliminate the cultural conditions caused by slavery that the freed slaves and their children faced in their everyday lives. The factors which led to the conversion of various African peoples into slaves were related not only to the work conditions they faced, the hours they spent in the fields, and other aspects of their physical circumstances, as some may think. The factor which most heavily contributed to the process of turning Africans into slaves were the efforts made to deny to them their status as their own beings. Africans knew, without doubt, that they were human before they were captured by whites and taken away from their lands of origin—there had never been reason to question their humanity before European contact—but after they were taken away from their own cultures, they found their very humanity had been drastically reduced by their captors, who relegated them to the ranks of contraband. The Africans captured into slavery became mere property owned by others who could buy and sell them as they pleased.

In his introduction to *"Race," Writing, and Difference,* Henry Louis Gates, Jr. (1986), examines the manner in which European intellectuals used the African's lack of education in Western letters as a means of justifying slavery. For one to be truly human, they claimed, one had to demonstrate the ability to reason, and for one to demonstrate the ability to reason, one had to offer discourse in the form of written letters.

Of course, enslaved Africans had little or no familiarity with the various Western modes of written discourse, having been taken from oral cultures where the spoken word was valued over all other forms of communication. Even so, it did not take long for various Africans to master English and other European languages, read the Western texts, and then compose their own.

Despite the various literary achievements of such individuals as Phillis Wheatley, Jupiter Hammon, John Marrant, Ottobah Cugoano, Olaudah Equiano, and others, questions about the human status of the people from Africa were still raised as a defense against attacks on slavery. When enslaved Africans first showed evidence of their ability to master the reading of Western texts, critics claimed it to be of little consequence since they could not write, meaning they lacked the facilities to reason. When they demonstrated the ability to reason in written discourse, that was also argued to be of hardly any significance since they could not write poetry. When Africans began to write poetry, many philosophers, statesmen, politicians, and representatives of other disciplines, such as Thomas Jefferson, suddenly took on the responsibility of serving as literary analysts and debated the literary values of their poetic works (Gates, *Figures in Black*, 1987). As soon as new challenges were raised concerning Africans' intellectual abilities, someone always stepped forth to answer them. Those who argued against the intellectual potential of the peoples taken from Africa, however, continued the tradition of creating myths disputing the African's capacity for intellect.

In order to remove all doubt concerning their status as human beings, the Africans stolen from their homelands were required to read and write as well as the leading Western scholars, the very ones standing in judgment against them, but were not allowed similar instruction or privileges, such as leisure time, to devote to the study of letters. In fact, in the antebellum South, laws were passed making educational instruction of enslaved Africans illegal. By totally denying slaves this right to learn to read and write, the proslavery factions found it easier to substantiate myths of their own invention regarding the intellectual deficiencies of the Africans held in bondage; they used the inability of most slaves to read and write as a major argument against granting them full human status.

Finding themselves denied access to education did not discourage enslaved blacks in the South, nor free blacks in the North, from seeking literacy; in fact, this exclusion encouraged it. As Thomas Holt has stated, "By the extraordinary efforts they made to keep blacks from learning, slave owners inadvertently acknowledged that learning was a powerful force in the world" (1990, p. 93). For the African slave and nonslave in the United States, education became the key to enlightenment, and enlightenment the key to freedom. Immediately after the Civil War ended, freedmen and freedwomen throughout the South organized schools in an effort to elevate their families, knowing that although they were supposed to be free, they would never be full citizens—fully realized beings—without education (Holt, 1990).

Long before Emancipation, slaves established a tradition of self-help education, which continued through the Reconstruction and post-Reconstruction periods. The ones who had somehow learned to read and write, even to a limited degree, shared what they knew with others in what Holt describes as "a chain of instruction" (1990, p. 94). This tradition of self-help was especially important in the post-Reconstruction period because African American disenfranchisement at this time eliminated many of the educational opportunities former slaves and their families received from state governments during the short period of change after the war. Furthermore, as Holt writes, in the post-Reconstruction period, whites from both the North and South found it in their economic interest to support an educational system for African Americans which would prepare them for lives as unskilled laborers in the southern labor system and nothing else (Holt, 1990). As a result, the former slaves and their children once again found themselves faced with inequitable human status due to barriers imposed to deny them access to education. When faced with a system that undermined all that they had previously believed education stood for—"that is to uplift, not keep down; to change things for the better, not to maintain the status quo; to educate for empowerment, not subordination" (Holt, 1990, p. 98)—the former African slaves, in many instances, built their own schools.

The black population shift from the South to the North which began in the later part of the nineteenth century and continued beyond World War I had a profound effect on African American attitudes toward education. Although many of the people who moved to the North were attracted by the hopes of a never-to-be-realized prosperity in the labor markets, the educational opportunities awaiting their children in free public schools was also an important factor in their relocation (Spear, 1967; Tuttle, 1970). In the black communities of cities such as Chicago, however, the enthusiasm for education was soon dampened because the quality of education received was not much better than what had been left behind in the southern school systems: the most important difference was that a larger percentage of the school-age population had the opportunity to go (Holt, 1990). In integrated schools, African

American students often found themselves placed in classes called "subnormal rooms" and classified as "mentally deficient" (Holt, 1990), simply because they were different; their southern speech and manners were frowned upon by school officials, who looked upon them as if they were backwards (Spear, 1967). When all-black communities began stretching out through the South Side into what eventually became known as the "Black Belt" (Drake & Clayton, 1970, p. 47), the racial makeup of the schools in those areas changed to reflect the neighborhoods. These schools, dominated by white principals, administrators, and teaching staffs, only provided a type of education which prepared students for little more than careers as menial laborers (Spear, 1967; Holt, 1990).

In *Frye Street and Environs* (1987), a collection of stories, many written and set in Chicago in the late 1920s and 1930s, Marita Bonner presents several interesting sketches of African American life in the emerging Black Belt. Although Bonner herself was a college graduate (Radcliffe) and served as a teacher in Washington, D.C., for eight years, for several of her characters an education in the Chicago school system was not considered a viable option for improving their lives. In Richard Wright's *Native Son* (1940), also set in Chicago's Black Belt, Bigger Thomas's first significant educational experience did not take place until after he found himself behind bars and on trial for murder.

However, despite the many discouragements they faced, African Americans in the North did continue the struggle for education that began when their ancestors were first taken into slavery and denied their status as human beings. The self-help tradition that had been established in the South was adapted for use in the ever-increasing all-black communities such as Chicago's Black Belt, where visible "Negro" elites developed, along with a class system which mirrored that of the dominant culture's. Even before the Great Depression, African Americans in Chicago and other northern cities began the process of developing institutions of every variety, including banks, insurance companies, newspapers, and other businesses, churches of every size and denomination, and even hospitals such as the black-owned and -operated Provident on Chicago's South Side (Spear, 1967).

The thrust of much of this institution building came from two distinct groups of men and women who formed the upper echelon of the Black Belt's social structure. Many of them came from families which had been free, educated, and already residing in the North before the waves of migrants from the South poured into the city; at one time, this elite made up the core of the city's domestic workers. Some of the city's early African American settlers had been escaped slaves, whereas others had never known slavery. Before finding themselves forced to live in segregated black neighborhoods, they lived in the white upper- and middle-class sections of the city where they worked, and where they often sent their children to the same schools their employers' children attended. Their presence was important in helping the fledgling Black Belt community develop a social, economic, and political structure not altogether unlike that of the larger city; in fact, many in the Black Belt considered it to be a city within the city (Spear, 1967; Tuttle, 1970).

Others who eventually assumed roles of importance within the Black Belt were migrants who were able to make quick fortunes through legal and extra-legal activities, ranging from running cosmetic businesses to the policy racket. Having a group of aristocratic-acting African American role models allowed the migrants who ascended to positions of importance within the community to emulate their social mores and behavior, and influenced many of those who became wealthy through shady means to clean up their affairs and become involved in more respectable activities (Spear, 1967; Tuttle, 1970). Therefore, in any comparison of the development of Bronzeville (see below) and Bluesville, the importance of Bronzeville having an already established "Negro elite" in its midst is something that cannot be overlooked. Because of the mass influx of migrants from the South, Bronzeville's elites found themselves with a significant consumer base which helped stimulate the development and growth of both businesses and institutions within the forming Black Belt (Spear, 1967).

An important event occurred in Chicago when the African American community gave itself a name—Bronzeville—and began holding annual elections for its own symbolic mayor (Drake & Clayton, 1970). Naming itself was an important act for Chicago's South Side because it showed the world that black Chicagoans were fully realized beings in their own right. Although not all of its citizens were fully literate (most, if nothing else, were functional enough to read the black newspapers, the Bible, and the daily numbers slips), as a community it had established its own cultural values for its citizens to adhere to: for one to be a functional Bronzeville resident, one had only to master the culture of Bronzeville and not a culture defined by the outside world. It mattered not if citizens of Bronzeville did not know the news of the day as reported in the *Tribune* or the *New York Times* because the *Chicago Defender* and the other African American newspapers carried everything Bronzeville residents needed or wanted to know, written in a manner that they best understood. No one cared about what musicians were performing downtown when all one had to do was read the black press to see that Louis Armstrong or another jazz great was appearing at the Regal Theater, which was located in the Bronzeville community. The scores of Cubs and White Sox games mattered little since the black press followed the teams of the Negro Baseball Leagues. In Bronzeville, even the politics of the city, state, and national governments took a backseat to the political races *within* the Black Belt; because of the influence of the black press, Bronzeville sent its own congressman to Washington as early as 1928, the first elected from a northern district, and it also elected its own aldermen, committeemen, and state legislators (Drake & Clayton, 1970).

Maybe Wright's *Native Son* (1940) did show how vulnerable a Bronzeville resident could be when forced to function in the outside world, but his novel was highly sensationalized, and Bigger Thomas, as a protagonist, was not truly representative of the average South Sider, just as Wright himself was not indigenous to Bronzeville. Nevertheless, his book, along with the poetry published by Gwendolyn Brooks, Lorraine Hansberry's critically acclaimed play *A Raisin in the Sun* (1959), and numerous other literary works by Bronzeville residents which used Chicago's South Side as a setting, gave the people living there a greater sense of pride of life and a greater sense of being. Bronzeville's tradition of achievement and community pride ultimately helped it to elect one of its own, Harold Washington, as mayor of the entire city.

On the other hand, communities such as Chicago's Bluesville are largely made up of people whose families did not leave the South, for various reasons, during the earlier migratory movements. Small pockets of African Americans lived in that part of the city, mostly on the *near* West Side, as early as World War I. They settled there because they could not afford to live in the Black Belt, where housing and the other necessities of life were much more expensive (Drake & Clayton, 1970). Of the droves of people who began to settle there during World War II, most came from the states which border the Mississippi River— Mississippi, Louisiana, Arkansas, Missouri, Tennessee, and Kentucky— with the vast majority of them coming from Mississippi. Most of these migrants were from rural areas and had little, if any, previous experience living in cities. Those who did come from southern urban areas such as Little Rock, Memphis, Louisville, and St. Louis, as well as those from other areas who owned their own businesses and property, were generally better educated than the typical migrant, and came with cash already in their pockets. They most often settled on the South Side, where housing and living conditions were better, or moved there after living on the West Side for short periods of time (Drake & Clayton, 1970).

Many of the new migrants, who were forced to settle on the West Side because of its cheaper and more available housing, had worked under the system of sharecropping in the South, which indicated that their parents and grandparents before them might not have possessed the means to leave the South sooner. The system of indentured servitude they had lived under prevented children who were physically able to work to attend schools for much of the year. As a result, large numbers of the new West Side residents were barely literate. Since they did leave the South soon after the system of sharecropping weakened, it is doubtful, as some have argued, that they remained there during earlier migrations in order to keep their roots intact, or out of loyalty to their southern ways of life. A more decisive factor was the cost involved in moving one's family across the country; it is possible that in earlier years, with no guarantees of housing and employment, they simply could not afford to go (Drake & Clayton, 1970). But lured by the many stories about African American life in the North, especially the big-city success stories of former black migrants, and drawn by labor shortages caused by the war abroad, large numbers were influenced to pack their belongings and head north (Drake & Clayton, 1970).

The African Americans who moved to Chicago in the later migration settled in the racially changing areas of the West Side, a section of the city that evolved from virtually all white and Jewish to African American in less than a decade. Not only were the migrants not acclimated to the ways of the North and living in large cities, but they found that they were also not welcomed with open arms by the older, already established community on the South Side, for several reasons; most important was the fact that the new migrants presented increased competition in a labor market that offered only limited opportunities for African Americans, especially after the troops returned from the war. Besides, the new migrants carried with them a laid-back, rural, southern way of life into a city whose established African American community had developed a jazzy, fast-paced, fairly sophisticated life-style. To many of the more conservative, longtime residents of Bronzeville, the new black Chicago residents, with their limited educational backgrounds and their "down home" style of living, posed a threat to much of what the Black Belt had gained over the years in terms of cultural advancement and overall respect in the eyes of the rest of the city.

Furthermore, before the newer migrants began flocking into some of the better areas of the West Side in mass numbers, some aspiring middle-class families from Bronzeville had already moved there. Like the Youngers in Hansberry's *Raisin in the Sun* (1959), they had moved into these less congested areas which were inhabited by whites, but soon after they had moved in, the whites moved to other, more remote all-white neighborhoods, or to segregated suburban areas. As a result, the Bronzeville families who thought they were resettling into better, more affluent areas of the city found themselves soon surrounded by poorer neighbors who had just moved up from the South. As soon as they could, they fled from their new neighbors just as the whites had fled from them, going back to the South Side, to other neighborhoods which whites had not yet abandoned (which, in cases such as Cicero, Illinois, resulted in riots and racial violence), or to black suburban areas such as Maywood, Illinois.

In African American culture, *literacy*, especially as related to the sociocultural implications of the word, has been one of the most important factors in drawing lines of class demarcation (Frazier, 1957). Although Bronzeville, it seems, might have developed a more sophisticated, jazz culture based on the importance of jazz music and the influence of those involved with a jazz life-style on the overall way of life of the community (including the musicians, deejays, club patrons, and hustlers), it is a culture that evolved over decades of living in the urban North. Its basic cultural roots, however, are the same as those which make up Bluesville's.

The people who came from the South to settle in both Bronzeville and Bluesville were steeped in a blues culture that involves much more than the way in which they express themselves in music. It is a vernacular culture which developed, to borrow an expression Houston A. Baker, Jr., uses in *Blues, Ideology, and Afro-American Literature*, as a response to the "economics of slavery" (1984, p. 3). It is an African-based culture that rose up in the cotton fields of the South as a race of people, relegated to the status of human contraband, were forced to work long hours in an alien environment while receiving no compensation for their labor. As contraband, they were forced to live in scanty quarters on big plantations, as well as on the lands of smaller farmsteads, where far too many were forced to dwell in lodgings which were very often fit for no one. After Emancipation, the economic situation of the vast majority of former slaves changed little, as the economics of slavery continued to shape every aspect of their emerging culture.

The influence of the economics of slavery extended into lumber camps, railroad work gangs, factories, migrant farm labor camps, and to other places where African American men, once freed from the direct bonds of slavery, had to travel in order to work for their own wages, and sometimes, but not always, to support the families they left behind.

Its influence was fled from by those who frequented the juke joints and early blues clubs, backwoods meeting places, moonshine shanties, prostitution houses, and other places where men and women gathered to mingle, get high, participate in the rituals of sex, or in other ways try to have a good time. Its influence extended into marriages, which were sometimes legal but more often of the common-law variety, and was also felt in the homes of single-parent families (where the men had gone off to find work, to make it on their own, or simply to seek a good time out of life), as well as in extended-family homes where grandparents, brothers, sisters, uncles, aunts, and cousins (as distant as third and fourth cousins) were taken in because they needed a place to stay or because their contributions were needed to help maintain the household. Those economics were the foundation of the system of sharecropping, which, as mentioned earlier, forced freedmen and women to work as long and hard as they did as in enslavement, providing them with none of the profits from their labor while taking advantage of the literacy skills they were lacking to fraudulently force them into deep and long-standing debt. This same system of economics provided the bitter taste experienced in every meal these people ate as they attempted to survive off the low nutrition of mere-subsistence rations; they ate the worst of foods but were forced to pay higher prices in order to get them. The economics of slavery even made its way into the shanty and open-air churches, where the rites of an Africanized form of Christian worship took root to give a people who cried out in, what was for them a strange new tongue, hope that a better day—a better economic reality—was there waiting for them just as soon as they could cross the River Jordan and head into Canaan. For the black migrants who fled the South and its cruel economics in both the early and later movements, the North was their symbol of Canaan.

Possibly the major disadvantage faced by the migrants who settled into what became a Bluesville on Chicago's West Side was the absence of a potential hierarchy of African American elites, such as was in the process of formation when the earlier migrants flocked to the South Side Black Belt. They found no role models with long-standing civic roots in the city, and no one with strong social and educational backgrounds for them to emulate. The lack of such a presence meant that the newcomers were left to fend for themselves, and instead of adapting quickly to the ways of urban life, many continued to live in a manner similar to what they were used to in the South. Long before African Americans settled on the West Side, Bronzeville had already developed the businesses, social service agencies, and cultural institutions necessary to aid its residents in their transition from a southern people living in the North to a northern African American community. The reputation it has built for itself allows it not only to maintain a position above its West Side cousin in the city's social hierarchy but also to compete with Chicago's other ethnic communities for political power.

Bronzeville's literary tradition dates back as far as Harlem's and has produced or claimed as its own such important African American literary figures as Fenton Johnson, Bonner, Wright, Brooks, Hansberry, Hoyt Fuller, Madhubuti, Carolyn Rodgers, Sam Greenlee, Sterling Plumpp (the only one who has actually lived on the West Side), Angela Jackson, Cyrus Colter, Leon Forrest, and many others. These writers have not only published while living in Bronzeville but have also used Chicago's South Side as a setting in their works. The literature these writers have created serves as more proof of Bronzeville's status as a vibrant cultural entity, and gives Chicago's South Side African American community a literary reputation that is known to people throughout the world.

On the other hand, even the very mention of the existence of the other African American community in the works of black Chicago writers has been rare. Finding its stories absent from the annals of a city revered for its African American cultural community makes Bluesville appear as if it has no cultural legacy of its own. For example, even though it was once the home of the Chicago blues music scene before it was taken over by white entrepreneurs and relocated in the upscale "yuppie" neighborhoods of the North Side, Bluesville has not developed viable institutions to commodify, promote, and profit from that aspect of its culture in relation to the outside world; nor has it developed institutions to preserve any other aspects of its history. Therefore, few of the young people growing up there know that the same Muddy Waters who influenced the Beatles and Rolling Stones and the music of the whole rock 'n' roll industry used to play for pennies in the bars of the neighborhood where he wrote and performed many of his most famous songs. They also have no way of knowing that Dr. Martin Luther King, Jr., during his Chicago campaign, made his home in an apartment building that is still standing on one of their streets, since there has been no movement to make this building a community shrine. Insufficient capital is a major problem hindering the building of institutions on the West Side, but not having people with the training necessary to organize and manage such efforts is an even larger one. As a result, the residents of the West Side who want to involve themselves with institutions that celebrate various aspects of African American culture find it necessary to go to the South Side to do so.

Finding themselves confined and isolated within one of the most economically depressed communities in the nation, many of the young adults fall prey to the vices—including gangs, drugs, alcoholism, and violent crime—which tempt them throughout their lives and trap them in bondage until they are of little use to even themselves. Those who do get away, such as the ones who earn grades and test scores good enough to allow them to escape to college, despite having attended schools which are operated more like juvenile detention centers than educational facilities, never return. As soon as they leave the community, they tend to disassociate themselves in an effort to discard their stigma of being from the *wrong* side of Chicago. If they do return, they are possible victims of a fate similar to the one suffered by Bailey in *Crimes in Bluesville* (1990), who, while on vacation from college, was stabbed to death in the streets of his old neighborhood for refusing to "loan" a junkie some money to get high.

James Baldwin, in *Notes of a Native Son* (1955), said that he had to write about his experiences as an African American because "it was the gate I had to unlock before I could write about anything else." Following his logic, it seems as if the most important step in the advancement of literacy in bluesville-type communities is the development of representative texts; it is as crucial for the bluesvilles, as it was for the bronzevilles, to have texts coming from out of their midst which explore the experiences of the people who live there before the eyes of the rest of the world. Then their citizens, especially the upcoming children, will not feel so isolated, as if no one beyond the boundaries of their neighborhoods knows they exist. Finding their world portrayed in written texts, they will then better see themselves as fully realized beings, a most important process in finally breaking the remaining yoke of slavery and its dehumanizing economics. In realizing the value of literacy in their lives, they will find themselves able to begin removing the barriers of their own limited geographic and cultural environments.

I can make no secret of the fact that the experiences of J. P. Bailey in my novel are closely related to my own. We both grew up as "closet poets," amassed large comic book collections, and did so "embarrassing well" in high school that we dropped out in an effort to better fit in with the tougher, more streetwise youths in our communities. Eventually, thanks to our efforts to conform to the standards of the streets, we both found ourselves in bondage to substance addictions as we attempted to escape the dehumanizing aspects of our Bluesville realities without ever making an effort to use our educational skills and talents as writers to help us leave. We were both aided by agents from the outside world who saw potential in us and helped us get our lives cleaned up, pushed us to get our high school degrees, arranged for us to take college entrance exams, and aided us in finding educational opportunity programs at colleges that would allow us to attend. Although I dropped out after a few quarters to take a summer job that lasted almost ten years, because of my experience of having once gone to college, when I felt the desire—*the calling*—to go back and write the text of Bluesville, I was better prepared to do so.

As children, what motivated both Bailey and myself to develop our reading skills were the books that each of us had in our households; our writing skills blossomed as a direct result of our reading habits. In Bailey's case, reading began with a box of books by African American writers, from Frederick Douglass to Gwendolyn Brooks's earlier works, and included many of those published by the writers of the Harlem Renaissance. They were the only possessions left to him from a deceased father that he had never known. He loved and cherished these possessions, read them constantly, and drew upon them when he set out to author his own text. With me, it began with a set of encyclopedias that my mother purchased on the installment plan not long after our family left the South and settled on the West Side in 1955.

My mother was a high school graduate who had attended a "Negro" college for a year, while my father, who was in the army when they met, was the son of an Arkansas sharecropper; as a child, he was not able to attend school beyond the sixth grade because the state placed more value in "colored boys" picking cotton than it placed on training them to read. He was sixty-five years old before he finally earned his high school degree. Theirs was a mixed marriage of sorts because of their different backgrounds, which, in earlier times in our family's history, influenced them to disagree concerning the usefulness of what my father called the "book reading" kind of education. He felt that practical skills were of much greater benefit to the children of colored families and that reading books would not lead to future employment. My mother, with what was then a middle-class Negro family background—her father had a respectable position as a Pullman porter in Louisville and was head of a stable, churchgoing family (see Frazier, 1957; Drake & Clayton, 1970)—was a greater influence on us because no black kids who desired places for themselves in the North wanted to be associated with poor southern states such as Arkansas and Mississippi or with degrading activities such as picking cotton, since they carried with them the stigma of slavery. (Bailey, on the other hand, never lived with either of his parents or with any adult male in his household, having been raised by his widowed Big Momma, who moved to Bluesville in the early 1950s to take a job doing domestic work;

in that sense, his family situation is much more typical of West Side youths than my own, since I grew up in a two-parent household.)

When we were children, whenever Negro actors and performers appeared on television, my mother gathered the family around to witness what was then a very rare sight. Because of that, while I was still in elementary school, I began reading through our encyclopedias for entries about famous Negro individuals, and about the race in general. I went from A to Z and through the annual editions covering 1960–1963, and found very little concerning my race. I learned a lot of information about the world that would benefit me throughout my life, but regarded it to be of little importance then because it was not my interest. Finally, when I was in the sixth grade, I started looking through the shelves in the school and public libraries until I went to the central branch downtown and found a book of poems by Langston Hughes and a collection of his Jesse B. Simple stories. I loved his work. I thought they were the "hippest" poems and stories ever written, since they used a type of language I had never before seen in books, the kind that my ears were used to hearing in my home and in the streets of my neighborhood. I felt as if his Harlem Renaissance works could have been written about life in the very streets where I lived, by someone who actually lived there. After reading his books and the few others I was able to find by Negro authors, I knew I wanted to write about the experiences of my community the way other Negro writers had written about theirs. Not long after, I started composing my first poems and stories.

Years later, influenced by that experience, I applied for and received a neighborhood block grant from the Chicago Office on Cultural Affairs for an artist to teach creative writing to elementary students in Lawndale, the West Side neighborhood I grew up in. Back then, my credentials as a writer were limited—I had only recently returned to college to start over as an undergraduate—but I was the only one from that area of the city to apply for such a grant, which is why it was awarded to me. I called my project "The *Lawndale Renaissance* Creative Writing Workshop." My main goal was to expose the young people in the community to Hughes and the other writers like him who influenced me while I was young, knowing that they were not being offered in the curriculum of the neighborhood's schools. I felt that if the students developed an affinity toward these works, it would motivate them to write about their own experiences and help them find greater value in the educational opportunities they had. Of the students who participated in the workshop (it was funded for a second year), at least seven now have college degrees in majors ranging from elementary education to nursing, and several others are still enrolled in various schools. Although I have lost touch with a handful of the former workshop students, nearly all of those who participated in either session have attended college.

By training elementary-school-age students to write about their experiences, I had hoped to establish the foundation of a literary tradition in Bluesville (the name Bluesville actually grew out of our workshop when we decided that it was important for the West Side to have its own descriptive name to identify itself; after telling the workshop about how the South Side once called itself Bronzeville, and that Gwendolyn Brooks even wrote a book called *A Street in Bronzeville* [1945], the name Bluesville seemed to evolve naturally). Although none of the former students have become creative writers, they have a thorough background in African American literature, and are book-buying consumers who will expose their children to the literature at an early age. They are, as I am myself, role models for those in Bluesville who are coming up behind us and who need to see visible examples of individuals who have made their way out.

After my eligibility to receive grant money ran out, and after a futile year of trying to fund Lawndale Renaissance/Bluesville on my own, I realized the importance of finishing school and earning the highest degree I could get. Knowing that no one from my neighborhood had ever earned a Ph.D., I decided that I would be the first. I knew that with a title after my name and the publications I could produce with advanced training as a writer, I would then be in a better position to help generate the renaissance needed in my old neighborhood to encourage its residents toward enlightenment. Although I now teach at a school located in another state, I am often a visitor in Bluesville schools, where I do readings, conduct workshops, and teach special classes. The children are usually in awe of me, asking such questions as "Are you really a *doctor*?" "You mean you wrote that story yourself?" and "Did you really live around here when you were growing up?" I now correspond with several young people who want to follow in my footsteps and become writers themselves.

In recent years, there has been a significant increase in the number of books and films which deal with the so-called black experience. Many of these are the products of African Americans who, because of their racial affiliation, are promoted by their publishers, film companies, other media, and even themselves as authorities on *the* black experience. These include figures with such atypical black experiences as Shelby Steele. The films, such as the popular ones produced and/or directed by Spike Lee, Robert Townsend, John Singleton, and others, have generated a tremendous response from nearly every segment of the greater African American community, but only rarely have books by African American writers made as much impact in lower-income ("lower-class") African American communities. The problem is not simply one of African American writers failing to create interest within these constituencies that they are assumed to represent; as writers, they compose for literate, book-buying audiences, meaning that their efforts are not necessarily directed toward people who live in bluesville-type community settings. Many African American writers come from more privileged social and economic backgrounds than the average bluesville resident and learned much of what they know about depressed, under-developed communities from books, and not their own experiences. Because of the artistic and economic realities they face, most African American writers have to appeal, to varying degrees, to an educated, multiracial audience in order to survive at their craft. Very few, if any, can support themselves off the sales earned exclusively from the African American book-buying public, especially considering the limited numbers among the African American educated elite.

For writers like myself who choose to leave bluesville-type communities to attend universities where we are trained by white professors, taught from texts nearly always written by whites, enrolled in classes where we are usually the only dark speck in a sea of white faces, we are forced to ask ourselves: Have we become too educated for our people? Must we find a way to purge ourselves of our *white* educational experiences, and the elevated social status we have received as a result in order for us to create a literature representative of the world we came from? We must answer ourselves with an emphatic no!

From the perspective of one who has not gone to college, and who has not left the bluesville-type community for any length of time to have significant experiences in the outside world, the works of college-trained African American writers, who find the marginalized, dispossessed, and disadvantaged of the race to be fertile ground for creative exploration, may not be accessible for various reasons. The language in these so-called black books might seem too literary, even pedantic; the plots too sensationalized, fabricated, or in other ways not truly representative of their lives; the characters too folksy, hip, or contrived; and even the themes too irrelevant to the lives of those who spend every day in this kind of a community setting. In fact, no matter how commendable might seem the efforts of these writers attempt to convey in their works various aspects of life in bluesville-type communities, what they produce, on the surface, might easily appear to have little, if any, effect on the lives of those who live there.

But these works are important; they force the greater society to pay critical attention to the existence of these people who are *still* heavily dominated by the same economics that has historically negated their status as fully realized beings. If I am successful in publishing *Crimes in Bluesville*, I realize that only a few of the current residents of Bluesville will ever read it because it is long, over 350 pages, includes a section of poetry from the protagonist's perspective (poetry is seldom read in bluesvilles), contains a complex narrative structure, and borrows other elements of literary technique—not just from African American writers such as Toomer, Hughes, Brooks, and Morrison, but also from the likes of Faulkner, Nabokov, Denevi, García Márquez, and others from around the world. The novel is about Bluesville, however, and is the creation not only of someone who came from out of that world, but of someone who has looked back to write about it. Knowing that I am a true native son of Bluesville, the community will find my text to be of value, as did Dorothy, because it records their name—and we must not forget the old slave axiom my maternal Great Aunt Nannie used to say: "You ain't nobody unless somebody's done written your name down somewhere."

Henry Louis Gates, Jr., has said that literacy is "the emblem that links racial alienation with economic alienation" (1986, p. 6). If this is true, it would seem that an economics of enlightenment is needed finally to tear down the boundaries created by the economics that has been used to keep the descendants of the African slave trade apart from the enlightened world. One must doubt, however, if such a new and affirmative economics will evolve anytime soon within a governing system still overwhelmingly controlled by the descendants of those who profited from the racial and economic alienation of slavery in the first place. Therefore, change is up to refugees from these communities, like myself, who have risen from the ranks of those kept in darkness, to continue the tradition of self-help education begun in slavery over a century ago. Although books have become more and more expensive commodities, meaning that those who earn the lowest incomes are the ones least likely to afford them, the people who populate the bluesville-type communities will find ways to obtain *particular* books, if they value them as *objects*, the way my mother provided her family with a set of encyclopedias. If they feel there are books which speak about them, which have their names in them, they will find a way to acquire them and put them in places of prominence in their homes where they will be seen. And if they are already in the house, the way Bailey's father's books and my mother's encyclopedias were, there's a good chance that somebody not only will come along and accept the challenge of reading

them but also will master them. To do so would only be to follow in
the tradition established centuries ago when Africans first challenged
the conditions of literacy which were used to deny them their humanity.
That is why I had to step out of the community where I grew up to
lend my hand in the process of creating that community's texts. That
was my calling and why I had to write about Bluesville.

Because of my level of education, I can, in a sense, no longer
consider myself among the ranks of those who remain in the Bluesville
community where I grew up (if I tried to move back there to live,
chances are I would also suffer a fate similar to J. P. Bailey's); therefore,
it is only through the memories of past experiences that I can identify
myself with the West Side of Chicago. But not even Frederick Douglass,
after he escaped from slavery in the South and became an articulate
spokesperson for the abolitionist movement, could have returned to
the life from which he came. In attempting to do so, he would have
been no more than an outsider to those with whom he once dwelled,
since he had evolved, because of his literacy, into something different
than what they were, and into someone different than what he used
to be (a process that actually began long before he escaped, and which
was actually the motivation behind it). Besides, by returning, he would
have been forced back into bondage, meaning that his voice would have
been silenced and his pen and paper taken away; far fewer slaves would
have benefited from a Douglass in shackles than they did from the one
who spoke from podiums and published in books and newspapers.
Considering the accomplishments of his struggle to liberate those he
left behind, he could never have done a fraction as much by going back
into enslavement. As a free man he could, however, draw on his past
experiences in bondage to compose works which helped give being to
the people he left behind.

I am conscious of the fact that this essay, even more so than my
novel, will be read by only a handful of African Americans—and they
will be well-trained, highly educated professionals in the field of
language studies. But there are others who will read it, including some
who train teachers, as well as individuals who influence *educational policy*
(and have the means to help influence a new economics of enlightenment), on local, state, and national levels. If what I have written here
is effective in its demonstration of reason, my hope is that this essay
will enable someone who was not informed of the truth to realize that
the African American experience has not been the same for everyone,
and that distinct segments of the African American population live
under varying economic conditions and suffer from different standards
of literacy as well. That is not to say that bronzeville-type communities

are havens which are no longer affected by the past racial and economic forms of alienation which were used to cast a shadow over the lives of African Americans in this country; it simply means that some segments of the African American population are more advanced and better developed than others—that is, they are visible to the eyes of the world that exists beyond their boundaries (and pockets of bluesville-type communities often exist *within* the geographic boundaries of bronzeville communities, including large segments of Chicago's South Side).

Dorothy, a woman who struggled to gain employment in a university on its clerical staff so that at least one person from the community would have a foot inside the halls of enlightenment, was there at UIC because she had faith that someone from Bluesville was bound to eventually come that way—and she wanted to be there to lend that person a helping hand. Upon its publication, I will send her a copy of this essay so that she will be able to place it next to the bound dissertation copy of *Crimes in Bluesville* that sits on the mantel in the front room of her home, so that both copies can sit there until others come along to read them, and then, in the future, place their own texts besides them. Until then, both will sit there as no more than symbolic objects, but as they do, they will serve to remind us that what she said while typing my thesis is in the process of coming true, and that people will no longer be able to ignore the existence of our world—because its name is on written record.

References

Baker, H. A., Jr. (1984). *Blues, ideology, and Afro-American literature: A vernacular theory.* Chicago: University of Chicago Press.

Baldwin, J. (1955). *Notes of a native son.* Boston: Beacon.

Bonner, M. (1987). *Frye street and environs.* Boston: Beacon.

Brooks, G. (1945). *A street in Bronzeville.* New York: Harper & Row.

Drake, S. C., & Clayton, H. R. (1970). *Black metropolis: A study of Negro life in a northern city.* Vols. 1 & 2. New York: Harcourt, Brace.

Frazier, E. F. (1957). *Black bourgeoisie.* New York: Macmillan.

Gates, H. L., Jr. (1986). *"Race," writing, and difference.* Chicago: University of Chicago Press.

Gates, H. L., Jr. (1987). *Figures in black.* New York: Oxford University Press.

Hansberry, L. (1959). *A raisin in the sun.* New York: Random House.

Holt, T. (1990). "Knowledge is power": The black struggle for literacy. In A. Lunsford, H. Moglen, & J. Slevin (Eds.), *The right to literacy* (pp. 91–102). New York: MLA.

Lee, D. L. (Haki Madhubuti). (1970). "Blackman/an unfinished history." In his *We walk the way of the new world* (pp. 20–23). Detroit: Broadside Press.

Spear, A. H. (1967). *Black Chicago: The making of a Negro ghetto, 1890–1920.* Chicago: University of Chicago Press.

Tuttle, W. M., Jr. (1970). *Race riot: Chicago in the red summer of 1919.* New York: Atheneum.

Travis, D. (1981). *An autobiography of Black Chicago.* Chicago: Urban Research Institute.

Wright, R. (1940). *Native son.* New York: Harper & Row.

Young, R. (1990). *Crimes in Bluesville.* (Doctoral dissertation, University of Illinois at Chicago). *Dissertation Abstracts International, 51/10A,* 3415.

4

A Stamp on the Envelope Upside Down Means Love; or, Literature and Literacy in the Multicultural Classroom

Barbara McCaskill

The library of Negro books in the sitting room is a trope of twentieth-century African American autobiography and life. For the distinguished historian John Hope Franklin (1990, p. 354), learning meant more than going to high school during the Depression in intolerant, segregated Tulsa. (In June 1921, homes and businesses of African Americans were looted and burned and Black citizens lynched in racial violence there.) Learning also meant learning at home, in the place where he was initiated into a different school of African American culture. His mother, herself a former elementary school teacher, exposed the young Franklin "to some of the great writers, especially Negro authors, such as Paul Laurence Dunbar and James Weldon Johnson, who were not a part of our studies at school" (1990, p. 354).

In this section, "Perspectives on Writing Literature," Reggie Young's essay introduces this trope, as well. Young recalls this icon of culture in his own autobiographical novel, when his character J. P. Bailey is bequeathed a box from his father that holds books by Frederick Douglass, Gwendolyn Brooks, and other African American writers. I myself grew up with such readings, as well as readings on the notables Benjamin Banneker, Toussaint L'Ouverture, Locke, Du Bois, Woodson, Crummell, Bunche, Terrell, and Bethune in a volume from the library entitled *Great Negroes Past and Present* (1963). The purpose of reading these books was threefold: to communicate the importance of liberation, self-definition, and preservation of community spirit and history. These are purposes of literacy that Welburn, Young, and Babb—all of the authors in "Defining Difference"—have emphasized.

In my own experiences teaching nineteenth- and twentieth-century African American literature in university classrooms, I convey these three intentions—of liberation, definition, and preservation—in several ways. Not only do I use written texts, such as the popular narratives of fugitive slaves, but also I call attention to other literacies through oral texts—spirituals, freedom songs, and work songs—and through visual icons from abolitionist, feminist, and other sociopolitical movements. Engaging another meaning of *literacy,* I relate to students my own family's literacies—for example, my family's readings of such postal signs as misdirected letters or unsigned cards or a stamp upside down on an envelope (which means love). Let me reflect upon the essays of Welburn, Young, and Babb in the custom in which I would engage my own African American literature class.

All three contributors to "Defining Difference" cite the connection between literacy and liberation, and they regard the narratives of former slaves, those such as Frederick Douglass's *Narrative* (1845) and Harriet Jacobs's *Incidents in the Life of a Slave Girl* (1861), as the written texts in which this connection between literacy and liberty is represented. As Valerie Babb observes, literacy's power in the narratives of former slaves is its power not only "to effect enfranchisement" and "to author a new self" but also "to explore issues of social justice." When such writers as Douglass and Jacobs link literacy and freedom, they do so as much to critique white American attitudes toward race as to celebrate a central step toward their own autonomy. Jacobs, for instance, blesses the memory of an early mistress, one who graciously, and dangerously, taught her "to read and spell." Jacobs implies that her mistress instructed her with the Bible as the sole primer book. "My mistress," she writes, "had taught me the precepts of God's Word: 'Thou shalt love thy neighbor as thyself.' 'Whatsoever ye would that men should do unto you, do ye even so unto them' " (p. 8). Jacobs's mistress must have known that this instruction of slaves was illegal and impertinent in antebellum North Carolina. To defy this law meant to challenge the conception that slavery was justified and right because Africans had been defined as intrinsically debased and intellectually inferior. To defy this law meant to denounce the institution of enslavement.

Immediately, however, Jacobs herself eliminates any notions of her mistress's charity. In the same paragraph in which she expresses gratitude for "this privilege" of literacy, a privilege that she observes "so rarely falls to the lot of the slave," Jacobs raises the issue of her own enslavement and devaluation. It was the *will* [emphasis mine] of my mistress for me to read" (p. 7), she remembers; and so she reminds her readers in the nineteenth-century North of her status and the statuses of other slave women as property: bodies, minds, and souls. And so these readers are reminded of how this "kindly" mistress bequeathed Jacobs, at twelve years old, to "her sister's daughter, a child of five years old" (p. 8). Lest a few still doubt that her mistress's tutorials arose from more than whimsy, or more than from a need to compensate for the blurring sight and shaky hand of illness or advancing age, Jacobs bluntly shares the following irony: "I was her slave, and I suppose [my mistress] did not recognize me as her neighbor" (p. 8). Jacobs exposes the racism that operates at the center of her encounter with literacy.

And Jacobs feminizes the injustice of her treatment when she places herself, an African and a captive, within a white matrilineage (mistress to sister to daughter). This female community disempowers Jacobs instead of nurturing her, and it is a community that commodifies her instead of acknowledging her subjecthood. This feminization of racism is one that Jacobs aims strategically at readers composed of "the women of the North." These Northern women readers might apprehend that slave-sustaining matrilineage themselves, in their own silence and noninvolvement in reform. These readers might recognize a sisterly obligation to support the abolitionist movement, once they had considered such statements by Jacobs of the (en)gendered miseries of "millions of women of the South, still in bondage, suffering what I suffered, and most of them far worse" (p. 1).

Signs not printed on the page also, and as often, have been "read" as "narratives" of enslavement. These visual "narratives" constitute literacy to stand for that which is shown and seen, and they again connect the meanings of literacy and liberation. Such visual signs from nineteenth-century African American culture include what contemporary Jamaican writer Michelle Cliff (1990) has assigned as the "mark[s] of the journey-man" (p. 52). These consist of the notches in wood, arrangements of stone, tracks upon the ground, or markings on the earth made by underground railroad "conductors" such as Harriet Tubman and Peg-leg Joe, made by that membership real and fictional, identified and anonymous, of Blacks and whites, of slaves and citizens, of women and men whose identities we never shall know. Toni Morrison's Stamp Paid, the journeyman in her *Beloved* (1987) who ferries "contraband humans" (p. 170) across the Ohio River to Kentucky and freedom, is a character whose fictional description commemorates these engravings on the landscape.

In the nineteenth century, the Black bodies of the fugitive slaves themselves most potently expanded definitions of literacy to include what is seen and shown. The exhibitions of the fugitives' mutilated flesh at abolitionist gatherings complemented the literary accounts and other visual symbols of enslavement and autonomy. Well known is the vignette of Sojourner Truth, baring her breasts to a hostile white heckler who expressed his doubt at the validity of her enslavement and the verity of her womanhood (Sterling, 1984, pp. 152–53). Her response can be likened to what Houston A. Baker, Jr., has called the "Negro exhibit." Baker states that escaped slaves, engaged to lecture on their servitude to white Northern audiences, chose not words but their bodies' own flesh to authenticate their gruesome ordeals:

> The fugitive slave turned his back to the audience and displayed his wounds and scars from floggings at the stake of slavery. His or her body, in all of its marked and visible clarity of wounding, made affective the metaphors of moral suasion propounded by white abolitionists. The fugitive slave silently turned his back to the audience. The fugitive slave was a silent, partially naked body turning to a predominantly white audience. The silent, fugitive slave's body became an erotic sign of servitude in the social, liberational discourse of white abolitionists and their predominantly white audiences. (1991, p. 13)

With these exhibits, the body of the silent slave made visible the African's membership among what Victor Turner (1969), influenced by Arnold Van Gennep, has called "liminal personae," those persons "possessing nothing" (and in the slaves' case, those who are themselves possessed), those persons who "wear only a strip of clothing, or even go naked, to demonstrate that as liminal beings they have no status, property, insignia, secular clothing indicating rank or role. . . ." (p. 95). With these exhibits the body of the silent slave exposed a Northern audience to truth and apprised them of the brutalities of enslavement as powerfully as any narrative or oratory.

Clothed, the fugitive slave was likewise "exhibited" as an intellectualized, civilized, colonized, and/or feminized sign. No longer undressed, debased, and scarred by whip, brand, and chain, the clothed African demonstrated the death of a captive identity and a resurrection of a willful self into freedom. The African's clothing was a swaddling clothes intended to persuade a preponderantly white audience of freed Black people's self-motivation, intelligence, and potential to succeed, as much as to persuade them of the degradation, speciousness, and moral insolvency of enslavement.

In her discussions of "American Africanism" in the literature composed by white Americans, Toni Morrison (1992) observes that "black people ignite critical moments of discovery or change or emphasis." In such literary works, Morrison writes, "black or colored people and symbolic figurations of blackness are markers for the benevolent and the wicked" (pp. viii, ix). In nineteenth-century America's visual "literature," Blackness ignited similar responses; and so the free African and the abolitionist manipulated these "figurations" of Black flesh and Black bodies in order to incite the enfranchisement of Black "property" still enslaved. One convention of the nineteenth-century slave narrative and broadsheet genre—and even apparent in volumes published by whites and published in the eighteenth century by enslaved African Americans—was the inclusion of a frontispiece drawing or interior illustration that depicted the Black author in garments symbolic of dignity, restraint, eloquence, reflection, and cultivation. All these were attributes that slaveholders deemed impossible for Africans, intrinsically wild and perverted, to attain.

If he were a man, essential to the writer's attire were topcoat, vest, and tie. Perhaps a hat or cane, symbols of maturity and manners, was observable. An epitome of this was the engraved commemoration of the escape of the Virginia slave Henry "Box" Brown (Figure 4.1). Printed in such classic abolitionist publications as William Still's *Underground Rail Road* (1872), this depiction captured Brown in hat, jacket, vest, and tie, rising from the stifling interior of a wooden crate. Brown is symbolically rising out of inhumanity, for he ascends from a crate which he has used to have himself mailed by antislavery sympathizers from Virginia into Philadelphia and into freedom. Three white men— identified as the abolitionists J. M. McKim, C. D. Cleveland, and Lewis Thompson—surround the crate (Blockson, 1987, p. 138). These abolitionists, prepared to rendezvous with Brown and to unnail his box before he suffocates or starves, confirm the civility that Brown's apparel represents with the coats and ties that they themselves wear. One gentleman in this tableau even sports a hat and cane.

A Black man, ostensibly free, who has assisted in removing the lid of the box, also decodes the symbolism of Brown's dress. This Black gentleman, the underground "conductor" and writer William Still (Blockson, 1987, p. 2), is appareled almost identically to his white colleagues in coat, tie, and vest. These foreshadow the visibility and empowerment—and literacy—that a fugitive such as Brown might find possible to attain in freedom. As if anointing Brown with the baptismal grace of freedom, Still haloes Brown with the lid of the crate, upon which has been written "This side up with care." Still himself was later to recall this scene as "the marvellous resurrection of Brown," and to remember that Brown emerged "as wet as if he had come up out of the Delaware" (Blockson, 1987, p. 138). As if he were an infant delivered

FIGURE 4.1

The Resurrection of Henry Box Brown.
Photographs and Prints Division
Schomburg Center for Research in Black Culture
The New York Public Library
Astor, Lenox and Tilden Foundations

into life, Brown struggled up to liberation: his umbilical cord the Undergound Railroad, his birth canal the Richmond-to-Philadelphia rail. Brown's clothing in the drawing of this rebirth presages the intellectual and psychological reconstitution that is his to engage in freedom. And a bookcase stands dimly behind Brown's box, a visual key to the interaction between literacy and liberation.

During the time contemporaneous with American enslavement, it was typical for the painted African—whether liberated or enslaved—to function as a sexually turbulent, socially uncivil, intellectually retarded foil to the white characters on the canvas. It was typical for such painters as Rossiter and Mignot to conventionalize the African as either absent or peripheral, crouched or enshadowed, feral or infantile, sporting in the dust or simmering under the darkness. Master and mistress, on the other hand, stood close to the icons of social order and national culture, close to Bible and flag, close to home and hearth. Central in the canvas, these white subjects claimed authority. Their presence and centrality underscored the marginality of the Africans in both moral and civic terms, and their presence and centrality erroneously depicted white America to be untainted by the attributes of racism that had warped the Africans' lives.

The classic scene of Henry "Box" Brown's escape subverts these racialized conventions of American visual art. Brown occupies the middle of the image, and all the gentlemen encircling him level their gazes, and direct the viewer's stare, to Henry's rising countenance. Brown's own eyes fix outward toward the viewer. His own upheld gaze counters the downcast pose assumed by "darkies" in typical images, and it challenges the assignation of "backwards" Africa to the penumbra of enlightened civilization.

If she were a woman, the African writer graced her frontispiece portrait or volume illustration in a corseted and girdled state. Her starched, enshawled dress draped her modestly (buttoned high, gliding close to the floor); her hair was pulled or braided smooth into a bun or cap: no savagery or sluttishness here! Bethany Veney's dictated Reconstruction-era narrative (1889) carries a portrait of her, brow benign and back straight, dressed—and dignified—in such a manner. Book or pen might be clutched or held aloft by narrators of either gender: the pensive Phillis Wheatley, becapped and beshawled, flourishing her pen over a page and book in the frontispiece of her *Poems* (1773), comes to mind. Wheatley's identification as impetuous, ignorant slave, as the "Negro Servant to Mr. John Wheatley, of Boston," according to the handwritten inscription seared around her portrait, belied the intrinsic thoughtfulness and urbanity represented by her garments and the accoutrements of her desk. Like the abolitionist emblems of the supplicant slave that historian Jean Fagan Yellin (1989) has discussed— emblems that depict the semi-nude African captive kneeling, fettered, and pleading for deliverance—the iconography of the clothed and literate African functioned as a visual discourse, in tandem with the written word. This iconography labeled as spurious the white supremacist governance and thought that had organized slavery as an institution and perpetuated its existence.

Crucial in this iconography to the fugitive's apparel of liberation was, ironically, a part of the body: the fugitive's mouth. Instead of the wide, gappy, watermelon span of the happy plantation darky, or the drippy, honey-and-sugar mammy's smack, or the heavy-lipped, rotten-toothed leer of the rapacious savage, the African writer, reconstituted from slave to seer, wore either a muted smile of self-respect and sagacity or else an ambiguous expression, one that might be "read" as both longing and satisfaction combined. Whatever the case, the Africans never exposed their teeth! Photohistorians might attribute this to the prevailing convention of the period: whites, too, posed closemouthed and sober for their portraits. Yet the former slaves must have recognized that the fallacious, grinning facial "costumes" of the stereotyped slave, the Uncle Ben and Aunt Jemima smiles deconstructed in Marlon Riggs's contemporary film *Ethnic Notions* (1986), were as much signs of servility and surrogacy as were the wounds on their denuded bodies that the abolitionists appropriated in their own publications and designs, wounds that in turn the Africans themselves elected to display.

For African women, exhibiting their freedom clothes allowed them to interrogate nineteenth-century middle-class standards of womanhood and to critique nineteenth-century whites' assumptions about African female sexuality. "In order to gain a public voice as orators or published writers," Hazel Carby (1987) explains, "black women had to confront the dominant domestic ideologies and literary conventions of womanhood which excluded them from the definition 'woman' " (p. 6). As Black women orators and writers presented visual images of themselves to public view, they faced battles over the same exclusionary ideologies and conventions of femininity. The nineteenth-century gospel of "true womanhood"—motherhood, wifehood, service, Christianity, fragility, intellectual deference to men—was problematized by visual images of Black women that implied that this mold was as stultifying and inauthentic as that of the unwomanly slave.

The visual "discourse" surrounding the story of Georgia fugitive Ellen Craft speaks to this difficulty, and it calls attention to how both picture and print conveyed the quandary that Black women faced as they attempted to disrupt their viewers' preconceptions about femininity. Craft prefigured the pop star Madonna as a visual icon of the incongruous expectations that women be two persons in one body: erotic and virginal, sophisticated and innocent, uninhibited and restrained, masculine and feminine. Craft's Blackness, however, destabilized this formula. Rather than being manipulated for her own profit, and being manipulated by her own design, Ellen Craft's personhood was confiscated for the cause of abolition by well-intentioned Northern sympathizers, and, in the name of proslavery, by diehard Southern slaveholders. In portraiture and in print, Craft's story illustrates the multiple jeopardies or marginalities that continually have ensnared Black women, the intersections of race and gender and class that have affected Black women's stories, as much as it exemplifies themes of liberty, self-definition, and the parallel impact of two kinds of literacies.

Most of what we know of Ellen Craft has been secondhand, from the story told by her husband, William, in his narrative entitled *Running a Thousand Miles for Freedom* (1860). In the 1840s this couple undertook a bold escape from their captivity in Georgia: the light-skinned Ellen disguised as an invalid Southern gentleman traveling to the Free States for a cure, and the darker William masqueraded as her loyal chattel and nurse. Audaciously, the Crafts traveled North, first-class, aboard steamships and trains jampacked with suspicious, sometimes confrontational, white slaveowners and passengers, hoteliers, and stationmasters. When finally they reached free Pennsylvania, their story was circulated as a cause célèbre of the abolitionist movement.

Just as the drawing of Henry "Box" Brown illustrates themes of enslavement and liberation, so, too, do drawings of Ellen Craft translate for the eye the issues of enslavement, liberation, racial stratification, and gender identification. An engraving of Craft as she must have looked in her furtive escape from Georgia, an engraving that configured her both as a white and as a man, spread wildly throughout antislavery newspapers in America and Great Britain, spread like the kudzu embracing the landscape of Ellen's Southern home (Figure 4.2). This portrayed her clad in the same kind of attire that Henry Brown wore in the tableau of his emancipation: the de rigueur white masculine signature of topcoat, tall hat, vest, and tie. Ostensibly, she has hidden her eyes with spectacles in order to cover from observant whites the fear and the caution that she feels and to cast aside any suspicion that her feminine facial features might arouse among skeptical observers. Just as well, her glasses might have functioned as an accessory that masculinized her, that suggested her to be educated, literate, aggressive and business oriented.

In spite of all of Craft's male imprimatur, the effect of the portrait was an androgynous one: it was *femininity* that this engraving of a masculine Ellen Craft also called into relief. Because they understood that they were encountering an African woman in white male disguise, viewers of this picture in the antislavery press might reflect upon the particular horrors that enslavement held for Black women. What could have been, what was, so monstrous, that Ellen Craft had violated the taboo of denying her own sex? What could have been, what was, so miserable, that she had appropriated the masculine privileges that women were neither spiritually elected nor intellectually endowed to exercise? Viewers might excuse Craft's intrepidity by presupposing that an *African* woman was intrinsically the opposite of female, a man, or at least the desexualized female that the mammy represented. These viewers might presume that the same attributes of the mammy— indifference and mannishness, those same traits that supposedly enabled female slaves to disregard their own children for the master's or to work

FIGURE 4.2

Ellen Craft in escape attire.
Photographs and Prints Division
Schomburg Center for Research in Black Culture
The New York Public Library
Astor, Lenox and Tilden Foundations

ILLusTrated
London News
Apr. 19, 1851

in the fields and the kitchens with their bodies exposed, without
blemish—these were traits that must have immured Craft to the
mortification and obscenity of her male costume. Yet these assumptions

were called into question by Craft's own swift and constant appearance in female attire once she and her husband arrived in the Northern states.

Female viewers who encountered this picture, white women, might gaze at Craft in her costume as if through a speculum that reflected insights into their own pedestaled positions. Distant and protected from the feminized perils of Southern enslavement—from rape, from homelessness, from the forced sale of their children, from the prohibition of marriage that made all intercourse illicit and immoral (William and Ellen's own marriage could be legally consummated only after they reached freedom)—white women contemplating Craft's male disguise might realize the gender-specific torments that made the lives of slave women nightmares of a living hell. For these white and womanly viewers, to reflect upon Craft's outfit of manhood, an outfit of authority and power, meant to recognize how enslavement divested African women of the protection of fathers, husbands, and sons, and demanded them freakishly to substitute themselves in the labors and decisions that the customs of the day inclined "naturally" to men. To reflect upon Craft's "debasement" meant for white and womanly viewers to realize how their own silence and complicity about enslavement deprivileged their darker sisters. The white female viewership that encountered Craft's disguise might understand, in a manner that no words could convey, that no prospect of escape from this living hell existed that was too forbidden or too desperate. Under these circumstances, Craft's was an escape that any woman would attempt. And such an escape meant high time for an end to enslavement.

This popular engraving of Ellen Craft also "speaks" to the efficacy of visual literacy, to the confluent themes that seeing and showing can distinguish, compare, and elaborate. This picture of Craft as a man enunciated the lives of enslaved African women at a time when the language of neither Victorian America nor Victorian Britain could express these dimensions with clarity and detail. Enslaved, a woman such as Ellen knew that mention of these unmentionables, even shared surreptitiously among the other captives, might result in death. As Harriet Jacobs (1861) lamented:

> The secrets of enslavement are concealed like those of the Inquisition. My master was, to my knowledge, the father of eleven slaves. But did the mothers dare to tell who was the father of their children? Did the other slaves dare to allude to it, except in whispers among themselves? No, indeed! They knew too well the terrible consequences. (p. 35)

Like the secrets of the Inquisition, the "secrets of enslavement" that Jacobs here implies found no easy expression in the euphemistic English of nineteenth-century Blacks and whites. Before language evolved and custom shifted to expose these "secrets," pictures like Ellen's "whispered," in modest yet audible tones, the "terrible consequences" of enslavement to shocked and apprehensive Northern audiences.

That Ellen Craft's picture was intended to communicate her multiple marginalizations—the racism and the sexism that cast her on the fringes of American society—is borne out in the textual descriptions that accompanied the famous engraving. Such instances concretized the notion that literacy involves both reading and seeing, both channels of printed and pictorial pages. *The Liberty Almanac*, one of the many annual, leather-bound souvenirs sold at bazaars to raise money for antislavery, combined written discussion and visual presentation of Ellen Craft's story as an example of this synchronous definition of literacy. By the time the 1852 edition of the *Almanac* was published, both of the Crafts had left the United States. In 1850 the Fugitive Slave Act had entitled slaveowners to recapture their escaped "property" in the Free States, and it had empowered judges, jailers, and officers of the law to assist in this enterprise. Harassed by mercenary bounty hunters, the Crafts had fled first to Canada, then England, where the *Almanac* reported that "they lived in peace, Craft working at his trade in his own 'hired house' " (p. 35).

Above this report of the couple's progress, the *Almanac* (p. 35) titillated its audiences with "a correct portrait of Ellen Craft. . .dressed in male attire." For those gazers who might have overlooked the caption, the report itself emphasized that the plan for escape had been that "*she* represented a young planter going to the North under advice of his physician. . . ." Just as this pictorial representation distinguished Craft's authentic feminine qualities from her fraudulent masculine ones, so too did the *Almanac* establish the Ellen in freedom to be womanly and wifely. The *Almanac* identified Ellen only in relational terms, as "wife of William Craft," as the Mrs. of "Mr Craft." In all other respects, it overlooked her and instead focused upon the public exploits of William. This report suggested that now "his wife" was protected and domestic, that now in liberty William's wife was able to exercise the feminine roles that a civilized society sanctioned and those roles that, even in enslavement, any "true woman" such as Ellen would desire. By omitting details of her life in freedom, this report returned Ellen Craft to the privacy of her home and family, away from the scrutiny of the crowds and the public attention that society deemed anomalous to the health and the inclinaton of the female gender.

Another textual companion piece to the manly Ellen of the drawing also appeared in 1852. Printed in London's *Anti-Slavery Advocate* (Craft, 1852, p. 22), this report at the same time encountered American audiences in the *Pennsylvania Freeman* (p. 207). In two ways, however, this report distinguished from the *Almanac* article: it included a rare letter from Ellen Craft herself, and it directly articulated the properties of womanhood that her masculine attire had alluded to. Out of a necessity to counteract "strange" and "erroneous" rumors that she "had grown tired of liberty," that "she had deserted her husband, and had placed herself under the protection of an American gentleman in London," Ellen Craft submitted a letter to the editor that set the record straight. She "very truly" contended:

> I write these few lines merely to say that the statement is entirely unfounded, for I have never had the slightest inclination whatever of returning to bondage; and God forbid that I should ever be so false to liberty as to prefer slavery in its stead. In fact, since my escape from slavery, I have gotten much better in every respect than I could possibly have anticipated. Though, had it been to the contrary, my feelings in regard to this would have been just the same, for I would much rather starve in England, a free woman, than be a slave for the best man that ever breathed upon the American continent. (p. 22)

Craft's response tied up literacy with liberation in a variety of ways. Because her letter demonstrated her own mastery of the skill of writing, she invalidated proslavers' claims of literacy to be superfluous to the African, like a diet sufficient in meat and dairy products or a workweek humane in duration and intensity. Because she wrote her own letter, she refuted the assumption that literacy, except upon a primary or imitative level, lay beyond the African's overreaching grasp. "I have gotten much better in every respect," Craft wrote, as if to recommend literacy both as an antidote to bondage and an assurance of lasting liberty.

And lest her detractors accused her of becoming corrupted by a literacy that she, as an African, could not possess without stepping out of place and risking further debasement, Craft punched a suasive stab at white Americans' own hypocrisy. "Slaves cannot breathe in England," William Cowper had rejoiced in 1785, "if their lungs / Receive our air, that moment they are free! / They touch our country, and their shackles fall" (*Task*, 1836–1837, Book II, line 40). By act of Parliament and official decree, England had emancipated the captives in its colonies; by the inaction of the American people, slavery was still operative in 1852! What, then, did it mean, Craft's letter implied, that both Northerners and Southerners participated in a country founded upon principles of justice and freedom, yet they did not truthfully practice those principles? What did it mean that England exercised these principles more fully than did its American nemesis? Craft's letter faulted those who had faulted her, and in her own voice she exposed and subverted the racialized subtext that her provocative male costume had critiqued.

Like her visual costume, Craft's written testimony of herself to a white audience attended to gender-specific dilemmas that African women in America confronted. In her analysis of contemporary African women writers, Carole Boyce Davies (1991) has used the term *symbolic effacement*, in part to refer to "the erasure, silence, and invisibility associated with motherhood" that is apparent in the African continent's canon of male literature (p. 256). Davies writes that the maternal and asexual roles to which the female subject in this male literature has been assigned are roles which symbolize the limitation and commodification of African women in real patriarchal orders (pp. 254–57). So, too, did Craft's letter call attention to this reduction of female identity and reconstruction of female sexuality by patriarchy.

Although Craft's letter admitted to have been composed by her own hand, her words had been both introduced and postscripted by commentary from the abolitionist press. Through its vocabulary and structure, this material elaborated not the voice of an African woman but that of a white man: through its vocabulary, Craft was constructed to be a dutiful mother and wife; through its structure, Craft was conceived to be illustrious and right only insofar as she deferred to the "protection" of white patriarchy. This material introduced Craft as a woman of "keen perceptions," as a woman who demonstrated the "refined feelings and vigorous understanding" that conventionally characterized all feminine and well-bred white women of the day. (In a similar description of Ellen Craft from a white woman with the pseudonym of "Mrs. L." [1858, p. 52], Craft showed "great self-control, such perfect sweetness of temper and grace of manner.") After Craft's own letter in the *Anti-Slavery Advocate* (1852, p. 22), the editorial voice again intervened, this time to include "that since the above letter was written, the noble woman has become the happy mother of a freeborn child."

Ellen's own writing literally was circumscribed here by the voice of white abolition that authorized her minor self to speak and that bestowed upon her identities—and *only* the identities—of mother, wife, and woman. "Of course, we did not believe this absurd calumny," the

Advocate's editors assured, and so they invigorated—and made ancillary—Craft's own denial of adultery. "Being personally acquainted with Mrs. Craft," the *Advocate*'s editors confided, "we know that such a course was impossible" (1852. p. 22). The presence and presentation of the abolitionist voice authenticated and legitimized Craft's own, in the same way that endorsements of slave narratives by prominent white women and men had underscored the accountability and veracity of the African author. Yet as much as this structure elevated Ellen Craft to respectable womanhood, it caricatured her, contained her, and eradicated other crucial aspects of her identity. Identities that her male outfit had problematized—her race, her conditioning to labor, her modesty—these identities were canceled by the *Advocate*'s determination, by the *Freeman*'s determination, and by the determined social dicta of "polite" Victorian manners, to reconfigure Craft in freedom as a silent and female subordinate.

Visual insignia of both containment and liberation similar to the Craft and Brown pictures have continued to circulate within African American communities, long after the demise of legally sanctioned, de jure enslavement in this country. The *X*'s on those baseball caps sported on the heads of Black consumers of the nineties communicate more than respect for the teachings and philosophy of Malcolm X—or that the wearer has viewed and enjoyed the Spike Lee movie! Those ubiquitous *X*'s do honor the struggle for enfranchisement, visibility, and self-determination that Malcolm's life and times embodied. These overtly politicized meanings are apparent in the discussion by Malcolm himself (1965) of the significance of his "X." He explains, "The Muslim's 'X' symbolized the true African family name that he never could know. For me, my 'X' replaced the white slave-master name of 'Little'. . . ." (p. 199). The X accommodates, like the wings of Mercury or the limp of Esu-Elegbara, the importance of both the messenger and the message. The *X*-caps that contemporary Malcolm fans wear also stimulate associations with names and naming that predate their hero's conversion to Islam: in enslavement the Africans had organized their own patterns of bestowing surnames, often composing names different from those of their owners (Gutman, 1976, pp. 230–56).

Additionally, the *X*-caps that Malcolm's progeny wear bear meanings of this sign that extend beyond those of dehumanization and enslavement. Because those *X*'s begin no word in particular and are seen everywhere, because those *X*'s call to all classes, colors, educational levels, professions, regions, and generations, the *X*-caps suggest—like the signals and markings of the Underground Railroad conductors—a signal of collective power and a marking of group cohesion, responsiveness, and strength. The X on the cap is also our most recent equivalent of the Protestant cross or Egyptian ankh, an abstract representation of a guiding spiritual force and an acquiescence to a transformative power greater than our individual selves. Like the cross or ankh, the X conveys that the aggregate energy of a people is a soul force that catalyzes imagination and energizes culture.

Yet just as easily, those X's can translate into question marks, into a collective hesitation and pause, into admonitions to the group of uncertainty, danger, and imminent risk, uncategorized and invisible, ahead. This X qualifies the themes of "indeterminacy, open-endedness, [and] ambiguity" that Henry Louis Gates, Jr., finds to be the themes that Esu, the Signifying Monkey, and other trickster figures "shared through time and space among certain black cultures in West Africa, South America, and the Caribbean" (1988, p. 6). Although it may be appropriated to designate such, this X is not merely the "Generation X" of Douglas Coupland's contemporary novel, a generation composed of middle-class white "twenty-nothings" consuming, copping out, and cursing the bankrupt America that they have inherited (1991). Instead, this X can evoke the equivalent to some mathematical invalidation or a scientific stamping out, an in-X-pressive sign of an "integrated" generation ignorant of both the directions it should take and the histories that have informed its directionlessness. And this Black X evokes the militant, angry stance of this country's disenchanted urban Black youth—youth of both genders who cannot recall a generation in which their families *owned* or gained gainful employment; youth who adopt life-styles that portend the statistical stay in prison, death by drugs and disease, or adolescent homicide on the streets; youth who cop whatever consuming and addictive attitudes they cop out of fear and impatience as much from victimization and abuse. This Black X (as if enclosed by periods at the ends of each line) encodes the latest dance step that Black youth might dance to. Graphically, it can be "read" as a depiction of a back-and-forth, side-to-side, let's-go-nowhere step that expresses the finite, confined, and other-defined status of Blacks in American society—in the same way that the conga emerged from the ankle-chained coffles of slaves, similar to the manner in which the Jim Crow shuffle, appropriated by white "blackface" singers, first developed from that Southern Black congeries whose Protestant ministers had prohibited it.

The meanings that the X-signias can convey are complicated and permutated by the backgrounds upon which they are displayed. And culture is the background most essential to pin down. "The problem of the Twentieth Century," said Du Bois in *Souls of Black Folk* (1903), "is the problem of the color line" (p. xi). Racism, "the color line," remains the slow cancer retarding our national culture. We need only to look at the persistence of middle- and upper-class schools and businesses and public and private recreational facilities segregated by race; at the frenzied, ridiculous surveillance of people of color shopping in both dime stores and exclusive boutiques; at the disproportionate amount of bank loans denied to credit-worthy nonwhite customers or interracial couples; at the refusal of taxicab drivers to accept nonwhite passengers, regardless of briefcase, coat-and-tie or checkbook; at the disparate paychecks of whites and Blacks with identical amounts of experience and education; at the de facto exclusion of people of color or interracial couples from mortgaging homes in "good" urban and suburban white neighborhoods; at the cross burnings, lynchings, vandalisms, and harassment that can result when people of color or interracial couples by quirks of fate do manage to reside in these "Good" white neighborhoods; at the numerous instances abounding. We need only look at these to challenge the assumption that in the U.S.A. affiliations of color do not matter anymore and the color line has disappeared.

As if to manifest the presence of this color line and to demarcate its racial divisions, X-caps are comprised of either black or white fabric upon which the solid black letter is superimposed. *Kente* backgrounds or solid and multicolor fabrics of red, yellow, and green—all to transmit meanings of Pan-African liberation—can be used. Often the X itself appears in Pan-African colors or in hues of gold, silver, grey, or white; and superimposed upon the X may be the name "Malcolm" or pins sporting photographs of Malcolm X, Marcus Garvey, Sojourner Truth, Nelson and Winnie Mandela, and other nationalist leaders. These reconfigure the X to be a symbol of global unity and cohesion among peoples of African descent. However, when worn in America, by Blacks *and* whites, in a society that denies the positive contributions of Black people, that denies the very humanity of Black people, these, too, acknowledge the persistence of racism and the psychological toll that white supremacy has exacted upon all Americans. The X-cap wearer who has not read Malcolm's *Autobiography* is walking testimony to this continual denial.

Finally, the Black X acknowledges another trope consistent among African American artistic forms. The Black X marks the crossroads spot that in African American oral and written literatures—and in African American musical and visual expression—symbolizes the intersection of many liabilities and potentials: of inhumanity and personhood, affliction and ease, poverty and affluence, silence and speech, political exclusion and social justice. X marks what Houston A. Baker, Jr. (1984), describes as the "matrix," the "point of ceaseless input and output, [the] web of intersecting, crisscrossing impulses" (p. 3) that elaborates African American culture and is an essential trope of African American song, art, and oral and written discourse. X connotes the crossroads that emblematizes the precarious and uneasy balance that exists between any of these polarities. Instead of a flag or an eagle, it is an X that inscribes the doorposts of Reggie Young's bluesvilles. An X heralds the "up south" that the bluesvilles of the "free North" revealed themselves to be, and its stamp is an assurance as well that the inhabitants of bluesvilles can enfranchise themselves through education, political action, and a variety of literacies.

More than the apparel and bodies of Blacks have stood as historical and psychological texts of autogenesis and as examples of the variety of literacies. In the nineteenth century the voices of women, and the audiences who heard these women's voices, generated another compelling strategy of transmitting culture and transforming lives. Ron Welburn calls attention to this definition of literacy that coincides with "orality and the oral tradition" as he recalls the various narrative styles of his family. The nineteenth century's fugitive slaves—Frederick Douglass, Josiah Henson, Harriet Jacobs, William Wells Brown—all preached their metamorphoses in this oral tradition. Through their lecture tours among abolitionist groups and religious congregations, they payed homage to the word as it is spoken and heard as another form of literacy.

It is not insignificant that the written works of antebellum African American women often commence with invocations of the word, of talk and speech, of the literacy that embodies the activites of speaking and listening. Harriet Jacobs's 1861 narrative, as an example, inclines the ears of white Northern women with a title-page exhortation from the book of Isaiah. " 'Rise up,' " Jacobs commands, " 'ye women that are at ease! Hear my voice, ye careless daughters! Give ear unto my speech' " (Isa. 32:9). Thirty years earlier, a similar strategy was applied in an antislavery tract composed by Boston's Maria Stewart (1831), who cautioned her African sisters:

> I am sensible of exposing myself to calumny and reproach; but shall I, for fear of feeble man who shall die, hold my peace? Shall I for fear of scoffs and frowns, refrain my tongue? Ah, no! I speak as one that must give an account at the awful bar of God; I speak as a dying mortal to dying mortals. O, ye daughters of Africa, awake! Awake! Arise! No longer sleep nor slumber, but distinguish yourselves. (p. 30)

Imperiously, both Jacobs and Stewart allude to Scripture to distinguish their cases. Exclaiming their wishes to a female crowd, both women challenge the shamed and decentered status that "feeble man" expects them as women and as Blacks to uphold. Once they have challenged this status quo and their "careless" sisters complicit in this system, in turn Jacobs and Stewart bestow visibility and voice upon those among their listeners who are marginalized and silent and female, who are Black and white. The singular possessives that they use—"my voice," "my speech," "my peace," "my tongue"—are not to suggest that their words and imaginative visions are their own. Rather, these possessives acknowledge both divine inspiration and the guidance of the collective voices and tongues of the abolitionist movement.

The assertion of female voice by these antebellum African women writers corresponds to that dignity, sanctity, urgency, and truth inherent in the testimonies of all black women. Girded and authorized by references to the omniscient voice of the Bible, this female voice affirmed the utility and power of oral literacies. The oratory of ex–New York slave Sojourner Truth—evangelist, abolitionist, suffragette—especially represents this literacy. "Mere fragments," Loewenberg and Bogin say, "of . . .Truth's compelling oratory survive. Never having learned to read and write, she spoke extemporaneously. Stenographic reporters or admiring friends from time to time recorded her words" (1976, p. 235). Yet Truth raised the spoken word to as contentious and formidable a level as the published narratives of former slaves that Babb and Young have cited. Her influence still on the African American oral tradition is a witnessing and a testament to this achievement.

It is an African American tradition to honor the fusion of words and energy, to exemplify Asante's theory of *nommo* or word-force, "the generative and productive power of the spoken word," which is a theory central to any discussion of African American oratory (Asante, 1987, p. 17). Commensorating this word-force is Bernice Johnson Reagon, an activist, a television commentator, a scholar at the Smithsonian Institution, and an acclaimed singer and founder of the a cappella ensemble Sweet Honey in the Rock. Reagon herself has articulated the concept of multiple literacies that the contributors of this section find essential in their development as writers and scholars. In her essay "Foreword: Nurturing Resistance," she reflects upon her own training as a community leader in the sixties—as a member of the Freedom Singers she traveled throughout the country—in order to end discrimination, lynching, and exclusion of Blacks from the voting booth. She demonstrates an understanding of sound and voice to be catalysts for action. And Reagon observes:

> Growing up in a traditionally based home and community, I had
> seen that it was important for leaders to also be cultural artists
> of great power. Content went beyond text; the virtuosity of delivery
> of a talk, sermon, or speech included both what was said and
> whether the speaker could tune her or his words with feeling.
> Information passed within the traditional forms of the African-
> American culture is concrete reality. . . .Our people respond when
> information is heard and felt. (1990, p. 3)

Although literacy means liberation, as the writers in this section affirm,
they themselves also concur that this statement cannot be true.
Litera*cies*, the abilities to encode and decipher meanings in what is
spoken and shown, are as necessary to liberation as reading and
writing.

In nineteenth- and twentieth-century African American traditions,
both written and read, spoken and told, the train emerges as a recurring
symbol of the necessity to master many literacies for both collective
empowerment and individual autonomy. In song and poster as well
as in text, the train has suggested to African American audiences the
multiplicity of literacies that have contributed to their survival and self-
determination. Examples abound—from the freedom songs of the
Southern slaves to the rhythm and blues ballads of the great Motown
groups, from the iconography of the radical abolitionists of the 1830s
to the Harlem Renaissance artists of the 1930s—that vivify this variety
of literacies. In the spirituals of the Southern slaves, a "heavenly train"
or a "glory train" riding through the wilderness was a coded phrase
for the savvy and wisdom to talk-fool the master, to quit the kitchen
or fields, and to hitch a ride on the Underground Railroad to quasi
freedom in the North. How different were these anonymous sounds
of determination and hope from those of the bluesmen and the ladies
of the blues, the rhythmfolk and bluesfolk who rode the rails and wrote
their songs like "Going to Kansas City" and "Midnight Train to
Georgia"? And this juxtaposition of trains and news, of trains and
information and dialogue, binds blues back to the legacy of the slaves'
organized resistance, back to phrases from the "Underground Railroad"
such as "conductor," "depot," and "pass" that determine both physical
and psychological freedom. And back again the train winds, to the
painting of Harlem Renaissance artist Jacob Lawrence, who in his
"Frederick Douglass Series" (1938–1939) and "Migration of the Negro
Series" (1940–1941) expressed the drama of striving for citizenship and
nationhood with the train as the symbol of Black optimism and energy.

The train suggests African Americans' quests for stability and home in the same way that our signs and sounds were among the few ways in which we could keep our cultures alive in enslavement. Angela Davis has observed that only through song were captive Black people "able to preserve their ethnic heritage, even as they were generations removed from their original homeland and perhaps even unaware that their songs bore witness to and affirmed their African cultural roots" (1990, p. 5). And when Black people conflate the activities of train riding and folk talking, we are invoking simultaneously ideas of appropriation and acculturation, of syncretism and change.

In the nineteenth-century narratives, recording family and community histories is another declaration of selfhood and authority for an African American writer, so much so that the stock beginning for a slave narrative is the recitation of all (and sometimes this means only several sentences) that the author can recall of biological parents and *their* histories, infancy and toddler years, and the inevitable auction of close relatives or extended family members. In the rare instance that the writer actually knows the date and/or location of birth, this information as well is meticulously pronounced. Welburn writes in this tradition when he begins with the stories of his father and his mother and other family members in his "Stories and Styles from Home." Some scholars have connected the standard nineteenth-century beginning—"I was born a slave. . ."—to the African *griot/te* or storyteller's tradition of acknowledging and honoring the lineage and great deeds of community before she or he begins to tell the tale; however, as South African poet Lewis Nkosi observes, "Writing laudatory verses [or praise] to the great and powerful was a fairly widespread practice in Europe and required no particular African predisposition" (1981, p. 110). At any rate, this structure does call attention to what the writers here in "Defining Difference" have observed as the literacy inherent in listening and telling as well as in reading and writing.

My mother's side of my own family provides rich examples of how "listening and telling" mean literacy and of how "rememory" works in one family's oral tradition, and inevitably our listeners are able to identify similar literacies in their own personal relationships. Listening and telling in my family often revolve around discussions of letters and letter writing. The following axioms on the letter form a continuum of childhood memories for me:

A stamp upside down on the envelope means the writer has fallen in love.

A signature incompletely formed implies the author is sneaky and duplicitous.

An undesired and unsolicited chain letter must be passed under running water before the recipient throws it away—else bad luck will occur.

Open an envelope carefully along its crease: fools and feckless folk tear ragged edges.

A dream of a letter is a straightforward omen of good tidings to come your way.

The irony in my family is that, though portents and admonishments on letters and letter writing abound, the entire maternal side of my family is now concentrated throughout the northern and middle tiers of Georgia. Proximity—and the convenience of the cordless phone!—renders many of these warnings idle. Obviously, they constitute one legacy of earlier, divided times: Civil War, economic stagnation, voluntary and temporary migration up North, involuntary and permanent Northern migration on the behest of white-hooded pursuers, passing for white, suffering and resisting enslavement and social injustice. It is significant that the proverbs and stories told person to person about letter writing and receiving have endured as firmly as the letters themselves. This stands as another testament to the premium our Black communities place on the effectiveness of the spoken word.

Perhaps I remember these proverbs because of their cogent connections to the experiences of the nineteenth-century writers whom I research. Though infrequent among the slaves, letters were also significant as means of liberation and cultural survival among nineteenth-century African American communities. Letters were smuggled from fugitives in the North to their family members still in Southern captivity, and letters were channeled out of enslavement and across the Mason-Dixon line with contents of ambrotypes, locks of hair, rings, and other small mementoes. Letters, such as those of Louisa Picquet, were passed between free Blacks and Southern slaveholders to negotiate for the sale of a mother or sibling: literal missives of freedom. Harriet Jacobs participated in such an exchange, receiving news after her escape from her grandmother in the South, who "could not write; but. . .employed others to write for her" (1861, p. 195). Babb also writes of how letter writing figured as a feminized expression of literacy in the pre–Civil War narrative of Harriet Jacobs. And when the Civil War ended, letter writing became one final strategy through which African Americans reassembled families and reconstructed community histories. Many times the letter writers did not read or write themselves: they dictated the words to discreet and empathetic white or free Black scribes. As historian Herbert Gutman (1976) affirms:

> Most adult slaves and former slaves, of course, could not write. But the letters' importance does not rest upon whether they were a common form of slave expression. They were not. What is important is their relationship to the beliefs and behavior of other slaves who left no such historical records. (p. 7)

As expressions of kinship and culture, these dialogues among "writers" and "readers" who oftentimes did not literally write and read are compelling and potent.

As the twenty-first century advances, African American artists across the disciplines—writers, musicians, dancers, painters, sculptors—are reviving in the meaning of literacy the African idea of communicating among generations unborn, living, and dead. This meaning, one easily overlooked in the hoopla surrounding "breakthrough" publications of multicultural literature, is explicitly conveyed by such titles as Mary Helen Washington's *Memory of Kin* (an anthology of short stories), Henry Louis Gates, Jr.'s, *Bearing Witness* (excerpts from Black autobiographies), Houston A. Baker, Jr.'s, *Workings of the Spirit* (essays and phototext on African American women's writing), and *Calling the Wind* (writer Clarence Major's collection of stories). These titles call attention to a literacy that encompasses more than written words and a literacy that extends through more than present time. This is a literacy that speaks to liberation, self-determination, history—what the nineteenth-century African American tradition alluded to and what contemporary artists in that tradition continue to convey.

References

A portion of the newspaper items mentioned in this article were compiled as a result of a 1987–88 American Fellowship that I received from the American Association of University Women Educational Foundation. I am grateful that this fellowship enabled me to travel to the Schomburg Center for Research in Black Culture of the New York Public Library, to the Olin Library of Cornell University, to Brooklyn College and to the University of Rochester in order to gather this information.

Adams, R. L. (1963). *Great Negroes, past and present*. Chicago: Afro-Am Publishing Company, Inc.

Asante, M. K. (1987). *The afrocentric idea*. Philadelphia: Temple University Press.

Baker, H. A., Jr. (1984). *Blues, ideology, and Afro-American literature: A vernacular theory*. Chicago: University of Chicago Press.

Baker, H. A., Jr. (1991). *Workings of the spirit: The poetics of Afro-American women's writing*. Chicago: University of Chicago Press.

Blockson, C. L. (1987). *The underground railroad: First-person narratives of escapes to freedom in the north*. New York: Prentice-Hall.

Carby, H. V. (1987). *Reconstructing womanhood: The emergence of the Afro-American woman novelist*. New York: Oxford University Press.

Cliff, M. (1990). A hanged man. In her *Bodies of water* (pp. 44–52). New York: Dutton.

Coupland, D. (1991). *Generation X: Tales for an accelerated culture*. New York: St. Martin's.

Cowper, W. (1836–1837). *The task*. In Robert Southey (Ed.), *The works of William Cowper* (vol. 9). London: Baldwin and Cradock.

Craft, E. (1852). Letter. *Anti-Slavery Advocate*, p. 22. Reprinted in December 1952 in *Pennsylvania Freeman*, p. 207.

Craft, E. (1852). Description of escape and illustration of male costume, in *The Liberty Almanac* (p. 35).

Craft, E. (1858). Letter by Mrs. L. In *The Liberty Bell* (p. 53). Boston: Prentiss.

Craft, W. (1860). *Running a thousand miles for freedom; Or, the escape of William and Ellen Craft from slavery*. London: William Tweedie.

Davies, C. B. (1991). Writing off marginality, minoring, and effacement. *Women's Studies International Forum, 14*(4), 249–263.

Davis, A. Y. (1990). Black women and music: A historical legacy of struggle. In J. Braxton et al. (Eds.), *Wild women in the whirlwind: Afra-American culture and the contemporary literary renaissance* (pp. 3–21). New Brunswick, NJ: Rutgers University Press.

Douglass, F. (1845). *The narrative of the life of Frederick Douglass, an American slave*. New York: Modern Library, 1984.

Du Bois, W. E. B. (1903). *The souls of Black folk*. New York: New American Library. 1982.

Franklin, J. H. (1990). A life of learning. In H. L. Gates, Jr. (Ed.), *Bearing witness: Selections from African-American autobiography in the twentieth century* (pp. 350–368). New York: Pantheon. (Reprinted from *Race and history: Selected essays 1938–1988*, [1989], pp. 277–291).

Gates, H. L., Jr. (1988). *The signifying monkey: A theory of Afro-American literary criticism*. New York: Oxford University Press.

Gutman, H. G. (1976). *The Black family in slavery and freedom, 1750–1925*. New York: Random House.

Jacobs, H. [Linda Brent]. (1861). *Incidents in the life of a slave girl. Written by herself*. Cambridge: Harvard University Press, 1987.

Loewenberg, B. J., & Bogin, R. (1976). *Black women in nineteenth-century American life: Their words, their thoughts, their feelings*. University Park: Pennsylvania State University Press.

Major, C. (1993). *Calling the wind: Twentieth-century African-American short stories*. New York: Harper Collins.

Malcolm X & Haley, A. (1965). *The autobiography of Malcolm X*. New York: Ballantine Books.

Morrison, T. (1987). *Beloved*. New York: Alfred Knopf.

Morrison, T. (1992). *Playing in the dark: Whiteness and the literary imagination*. Cambridge: Harvard University Press.

Nkosi, L. (1981). *Tasks and masks: Themes and styles of African literature*. London: Longman.

Reagon, B. J. (1990). Foreword: Nurturing resistance. In C. Little et al. (Eds.), *Reimaging America: The arts of social change* (pp. 1–8). Philadelphia: New Society Publishers.

Riggs, M. (1986). *Ethnic notions: Black people in white minds*. San Francisco: California Newsreel.

Sterling, D. (Ed.). (1984). *We are your sisters: Black women in the nineteenth century*. New York: Norton.

Stewart, M. (1831). Religion and the pure principles of morality, The sure foundation on which we must build. In M. Richardson (Ed.), *Maria W. Stewart: America's first black woman political writer: essays and speeches*, (pp. 28–32). Bloomington: Indiana University Press, 1987.

Still, W. (1872). *The underground rail road*. New York: Arno Press and *New York Times*, 1968.

Turner, V. (1969). *The ritual process: Structure and anti-structure*. Chicago: Aldine.

Veney, B. (1889). *The narrative of Bethany Veney: A slave woman*. Worcester, MA. In H. L. Gates, Jr., (Ed.), *Collected Black women's narratives*. New York: Oxford University Press, 1988.

Washington, M. H. (1991). *Memory of kin: Stories about family by Black writers.* New York: Anchor Books/Doubleday.

Wheatley, P. (1733). *Poems on various subjects, religious and moral.* In J. C. Shields (Ed.), *The collected works of Phillis Wheatley* (pp. 1–128). New York: Oxford University Press, 1988.

Yellin, J. F. (1989). *Women and sisters: The antislavery feminists in American culture.* New Haven: Yale University Press.

Part II

Making Space:
Perspectives on Writing Policy

5

The Ideology of Canons and Cultural Concerns in the Literature Curriculum

Alan C. Purves

Demetrius of Phalerum, as keeper of the king's library, received large grants of public money with a view to his collecting, if possible, all the books in the world; and by purchases and transcriptions he to the best of his ability carried the king's purpose into execution. Being asked once in his presence, about how many thousand of books were already collected, he replied: "More than two hundred thousand, O king; and I will ere long make diligent search for the remainder, so that a total of half a million may be reached. I am informed that the Jews also have certain laws which are deserving of transcription and place in the library."

"What is to hinder them then," replied the king, "in this task? For all the necessary means are at thy service." And Demetrius answered: "Translation is also required. For in the Jews' land they use a peculiar script...." And when the king had learnt all the facts, he gave command that a letter should be written to the high priest of the Jews, in order that the proposal [of Demetrius] above mentioned might be carried into effect.

— The Letter of Aristeas, Parsons, 1952, 94–95

Educational Goals and Diverse Cultures

In this paper I will survey some of the issues that face those who must plan curricula in literature and who wish to do so with a full respect for the diverse groups that comprise our society. Although at one time we may have thought that the United States was a melting pot resulting in a single national culture, we have found that that metaphor does not hold and that it fails to respect even those groups that we thought had been assimilated. Our situation is not unlike that described in the epigraph, which treats of the world of letters at the time of the development of the Library at Alexandria over two thousand years ago. A close reading of that description tells us a great deal about our predecessors and ourselves. Like the Hellenistic peoples who first thought "the world" was Greek only, but who came to realize there were cultures other than the Greek, we have also found that the "Western heritage" was an artifact that limited our perspective on the world. This situation has been paralleled in China and Japan as well as other societies. What may have worked for an age of insular nationalism without electronic media does not suffice in a global village where all inhabitants claim equal status.

The current way to think of this new vision in setting policy for literature instruction is in terms of the canon: what works are to be read by whom and in what order? I shall explore this notion in the first part of this chapter, and shall attempt to show how this approach may lead to various dead ends. In the final part of the chapter, I shall offer an alternative view that may be more pedagogically sound.

Education and Acculturation

As Torsten Husén (1990) has noted, education is, by its very nature, ethnocentric. From the very first schools of which we have knowledge to the present, the school system has been in the business of bringing young people into the local, regional, or national culture. For many systems, this function is most clearly realized in the fields of language and literacy study and of history, which is itself a consequence of literacy. Although there has been a recent tendency to think of literacy as a neutral skill, those who promote such a view neglect the fact that people learn to read and write texts and that texts are necessarily about something. Willy-nilly one learns a skill and acquires knowledge; such a truth was well known in Lutheran Sweden, nineteenth-century America, and Castro's Cuba. We deny it at our children's peril. Education in literacy and particularly literature and history leads people away from their individual or familiar past into something broader, a literate community with its own models and norms; it is the main agent of acculturation.

Culture has a variety of meanings, depending upon the bias of the definer; for the purposes of this paper I shall stipulate it to stand for a combination of (a) a set of intellectual beliefs and social practices of a self-defined group of people, and (b) the arts that embody those beliefs. This group can be an ethnic or geographic group. It can also be a group that defines itself by gender, sexual preference, or some other characteristic. Edward Said has noted that "culture is used to designate not merely something to which one belongs but something that one possesses, and along with that proprietary process, culture also designates a boundary by which the concepts of what is extrinsic or intrinsic to the culture comes into forceful play" (Said, 1983, pp. 8–9). Any culture serves to distinguish its members from those of other cultures, and any culture is elitist in some senses; as Said points out, "What is more important in culture is that it is a system of values saturating downward almost everything within its purview; yet paradoxically culture dominates from above without at the same time being available to everything and everyone that it dominates" (Said, 1983, p. 9). Cultures are exclusionary by definition; people who have a culture see others as outside, above, or beneath them; and certainly very few people transcend cultures to become cosmopolites.

Judit Kádár-Fülop (1988) has written that there are three major functions of the literacy curriculum in school as a cultural instrument, and I shall adapt them to the particulars of the literature curriculum. The first of these functions is the promotion of cultural communication so as to enable the individual to communicate with a wider circle than the home, the peers, or the village. Such a function clearly calls for the individual to learn the literature and lore of the culture, the texts valued by the culture. The second function is the promotion of cultural identity, which includes the accepting and valuing of those texts and the inculcation of a desire to have them remain as "classics." The third function of literacy education is the development of individuality. Once one has learned to communicate within the culture and developed a loyalty to it, then one is able to become independent of it. In terms of literature, after one accepts the cultural "classics," one can develop individual tastes and interests. Some societies do not encourage this third step.

Education fulfills these functions not without cost; again to cite the comments of Edward Said: "When our students are taught such things as 'the humanities' they are almost always taught that these classic texts embody, express, represent what is best in our, that is, the only, tradition. Moreover, they are taught that such fields as the humanities and such subfields as 'literature' exist in a relatively neutral political element, that they are to be appreciated and venerated, that they define the limits of what is acceptable, appropriate, and legitimate as far as culture is concerned" (Said, 1983, p. 21). Said, it should be noted, is writing as a scholar and professor of English literature who is also a Palestinian and is recognizing the paradox in his own life. This paradox has been noted by many others who have grown up in a postcolonial world. We can see the irony in the letter of Aristeas and its many parallels across the globe today.

Recognizing Other Cultures

We live in a time when cultural definitions shift either through an influx of new cultural groups, the breaking up of larger polities, or the belated recognition of existing but suppressed cultural groups. Monolithic national cultures have been challenged by ethnic groups across the world. They have also been challenged by the self-definition of groups like women, by the arrival of new artists of mixed backgrounds, and by the very existence of a popular culture.

The educational solutions to this situation, which is more an ideological than a curricular issue, vary according to the ideological beliefs of those in power. In many parts of the world the issue is one of language policy, which is to say political policy (Foster, 1991). The options have included a program planned to assimilate the new groups into the existing one, as was the case in the United States in the early part of the twentieth century (Bell, 1965) and as seems to be the case in France and its colonies; a program designed to create a new unifying "culture," as is the case of Indonesia; a program planned to ignore the subgroup as uneducable, as has been the case of the treatment of the Gypsies in countries like Finland, Hungary, and other European countries as well as in Indonesia with respect to the Chinese; one planned to establish separate educational systems, as was the case with many immigrant groups in the United States and can be seen today with a group like the Amish as well as in a country like Belgium, which has evolved two school systems for the Walloons and the Flemish; or one planned to meet the demand on the educational system that it accommodate the new populations by including their culture in the curriculum and thus redefining culture. The last example is the situation in the United States today, and is paralleled in countries like Canada, New Zealand, and England. The situation in the United States and Canada, I believe, differs from that in Europe or England or in other former colonies because the dominant cultures in Canada and the United States are themselves immigrant cultures and they themselves are culturally and linguistically diverse. In the United States as well as other parts of the world, there the fact is that some of the minority cultures are what Ogbu (1978) calls "caste cultures," peoples who came or were brought as slaves or lower-caste workers. Although they could be compared to the "guest workers" of Europe, I believe their status is actually quite different. The Turkish population of Germany views itself and is viewed as temporary residents; such was not the case of the African slaves or the Chinese laboring force.

To pursue the alternative of accommodating to the new populations rather than ignoring them, I would argue that the educational system has generally approached it by adding the classics of any newly recognized culture and thus changing the canon by evolution; thus white American texts were added to British ones in the late nineteenth and early twentieth century, and African American texts to the American in the mid-twentieth century, and so on. It is a slow process similar to the gradual addition to the British canon of colonial writers or to the French of the francophone. The alternative that has emerged since the 1960s has been to create separate canons for various groups (the practice had occurred within the groups themselves but was often not recognized by the official curriculum, as the Irish group lead by Yeats testifies). Educational planners are now being asked by many groups to speed up the evolutionary process, to incorporate the separatist movement into the official curriculum, or to do both. This demand comes under the umbrella term *multiculturalism*. The call for multiculturalism in the schools of the United States is to include in significant numbers representative texts and authors that may be defined by ethnic membership, in particular Hispanic, African American, Native American, and Asian. To this group have been added women, and there have been voices calling for the inclusion of homosexuals and those with distinct physical characteristics. One should carefully note that the issue does not concern "world literature"; in that sense, for the United States, multiculturalism remains ethnocentric.

The practical issues raised by this call include problems of canon definition, problems of time, and problems of access to materials, including such matters as cost and censorship. To my mind these issues can be separated for the purposes of discussion, but in the real world of the schools and curriculum making, they often impinge upon each other and combine in various ways to force decisions on teachers and curriculum planners that are other than what they would have in an ideal world. In making my arguments, I will focus primarily on the theoretical issues and on the U.S. situation, but will occasionally refer to that in Canada, England, and New Zealand, as well as some European countries of which I have knowledge.

The major theoretical issue that the various parties to the controversy argue is how to approach literature and its reading in the light of cultural diversity and of the structure of the curriculum in terms of how it is taught, not of what is taught. In making their various canonical decisions, they proceed to conceive of literature instruction in the same terms as when the canon was seemingly one.

Looking at the Canon Wars

As it has been portrayed, the overwhelming issue in the admission of "new" cultures such as the African American, female, or Latino/a to the literature curriculum is that of the determination of the appropriate canon to represent a culture and how to place that canon in relation to the existing one. The questions surrounding a canon of literature are not new, and they have been ideological rather than pedagogical issues, or even literary issues, as Northrop Frye has been so patiently telling us for over thirty years (Frye, 1957). There was the question of the canon of Scripture in many religions, setting forth what is canonical and what is apocryphal. In his brilliant essay, Wendell Harris (1991) observes that despite the etymology of *canon*, biblical canonicity is not an appropriate model for our thinking about literature. More important for our purposes were the issues surrounding the Library at Alexandria, that monument of Hellenistic Greece wherein all of the major Greek texts were collected as well as various works that were donated to it or which came from muniments left the library. To these were added many Jewish texts as well as those from other Eastern cultures; as the epigraph notes, the addition was not what was originally planned. It was a diverse and rich collection, and one of the problems facing the librarians was what to preserve, for much was on papyrus, a fragile medium. As Parsons (1952) has written,

> Before Alexandria, men had considered Aeschylus, Sophocles, and Euripedes as the greatest tragic writers and Homer as the greatest Epic writer, if not the greatest of all writers, and these, perhaps individual, preferences had a public approval. But it was apparently reserved for the scholars of the Museum-Library to select in their literary laboratory the foremost writers and to construct lists or canons of their selection. (p. 224)

The origin of the word *canon* means "rule or measure," so that the lists serve as criteria for selection rather than as fixed boundaries. The scholars made their selection, fallible as they were, and it remained, although added to from time to time, and it is from that canon that we know Greek culture, as well as what the Hellenes included from the "barbarian" world surrounding theirs. Archeology has given us a taste of what was not included (the Gilgamesh epic), either because unknown to or spurned by the scholars.

Every society and culture has a canon, that body of artistic works which are considered central to a group's self-definition; some were formed as deliberately as that of the Alexandrian Library; others formed much more haphazardly. Petrarch and his successors formed the canon of Roman and later Greek literature by what they could salvage from monasteries and nunneries. Their success depended upon happenstance and the vagaries of the abbots and prioresses as well as the ability of the searchers to copy materials quickly before they deteriorated or were destroyed (Deuel, 1965). As Harris (1991) observes, there are several operating definitions of *canon*, each of which can be seen as the fruit of an individual or a group defining a body of texts that serves a particular function. In a sense, the term is as slippery as *culture*. It may be cynically seen as what we believe should be read, viewed, seen, or listened to by those who would join us. What makes it problematic and political is that it has come to be part of a national debate on the nature of our society and the government's role in defining that society. It has become reified in a way that far exceeds the historical reality of what we know about canons.

How Canons Are Really Made

In few cases is there a consensus as to what belongs in the canon, what is excluded, and what is marginal. The makers of canons include editors, reviewers, librarians, historians, and others concerned with the determination of what shall be known of a culture or a society. In our society, literary canons are determined by diverse forces; Janice Radway painstakingly describes canon formation among a group of midwestern women (Radway, 1984) who meet through a bookseller to determine the "classic" romances. Others have described the ways by which the canons of popular culture such as film, television, and music are created through combinations of market research and promotion. These too have the aspects of canons, as do comic books and commercial juvenile and adolescent literature.

At times, as in Radway's example, those who set a canon are members of a culture; often they are from without. Such is true of the Renaissance scholars and the later archeologists who had to be content with what they could find and decipher. All we have of the "literary canon" of certain Mesopotamian cultures is a collection of tables of the price of corn. Let us hope that those who could read had something else to amuse themselves with and that mothers had other tales for their children.

Another group of external definers of a canon includes the folklorist-anthropologists who determined what they would preserve of various dying cultures and societies throughout the world. At times they made selections; most other times the selection was determined by their informants, who might have had many motives for their selection. We must remember that for many societies the very idea of recording folktales and folksongs is new, less than a century old; what is recorded is but the tip of an iceberg and it probably is not revealing of a full culture.

If we examine the body of texts from the past two centuries in the United States to select representative texts of a cultural group, we are again at the mercy of printers and booksellers, of magazine and newspaper publishers, and of the marketplace. Even in the "dominant culture," canon formation is about as scientific as the stock market or the top forty in pop records (itself a "nonce" canon, to use Harris's term). Whether it represents the best or the "classic," the most representative, or the popular is arguable. We know that in England F. R. Leavis led a propaganda campaign to get Lawrence into the curriculum and Tennyson out of it; similar campaigns have been waged in this country. Scott, Hardy, and George Eliot have been driven out of the school curriculum by various groups. The inclusion of one writer is subject to fashion, and writers blossom and fade based on the taste of editors and teachers, not to mention students. Contemporary writers, particularly of children's and adolescent literature, are promoted and sold by cartels of publishers, reviewers, teachers, and librarians.

Canons are capricious human selections among artifacts and are subject to change as the criteria change. Matthew Arnold's list of the "best that has been thought or said" contains holes such as the works of the eighteenth century. T. S. Eliot and Archibald MacLeish helped bring Donne and the metaphysical poets back into favor. Whatever approach to the literature curriculum one adopts, one is always subject to criticism on specific authors and titles, and one can never *fix* what is most important for young people to read from whatever heritage. A particular canon is probably not adequate to the culture at large nor even to the "elite" within that culture. Curriculum planners need to acknowledge and accept the limitation of what is selected; they should never be seduced into defending it, as William Bennett and Allan Bloom did, as the best and enduring monuments, nor attacking it as being a monolith that excluded minorities, women, and homosexuals, as some of the critics of Bloom and Bennett have done. Some texts and writers have greater staying power than others; that is about all we can say. Why they stay is partly a matter of intrinsic quality but mostly the result of fashion. Because of their staying power, they have had greater influence on other artists and on the culture. Curriculum planners should simply say: "These are the works that we think best represent and define the cultures of the world in which our students live and the larger world culture. The list represents our judgment and it is subject to revision."

Educational Time and Access to Cultural Materials

Our main concern in this paper is what Harris calls the "pedagogical canon": If we take Fowler's (1979) official canon to mean something like all the authors and titles in whatever reasonably comprehensive literary histories are standard at a given time and if we accept his definition of the critical canon as the texts most written about at the time, the list of works commonly taught in high school and undergraduate courses will be not only much shorter than the official canon but also unlikely to correspond exactly to the critical canon (Harris, 1991, pp. 112–113). The reason for the discrepancy stems from practical problems of canon implementation that include those of fitting new materials into a crowded school day and calendar. In colleges and universities, where the approach to the curriculum is that of the cafeteria, the problem is not great. Anyone can add a course and with perseverance turn it into a department. The primary and secondary schools are another matter. Legislatures continually mandate new topics to be inserted into the curriculum; they seldom mandate the deletion of a topic. If they talk about lengthening the school day or the school year, it is to boost the amount of science and mathematics and not to allow teachers and students time to consider matters of culture. So those who plan the day-to-day lives of school find themselves having to use thinner and thinner shoehorns to make the shoe fit. As the demands for cultural inclusion mount, the school must take something out. But the teachers are often conservative and do not want to give up what they have been teaching. Teachers are particularly reluctant to work on interdisciplinary projects, a sad fact at all levels of education from the grade school to the graduate school; departmental and disciplinary tugs are much too strong. The plea that is often given for not taking a more active part in these efforts is time, daily time, yearly time, or time in the total program of education. To add works representing new canons to the existing course or to add new courses or units represents a disruption of time; innovators insist that time be sacrificed for a new look at the world and ourselves.

A current example at the college level can be seen in the new *Heath Anthology of American Literature* (Lauter, 1990; see also Edmundson, 1990). The anthology intends to be comprehensive and representative of cultural diversity, including Native American traditions, as well as Africana, Hispanic, Asian, and a broader representation of women and of new contemporary writers. As Mark Edmundson notes in his review, "The *Heath* aspires to be simultaneously an ideal political image of America, and a celebration of artistic achievement" (Edmundson, 1990, p. 1133). At the same time, it slights other American groups, such as the Middle Eastern and Eastern European. The problem that this admirable anthology presents for the curriculum is that it contains about six thousand pages. How can that be fitted into a year's course, much less a semester's, at better than a sprint through the pages? It is likely that the faculty will select, and the selection may well fail to meet the compromise. As Harris writes, "Recent textbook anthologies have fattened noticeably in their editors' attempts to represent greater cultural diversity, but the length of the semesters has unfortunately remained the same" (Harris, 1991, p. 118).

The second set of constraints upon implementing programs that deliberately set out to introduce students to the canons of various groups, either through separate units or the integration of these groups into a broader survey, is that of availability of materials. Many of the texts that would be taught in multicultural programs are relatively new; as such they present problems of permissions cost, availability, and censorship. The first of these is a problem for the publisher or editor who would create an anthology. The *Heath* volumes cost about $50. I was editor of a 7–12 series in the 1970s that strove to increase the representations of African Americans, Latinos, women, and contemporary world literature. The series went out of print quickly, but I and my colleagues still owe the publisher about $500,000 in permissions costs—most of it for the material I mention above. We, none of us, begrudged the authors receiving this money—but we doubted whether they would get it. Such costs, however, represent a major expense to a publisher and are daunting to editors and schools, for the increased cost must be shared.

The series went out of print quickly for the other reason that provides a curb on multicultural programs—censorship. Our series provided a target for the "religious right," which was just then flexing its muscle, and we were quickly put on the blacklist. The ostensible reason was not that we were publishing works by minority populations (although it was remarkable that the works cited for language, sex, drugs, violence, attacks on the police, and the like happened to be by African Americans, Native Americans, and Latinos, both female and male). In part, many works of contemporary literature from various cultures touch upon contemporary topics and issues. Because these topics are so prevalent in our society, works that deal with them are paradoxically grist for the censor's mill. What many seem to tolerate on television and in the popular press they will not tolerate in the schools. The problem for the editor and curriculum planner is how to deal with this paradox of our society. It is not a new paradox; Shakespeare, Milton, and Shelley faced it and so did Wilde, each of whom is now "safe."

The issues of time, availability, and use of materials are real problems for the implementation of literature programs that seek to represent diverse cultures. They are tangible problems and manageable ones. The more intangible problems are those of purpose and program development, both of which are thorny and made more problematic by the practical issues to which I have referred in this section.

Parallelism or Integration in the Pedagogical Canon

In 1989, the New York Task Force on Multicultural Education issued a statement concerning the school curriculum which they titled "A Curriculum of Inclusion." Although it focuses on social studies, that report raises many of the issues that frame the curricular debate. The task force espouses a program that segments selected ethnic cultures into their own units or courses. It suggests a structure that would have a block of curricular time devoted to each group, particularly African and Hispanic, and would have each course taught independently. Opposed to this is an approach that would seek to bring these different cultures under a single umbrella and teach them interdependently. This is what is proposed in California and in other settings.

What is suggested in the New York plan is what Diane Ravitch (1990) calls "particularism," which she sees as a deliberate attempt to divide the polymorphous American cultural democracy into a series of ghettoized cultures. She attacks such an approach on intellectual grounds and sets up the integrated approach as a desirable solution to the curriculum. She believes it to be truer to a historical reality. The debate between Ravitch and her opponents over the New York plan is a debate about the curriculum in history.

When we transfer this debate to the literature curriculum in the elementary and secondary schools, we see, I would argue, difficulties in both options. The separatist approach presents grave logistical problems of whom or what to include in whatever brief time is allotted; but then so does the integrated approach. The separatist approach tends to valorize particular minority cultures and denies the fact that literary texts from the "minority" cultures play against the "majority" culture, as the poetry and drama of a writer like Baraka so clearly shows. That being so, the students may be at a loss as to what is going on in those works. On the other hand, the integrated approach may fail to point out the specific cultural roots of a particular text. The debate concerning the approach to literature seems to me to be a debate among scholars rather than a debate among educators. It also seems a debate that may have some liveliness at the college level, but which is finally a nondebate since the college operates on the caveat emptor approach to curriculum, but which becomes obscure and precious when applied to the common school, where everyone has to take everything.

The Futility of the Canon Wars

Both sides in the debate are elitist, urging an approach to the curriculum that seeks to teach some "canon" that emerges from the academy (usually the literary academy, although, in the case of folklore, the anthropological academy also sanctions a canon). Against them stands the culture of the students, children who have been raised in the broader culture of television and other media that has an ambiguous relationship to either the traditional Euro-American or the valorized ethnic cultures. The media tend to homogenize culture into a world of The Simpsons, Madonna, Richie Valens, Oprah Winfrey, Michael Jackson, and Vanilla Ice, a world where color, race, ethnicity, and gender are commodities. At times the works of these cultural figures play against a "school" culture of the traditional canon much as does the humor of *Mad Magazine, Sesame Street,* and *Bugs Bunny.* They allude both to the stalwarts of the traditional and some of the ethnic canons as well as to the canons of film, music, and television. Media culture has brought with it the merging of ethnic and cultural strands in food, dance, music, drama, and dress. Advertisers and producers change the color or the language of their commercials, but they do not change the content.

Such a broad culture is the culture of the students. It is the one they have been sold whether they live on an Amish farm in Illinois, a barrio in Miami, or a reservation; it has become internationalized as well. The school represents a culture distinct from these students and their families, no matter how the school tries to represent itself. School literature is distinct from many people's culture, no matter how hard it tries to present the heritage of the people in glossy courses whether separatist or integrationist. The texts presented represent a canon of "high" culture, not one of "mass" culture (I am using these two not as values but as indices of the source of the canon). Many students see school literature as "texts that teachers like." The school takes literature and makes it a matter of study and testing. The commercial culture makes no such demands on the students; they can become part of it, learn it, and even become experts in it without taking any tests, seeing coercion, or feeling the threat of failure behind the invitation to partake in it.

It seems to me that the debate over the canon and the curriculum is a debate in Laputa. The schools lie under that floating island in a world inhabited by people who read, listen, and view other materials that have been touched by, but are nearly independent of, the ethereal culture of English, African, Hispanic, or feminist studies. The world on the mainland is a multicultural world indeed; its inhabitants have all sorts of roots and histories. Those histories have been touched by the arts and the literature of the academy, but the cultural icons are popular and not academic. At the same time serious artists have their feet planted firmly in both the popular and the academic worlds; only a few in any society are so esoteric as to be oblivious of the world around them.

The schools of our society are asked to help people get in touch with the higher cultures and are often enjoined to criticize the popular culture. In responding to this request, the schools ride into the canon wars and get attacked by everyone. Those who attack with their feet and minds are the students to whom whatever literature the schools offer is simply a vehicle for testing and sorting. If it is to be read, it is not to allow them to explore the culture or the society of an ethnic group or of the broader world. It exists to be the object of searches for literal meaning or the springboard for the development of critical talk. It exists apart from the world outside of school and the culture that the students (and their parents) inhabit.

The canon wars are political wars that attack the schools and perhaps tear them apart. I question whether they will affect the lives and cultures of most of our students. The previous debates on the canon have had relatively little impact on the culture of our society; I doubt if this one will, but I think that the canon wars have raised a deeper issue: the nature of what it is we are about when we teach literature.

Looking at the Underlying Issues

A literature curriculum is not simply a matter of a canon. As I have argued for years (Purves, 1988; Purves, Rogers, & Söter, 1990), a literature curriculum embodies a theory of the text and seeks to do more than simply have students read works. They must talk, write, and otherwise display their responses to what is read by expressing either their understandings, their attitudes, or their beliefs and judgments. As Kádár-Fülop (1988) noted, the literacy curriculum seeks to promote cultural communication and cultural identification, to socialize and humanize students through the reading and discussing of texts, and these two goals exhibit themselves not only in what is read but the way in which it is read and understood.

Cultural Literacy and Acculturation as Issues Defining the Literature Curriculum

The following statement from the New York Task Force described earlier sets the terms of the issue of the ends of a multicultural curriculum. "A restructuring of the entire curriculum must be done not in a piecemeal fashion but rather in a fundamental manner to insure that the pluralistic nature of our society is clearly represented and that students of all [sic] cultures are properly educated. Aspects of cooperation and amicability among all cultures should be stressed over conflict and violence" (Sobol, 1989, p. 40). The last sentence of the paragraph can be construed as saying that the literature as well as the history of the various cultural groups should deny the strife, oppression, and resistance that has existed among and between them; history should be rewritten in order to affect the students' attitudes. A sharper example can be found in the executive summary:

> The Task Force promotes the idea that all curricular materials be prepared on the basis of multicultural contributions to the development of all aspects of our society. Such a balanced, integrated approach is seen as serving the interests of all children from all cultures: children from Native American, Puerto Rican/Latino, Asian American, and African American cultures will have higher

self-esteem and self-respect, while children from European cultures will have a less arrogant perspective of being part of the group that has done it all. (Sobol, 1989, p. 4)

Again the text clearly suggests that a major focus of the curriculum is to affect the beliefs and attitudes of the children, to "raise" or "change" their consciousness, which is to say it is to acculturate the children. One can quarrel with the substance of the last clause, which suggests— contrary to reality—that all European immigrant cultures share the arrogance of the Anglo-Saxon. Clearly, the intent of the curriculum is to effect a sea change in ethnic and cultural attitudes and beliefs, which I find frightening and as tyrannical an approach to culture as that of the Anglo-Saxon approach. However, the question I would raise here is less that of desirability of the goal than that of the feasibility of its success.

The formation of such a goal is based on the idea of literature's moral or affective force. Such a belief permeates American thinking about literature and is the basis for, among other things, censorship; it lies behind the recent trials of the Cincinnati Arts Center and 2 Live Crew. There has been some research on the capacity of literature to accomplish this goal: some of it has dealt with cultural attitudes, some with moral beliefs, and some with personal codes and attitudes toward issues such as death or divorce. The results suggest that the reading of literature tends to reinforce attitudes and beliefs rather than to effect conversions (Beach & Hynds, 1990; Purves & Beach, 1972). Such is also the position of reader-response theory, which tells us that readers bring their heads and hearts to the text and create meanings rather than simply abstract them from the unvarying message of the text. The reader is not a passive recipient of the text and the cultural values it embodies. Research and theory, then, tend to cast doubt on the capacity of a text by itself to acculturate peoples to a culture that is not the one to which they are accustomed as filiated members or one about which they are predisposed to understand and appreciate.

On the other hand, there is a body of research that suggests that schooling, particularly schooling in literacy, has a strong influence on habits of mind and creates the mental conditions that help to define cultural practices (Langer, 1990; Purves, 1973, 1990). Being asked to approach texts the same way from the first day of school to the last breeds a way of responding to texts that pervades an individual's outlook and that clearly can be seen as a cultural artifact. Similarly, by being exposed to only one type of literary text (such as rhymed poetry or stories that have only happy endings), students probably come to recognize these as somehow sanctioned and other kinds of texts as less sanctioned or as not being literature. The empirical evidence for the last point is not as clear as for the first, that dealing with type of response; yet it would follow that the two points have equal force. If students learn to see that one approach to a text is culturally approved, they can also learn to see that one form of text receives such approval. We do not know whether extensive exposure to texts from one culture can limit the vision of readers over time. But such is the argument for the cultural pluralists, and it would seem to have some support.

How can we put together these two findings about acculturation that appear to be diametrically opposed? On the one hand, it seems clear that simply reading a few texts that show a culture in a particular light or that espouse a particular viewpoint will do little to affect the attitudes and beliefs of readers other than to reinforce existing beliefs; on the other hand, prolonged exposure to a particular type of literature or a particular approach to literature will have an effect on the beliefs of students and readers.

Acculturation, it would seem, results from a deliberate and prolonged immersion into a culture; it cannot be accomplished on an hour-a-day basis for a semester. This being so, it would seem that if one is concerned with acculturation, one must look at the K–16 curriculum in reading, history, and literature, and determine what its potential long-term effects might be. To examine simply a unit, a course in the middle school, or the American literature curriculum in the eleventh grade will not suffice. Second, one must reexamine the approach to text that imbues the curriculum, and it is here, I think, that the problem and the solution lie. If we do not change our way of teaching literature, then the goal of attitude change and indoctrination should probably be abandoned for the more modest one of introduction. It may be prudent to settle for teaching students about a culture such as the Native American, for making them aware of the depth and strength and pride of that culture, its uniqueness and its common concerns with other cultures. Surely such knowledge and appreciation cannot hurt those who are not Native Americans; and it will probably serve to reinforce the self-esteem of those who are.

The Double Vision:
An Alternate Approach to the Canon Dilemma

I should like, however, to propose an alternative way of thinking about the problem that arises from the point I have just made. Although it will not go away, the issue of text selection cannot be divorced from that of the perspective by which one approaches literature. The current approach to the teaching of literature has, paradoxically, led to the canon wars, and these wars have, as we have seen, confined themselves to the texts and to the ways in which the texts are read. The canon issues are issues of taste and ideology, and such issues can never be resolved. To return to Said's criticism of the supposed neutrality of the current view of the humanities and the single canon, that view stems from an ideology that holds the text autonomous and the reader clever but ignorant.

The view of literature instruction in vogue in the United States for the past sixty years is one which sees the literary text as detached from its author and its culture. In 1929, I. A. Richards suggested that the problem many students had in reading literature stemmed from the fact that they could not read poems when those poems were detached from author and history. To prove his point, he gave students poems without any external information, asked students to write about them, and showed the varied nature of their misreadings (Richards, 1929). One can argue that his experiment was doomed to success. Richards magnificently showed that many of the problems readers had resulted from lack of knowledge about the circumstances of the poem, from cognitive failure, and from the attempt to fit the text to various critical, emotional, and topical preconceptions. The result of his study was to lead critics and teachers to dismiss the first cause (ignorance) and to develop curricula which would help students read texts that they knew nothing about, and from whom background knowledge was barred. In the heyday of this approach, some poetry anthologies went to great length to hide the names of the authors from the reader so as to minimize the influence of knowledge.

At the college level, critics and teachers turned to a variety of strategies: the New Criticism, rhetorical criticism, reader-response theory, structuralism, poststructuralism, semiotics, myth criticism, Freudian criticism, and the like. In most cases these approaches took the famous triangle of writer-text-reader, and lopped off the right-hand term. They took either objective or pragmatic approaches to criticism (Abrams, 1953). Varied as they may be, they have all subscribed to the "authorless" text and the "ignorant but clever" reader. One of the most famous essays of the fifties attacked the "intentional fallacy" as leading away from the understanding of the text as a "verbal icon" (Wimsatt & Beardsley, 1946). Terms have abounded for the authorless text: *persona, implied author, mask*. They have also abounded for the innocent reader: *subjective criticism, reader-response, reading from context, new critic*.

These ideas concerning text and reader filtered to the secondary school; for years articles in *English Journal* as well as more scholarly works have derided the presence of biographical information in the anthologies (in part because it is detached from the reading of the text). The idea of the authorless text has permeated even to the field of reading, where experts hold that the reader should determine meaning, as one camp has it, by "word attack," or, as another has it, by "gathering meaning from context." Even cognitive psychology has been focused on text and reader, with its limitation of "schema theory" to the reader's knowledge of the content and structure of the text rather than to the idea of the author and intention.

Into this framework, the importance of the gender and race of the writer has exploded along with the politics of culture. If the canon wars and their ideological frameworks become important, and if at the same time literature is to be taught within the ideology that holds that writers, canons, and cultures didn't exist, then the result is confusion. In reading and literature instruction as well as in curriculum, the focus has been on text and reader. Instead of the intentional fallacy, the current approach to criticism and teaching commits what I would call the *fallacy of anonymity*. It assumes that the text is a self-contained artifact which we can probe and analyze and which we can see in terms of our experience. The experience of the writer and the experiences which surround the text are immaterial because they are unverifiable. All we can verify is our individual and perhaps group experience of the object. Ignorance of history and culture, ignorance of the author and her world, are the outcomes and the hallmark of the "good" reader.

The advocates of feminist, African American, Hispanic, and other cultural studies to whom I have talked, however, are saying that such a view is myopic. As other essays in this volume proclaim, texts come from writers who inhabit cultural contexts which shape their writing. The text is simultaneously an individual aesthetic object and a cultural document, a part of the legacy of an individual and a group. The literature of a country is the literature of men and women of all sorts of subcultures—racial, ethnic, national, regional, and local. Such texts should be read not as disembodied from their creators but as intimate parts of their culture. Reading the text is to read it in the light of what Hazlitt called the "spirit of the age" or of the culture. Such reading is to affirm in principle the distinction between what E. D. Hirsch, Jr. (1976), called the "meaning" of a text, that which refers to the text in cultural and authorial context, as opposed to the "significance" of the text, that which we, distant from that culture, make of it. That Shakespeare "writ not for an age but for all time" must be recast as

"Shakespeare wrote both for an age and for all time," and so does Chinua Achebe and Margaret Atwood.

If we adopt a broader view of literature and its teaching, the canon wars take on a different nature. Special courses and departments have their place at the university, but in that arena that we call general education, it may be better to take a different approach. We should start from the premise that, like other pieces of art, literary texts have creators who inhabit and half-create the various cultures of the world. If we remember that simple fact, then we have reinstated the author and we see that texts come from a context that is rich and complex; they can best be understood within that context. As we read the text, we build that context and we also use that context to help us read the text. We are not to be ignorant, but clever readers, relying on our own wits to come up with the clever interpretation. We are readers who strive to be more fully aware of the writer's world and the text's relation to that world. We make connections among texts and build our canons and examine the mosaic of cultures that constitute our world.

What is important in the curriculum, particularly at the secondary level, is to provide a broad variety of texts from around the world (with some focus on the United States, but not a myopic view of even our own country that the Sobol report endorses). Such a view is that of Northrop Frye (1957), who held that all works of literature are to be held as equally valid, and that it is not the role of criticism or the schools to rank them. In one of his last writings he summarized his definition of literature:

> ...where the organizing principles are myth, that is, story or narrative, and metaphor, that is, figured language. Here we are in a completely liberal world, the world of the free movement of the spirit. If we read a story there is no pressure to believe in it or act upon it; if we encounter metaphors in poetry, we need not worry about their factual absurdity. Literature incorporates our ideological concerns, but it devotes itself mainly to the primary ones, in both physical and spiritual forms: its fictions show human beings in the primary throes of surviving, loving, prospering, and fighting with the frustrations that block those things. It is at once a world of relaxation, where even the most terrible tragedies are still called plays, and a world of far greater intensity than ordinary life affords. In short it does everything that can be done for people except transform them. It creates a world that the spirit can live in, but it does not make us spiritual beings. (Frye, 1991, p. 16)

In taking such a definition, we see that an individual work is a part of the totality of myth; at the same time it is situated in the world from which it came. This double vision must hold and must be taught.

In transforming this double vision to the curriculum, we must recognize the pressures of the world in which teachers and students reside. To be sure, there must be constraints to ensure a breadth of selection from the totality of literature—Sappho to Narayan; tales of the First Nations of this continent to those of Stan Lee, Harper Lee, and Spike Lee. These works might be grouped at times by the cultures of the authors, but at times texts from disparate cultures might be yoked so they can be compared and contrasted. Both groupings help students learn to look at texts both as individual worlds of the larger universe of myth and metaphor and as written by people who have real lives and real backgrounds, and who express in manifold ways their culture, whether it be a mainstream culture or a marginalized culture, whether it be a culture of race, gender, sexuality, or physical difference. We can read John Milton's poetry as the work of an Englishman, a defeated and disgraced Protestant radical, a man, and a blind person. All of these additions to our knowledge help us to see a work like *Samson Agonistes* more clearly than if we treated it as anonymous. But we cannot forget it is also part of the larger matrix of drama. We can make the same claim about Gwendolyn Brooks, American, African American, woman, urbanite, midwesterner, caught up in the Civil Rights movement of the 1960s both in the South, in Chicago, and in its suburbs. To know these facets of the poet is to help us read "The Ballad of Rudolph Reed." But we must also read it as a ballad, a poetic object.

In my own teaching of poetry at the college level, I have moved away from an approach that focuses solely on the students' naked responses to the texts, not that these are unimportant but that they serve to raise questions about the text and where it comes from as well as who it comes from. I now suggest that when they read a poem they should find out something about the poet and test how that knowledge brings them a newer or deeper understanding of the text. The course title is "Reading Poetry"; I have mentally changed it to "Reading Poets." We consider the gender and ethnicity of the poets and how that may affect their and our perspective on the subject. We have looked at Swift as an Irish poet in a London that had ground down his people, and at Yeats as an Irish poet in a different age. We have looked at Audre Lorde as an African American woman and a lesbian, at Leslie Silko as a Native American, and at Josephine Miles as a woman crippled by rheumatoid arthritis.

As a final examination I have given the students some poems by Ron Welburn and a portion of his essay on his writing and asked how reading the essay has helped them. Their responses made many different kinds of connections. One said, "The essay helped me see how bitterness can become art." Another wrote that although her feelings about them did not change, she could now "understand the poems more fully." Another mentioned the ways in which the essay made her look at the legends behind the poems. One connected the loss of culture in the poems to Welburn's personal statement of his attempt to regain it. Another found that the essay led him to look at the storytelling elements in the poems. Another wrote of the ways in which the essay forced him to reexamine the imagery in the poem. One connected Welburn's poems to poems written by an Irish ancestor of hers who was forced off the land in the nineteenth century. Each of these and the others find that the information does not limit their response, but that it does make it deeper and, I suspect, more lasting.

I would argue that in order to celebrate the cultures of our world, it is not enough to have courses or units on these cultures and treat the texts as if the writer is nonexistent and as if the reader can look only at her response to the naked text. We must take off the mask of ignorance in our teaching of literature. We must not expect the naive reader to understand cultural difference if we treat all texts as contemporary, genderless, and mainstream. We must not fool ourselves with the fallacy of anonymity. To look at texts as the works of human beings who have a past and a culture is to see literature, ourselves, and our culture whole. The texts build upon other texts and they do indeed both emerge from and reshape a culture or a subculture. To adopt such a view is to make the canon wars recede; it may even help our students become serious readers of texts and the cultures from which they spring.

References

Abrams, M. (1953). *The mirror and the lamp: Romantic theory and the critical tradition.* New York: Norton.

Beach, R., & Hynds, S. (1990). Research on response to literature. In E. J. Farrell & J. Squire (Eds.), *Transactions with literature: A fifty-year perspective.* Urbana, IL: National Council of Teachers of English.

Bell, D. (1966). *The preforming of general education.* New York and London: Columbia University Press.

Deuel, L. (1965). *Testaments of time: The search for lost manuscripts and records.* New York: Alfred Knopf.

Edmundson, M. (1990, October 25). Dangers of democracy. *London Times Literary Supplement,* p. 1133.

Foster, P. (1991). Literacy and the politics of language. In E. M. Jennings & A. C. Purves (Eds.), *Literate systems and individual lives: Perspectives on literacy and schooling* (pp. 37–50). Albany, NY: SUNY Press.

Fowler, A. (1979). Genre and the literary canon. *New Literary History, 11,* 97–119.

Frye. N. (1957). *The anatomy of criticism.* Princeton: Princeton University Press.

Frye, N. (1991). *The double vision: Language and meaning in religion.* Toronto: University of Toronto Press.

Harris, W. (1991). Canonicity. *PMLA, 106,* 110–121.

Hirsch, E. D., Jr. (1976). *The aims of interpretation.* Chicago: University of Chicago Press.

Husén, T. (Ed.). (1990). *Education and the global concerns.* Oxford: Pergamon Press.

Kádár-Fülop, J. (1988). Culture, writing, curriculum. In A. C. Purves (Ed.), *Languages and cultures: Issues in contrastive rhetoric.* Newbury Park, CA: Sage.

Langer, J. A. (1990). *The process of understanding literature.* (Report Series no. 2.1). Albany, NY: Center for the Learning and Teaching of Literature, State University of New York, University at Albany.

Lauter, P. (Ed.). (1990). *The Heath anthology of American literature* (2 vols.). Lexington, MA: D.C. Heath.

Ogbu, J. U. (1978). *Minority education and caste: The American system.* New York: Academic Press.

Parsons, E. A. (1952). *The Alexandrian library, glory of the Hellenic world: Its rise, antiques, and destruction* (pp. 94–95). Amsterdam: The Elsevir Press.

Purves, A. C. (1973). *Literature education in ten countries: An empirical study.* New York: Wiley.

Purves, A. C. (1988). Literacy, culture and community. In D. Wagner (Ed.), *The future of literacy in a changing world* (pp. 216–232). Oxford: Pergamon Press.

Purves, A. C. (1990). *Scribal society: An essay on literacy and schooling in the information age.* New York: Longman.

Purves A., & Beach, R. (1972). *Literature and the reader.* Urbana, IL: National Council of Teachers of English.

Purves, A., Rogers, T., & Söter, A. (1990). *How porcupines make love, II: Teaching a response-centered literature curriculum*. White Plains, NY: Longman.

Radway, J. A. (1984). *Reading the romance: Women, patriarchy, and popular literature*. Chapel Hill, NC: University of North Carolina Press.

Ravitch, D. (1990). Multiculturalism: E pluribus plures. *The American Scholar, 59*, 337–354.

Richards, I. A. (1929). *Practical criticism*. New York: Harcourt Brace.

Sobol, T. (1989). *A curriculum of inclusion: Report of the commissioners' task force on minorities: Equity and excellence*. Albany, NY: The State Education Department.

Wimsatt, W. K., & Beardsley, M. (1946). The intentional fallacy. *Sewanee Review,* University of the South, Sewanee, TN, *54*, 60–68.

6

Finding a Common Ground: Integrating Texts and Traditions

Suzanne K. Sutherland

While many argue that there is one culture, the reality is that there are a myriad who have shaped that "one."

Dr. James Pipkin, Common Ground program director,
University of Houston (1991)

Public education is receiving its harshest criticism, and educators are serving a more dynamic population of students than ever before. And just as school populations have become more diverse, including students of many backgrounds, so schools have grown in size and complexity. One race and one culture as a dominant focus has become a part of the past; educators are realizing now more than ever that teaching is the most dynamic task a person can do. Education reformers have been initiating change to meet the needs of this dynamic population of learners; ultimately, with understanding and wise actions, we may transform traditional classroom practices and text lists to serve these cultural and ethnic groups.

A reform project serving the Houston teachers is Common Ground, a project funded by the National Endowment for the Humanities (NEH) and designed to close the once-widening gaps between the schools and universities, as well as between the teacher and student and between cultures. Though just beginning, and with a great distance yet to travel, the Houston Independent School District (Houston ISD) does hold tight to the ideal of providing the setting and support for a diverse population of students and cultures in our classrooms.

The need for reform in multicultural literacy and literature is great, yet the process of change takes time in so large a district. The Houston schools encompass 312 square miles and serve a population of 1.73 million people. With a student population of 196,000, Houston ISD is the largest school district in the state of Texas and the fifth largest in the nation.

Because of Houston's rich diversity, many opportunities exist for children to encounter a variety of cultures and races before entering the public school system. Over ninety countries are represented in Houston schools, and sixty-seven different languages are spoken among its students. Presently, the student population consists of 44.9 percent Hispanic, 38.1 percent Black, 14.3 percent Caucasian, 2.6 percent Asian/Pacific Island, and 0.1 percent American Indian/Alaskan. Enrollment has steadily increased over the past five years in the district's 238 schools (169 elementary schools, 36 middle schools, and 33 high schools). A handful of neighborhood elementary schools have remained predominantly one race, but the majority of elementary and secondary schools reflect a culturally and racially integrated city population. Students have the option of attending their neighborhood schools or selecting from a variety of alternative and magnet schools. Thus Houston is that unique system where cultures meet and crisscross: a fertile ground for reform for a multicultural society.

To support an ever-changing society, the city of Houston has created a rich source of commercial and cultural exchanges. Houston is home to several universities, one of which is the University of Houston, an environment where many Houston teachers have received their degrees and have returned for advanced studies. The Houston ISD and the University of Houston have joined as partners to assist teachers in meeting the many challenges of today's classrooms. Because of this partnership, the NEH awarded funds to create a professional relationship between the university teachers of English and secondary school teachers of English.

In designing the project, university and school district administrators wanted to bridge the gaps that exist between the secondary school and university teachers of English and ultimately those between teacher and student and cultures. The College of Humanities and Fine Arts at the University of Houston and the Houston ISD developed Common Ground as a result, and based this program upon the belief that the common ground shared among these public school and university teachers is the *text*, the major classic or contemporary works of literature that help to illuminate culture and self. Because literature generally is what brings English teachers into the educational profession, a literary dialogue was to serve as a source of renewal as well as an approach to teaching literature that could be used at both the university and secondary school levels. By pairing classical and contemporary works by white and minority writers, participants were to trace themes common to American culture as a whole and discover ways to integrate significant works by minority writers into a literary tradition. At a time when there is an increasing concern over the quality of the preparation high school students are receiving for college, and at a time when some intellectuals have issued a call for the return to a classical education with emphasis on the humanities, this project has chosen to challenge tradition.

Common Ground was designed with four initial stages: (1) the familiarization of the university faculty with the high school curricula; (2) seminars for the university faculty taught by an expert in the American literary tradition; (3) an intensive two-week summer institute by the university faculty for the Houston ISD secondary teachers; and (4) a series of in-service workshops by these same secondary teachers for their colleagues during the academic school year. Originally funded for one year, this project has received additional NEH support to continue through 1993. Thus Common Ground is intended to create a common ground across the many variables of race and culture and education of our literary heritage.

In phase 1 of the project, eight University of Houston English teachers familiarized themselves with the culture of the public school system. After visiting classrooms, these teachers discovered the high energy and demands of high school students, the staggering number of students each teacher is responsible for, and the complex daily routine of public school teachers. It became evident that an array of challenges can be found in today's public school classrooms. As many have found, the reality of the classroom experience differs from the philosophical expectations and the theoretical teachings at the university.

In addition to classroom visitations, these same teachers surveyed secondary school teachers to learn about their curriculum and textbooks. They found texts to contain some examples of multicultural literature, but these texts did not seem to have the diversity hoped for. The classroom visits proved to be most beneficial for gleaning the essence of the public school culture and for developing the beginnings of a collegiality based on shared concerns.

The classroom teachers who were visited found the university teachers to be supportive and reassuring. For many it was the first time that they had connected with a professor outside the university classroom. New relationships developed, and this new sense of comradery was captivating. Several teachers even commented about the equality they felt. An illustration was the unanimous agreement that the term *teacher* was to be used to describe the classroom teacher as well as the university teacher. *Professor* was seen as a continuation of a hierarchy between the secondary school and the university, one that had no place in this project.

Phase 2 of the project involved the eight University of Houston teachers in a two-week seminar offered by Dr. Michael Cooke, Housum professor of English at Yale University and the former chair of the Yale-New Haven Teachers Institute. It is at this phase that these university teachers found themselves in a learning situation not unlike that of the public school teacher. This seminar's guiding paradigm was the pairing of the minority and white literatures. Dr. Cooke fostered a stimulating and collegial environment that became an important attribute of the entire project. The seminar proved to be rigorous and demanding, yet one that offered the University of Houston "eight" a firm understanding of some literary texts with which they had been unfamiliar.

The third phase involved the selection and "training" of fifty-four secondary English teachers, representing twenty-eight of the Houston ISD's thirty-three campuses. Uncertain of the cultural content and the method of presentation, some teachers entered this phase with hesitancy and apprehension. These teachers were placed in a two-week seminar based on self-selection of course topics (Appendix A). Here they examined paired literary texts. Each group considered one text per day, wrote sustained journal entries, and met individually with their seminar leaders to delve more deeply into individual ideas. An intellectual rigor developed as a result of the very nature of the concept of the pairings and the way the pairings helped to open discussions of the literary texts. This concept of pairing also emphasized that literature, not pedagogy, was the central subject of inquiry.

The summer institute clearly narrowed the gap between the secondary and university teachers by providing enriching experiences for individuals and a forum to find and discuss commonalities. Individuals were certainly moved, and attitudes changed through this experience. In fact, it was likened to a "spiritual awakening." With unanimous agreement, these teachers felt this third phase to be one of the most rewarding experiences of their professional and personal lives.

In the fourth phase of the project, however, the teachers achieved the most success. Through the teamwork of the teachers, the University of Houston English eight, and the administrators of the Houston ISD's English-Language Arts Department, the ideals of the project influenced other teachers in the district. In a collaborative effort to include more high school English teachers in the ideals of the project, project teachers attended planning meetings to discuss how the ideals and spirit of Common Ground could be implemented. The project's participants designed four half-day sessions for fall and spring semesters that would be open to the four hundred secondary English teachers. The project teachers arranged themselves into literary teams according to interests, favorite literature pairings, and/or campus proximity. These teams further designed their pairings and divided the tasks of planning their individual sessions. Tasks included location arrangements, presentations, future meetings, materials and texts, and advertising. In fact, each team planned everything from mailings to discussion questions to evaluations of the project.

To assist in advertising, one group designed a flyer which was distributed to all high schools. This announced, "Come join in the revision of the canon" to high school principals, deans of instruction, and English department chairpersons. This information was also published in a communications document which reached every department and school in the district.

Monies set aside by the school district were used to purchase the texts to be read, so that each attending participant would have texts for their immediate use. These texts included *Bless Me, Ultima* (1972) by Rudolfo Anaya, Tonatiuh-Quinto Sol Publishers; *Their Eyes Were Watching God* (1937) by Zora Neale Hurston, University of Illinois Press; *The Awakening* (1899) by Kate Chopin, Avon Book Publishers; and *The House on Mango Street* (1983) by Sandra Cisneros, Arte Público Press.

Each Saturday session began with a published author/educator as a keynote speaker. Then participants met in small group sessions to discuss literature that had been previously read. Discussions were based on the themes of Death and Alienation; Diverse Voices and Displaced Persons; Family—Fate. . .Failure. . .Future; New World/Nuevo Mundo; Outsider's Search for Acceptance in Society; Rage, Ritual and Resolution; A Search for Identity: Who Am I? Where Am I? Where Am I Going?; Society's Misfits; and Joining the Melting Pot Without Melting. Teacher participants attending these Saturday discussion sessions received recognition of Advanced Academic Training for the state's career ladder benefits, had the advantage of being introduced to a literature selection not previously read, and cultivated a renewed spirit for the teaching of literature.

Overall reactions were positive; the numbers of participants were consistent and growing; commitment by discussion leaders varied; and attitudes changed. For example, 108 people from twenty-eight campuses signed up to attend the first Saturday session, with 67 actually attending. An additional 24 more people signed up for the second session, with a total of 91 people attending. Throughout the year, the numbers of participants attending sessions consistently rose with each session.

A change in attitude has been reflected by every single participant. Each has shown more sensitivity to the diversity of cultures in the classroom, and many have come to believe that the cultural diversity of Houston ISD students should be reflected in the literature that students read. For a variety of reasons, this may not be reflected through explicit pairings of texts in the classroom, but it can be sensed in the sessions where these ideas are discussed.

To assist classroom teachers and others who have shown an interest in the concept of pairing classical pieces with contemporary selections and white-authored pieces with those by persons of color, the school district has purchased class sets of the texts studied in the summer institute and in the Saturday sessions. Teachers were asked, after reading a variety of selections, which texts they would like to have purchased for their students. *Bless Me, Ultima* (1972) by Rudolfo Anaya, *The House on Mango Street* (1983) by Sandra Cisneros, *I Know Why the Caged Bird Sings* (1969) by Maya Angelou, *A Raisin in the Sun* (1959) by Lorraine Hansberry, and *Their Eyes Were Watching God* (1937) by Zora Neale Hurston were by far the most popular and versatile. The class sets of thirty texts have been purchased for each of Houston's thirty-three high schools. Overall with these selections, teachers and students are able to gain a new understanding of each other and other cultures through texts that have a level of comfort and that are understandable.

Common Ground is not only changing how teachers are viewing themselves and their favorite literary selections, it is also affecting how teachers view their students and their students' interests. By expanding the canon to include significant works by persons of color, literary discussions are themselves expanding to include discussions of social, cultural, and political issues and behaviors. Teachers, too, are finding uncomfortable the traditional lecture and questioning practices. Instead, a more cooperative practice has become evident in these teachers' classrooms. A pairing may bring into focus a moral or cultural aspect that is not easily explained and that lends itself to further discussion and readings. Although this may seem common sense to some, traditionally secondary literature and composition courses have been taught in an arena where only the teacher is knowledgeable. This project includes a group of teachers who now question their own motives and methodologies, the variety of textbook selections (or lack thereof), and alternatives to using the textbook.

These teachers continue to be concerned about the lack of a variety of classroom sets of texts written by persons of color, the difficulty of planning paired texts, and their own inexperience in pedagogy, especially when using guided discussion and inquiry as strategies. Tools for literature "observations" (portfolios, journals, sketchbooks) are becoming more prevalent as a means to record processes, long-term developments, and reflections, all so important for today's youth as they balance academic discipline with the cultural and creative stimuli necessary for self-expression.

Through the support of Common Ground, students are discovering the incomparable recordings of our past, a common culture and expression of the values cherished, the depth and complexity of human nature, and the freedom to enjoy the best of the literature and arts which enhance our lives. Thus the gap between the secondary teacher and student is closing in Houston.

The benefits of this project have been evident with the fifty-two participants and the curriculum they have been able to affect. This first step toward more thoughtful and relevant instruction has some drawbacks, but overall the results have been positive and rewarding. Project teachers have a renewed spirit for the teaching of literature. This project has changed how teachers are viewing themselves, their favorite literary selections, and their students. A deeper sense of culture and cultural literacy is replacing superficial literature assignments, and this can only enhance students' self-awareness and their awareness of others.

Project drawbacks have been few, yet important. Teachers have had great difficulty replicating the open discussions of the summer seminar in their classrooms. This is due to an uncertainty about cultural distinctions, an unfamiliarity with the texts, and a reluctance to try the unknown with students. Many have confided that they find themselves returning to the "tried and true" when there is discomfort. In addition, students have been passive receivers of information for so long that they are somewhat uncomfortable with active participation. Since pedagogy took a backseat in this project, the lack of response has been felt in the classroom. It has been difficult for many to use a variety of teaching methods. Lecture has been the predominant mode of presentation for a long time.

In addition, through trial and error, teachers must discover which texts would best be left to adult discussions and which are appropriate for high school students, whether because of content or reading level. This becomes a problem caused by a shortage of district funds for the purchase of multiple class sets of books. If a teacher has selected a title that is found to be inappropriate, that is a loss of an entire set of texts for that classroom until other funds can be located to purchase anew.

Finally, since this is a relatively new project, the Houston ISD is much too large to feel an immediate impact. School-based administrators expect results that take time to achieve. At the same time, the fifty-two NEH-trained teachers have had varying degrees of commitment to sharing this training with their fellow Houston ISD teachers. Some are committed to the vision of pairing texts and sharing that vision with peers and students. This is evident by the number who are attending discussions conducted on their own time and by the number who are holding discussions with co-workers. Some are able to openly discuss successes and failures in their own discussion groups and in their classrooms, as well as to seek out additional selections to read. Others have had less of a commitment to ensuring the success of Common Ground for the classroom. They participated in ongoing literary discussions but have chosen not to use these texts with their students. Excuses range from the textbook being a sufficient resource to the difficulty of using these texts in the classroom.

To date, the greatest progress lies in the collegial relationship between the University of Houston and Houston ISD teachers. They have maintained a close relationship throughout this project, and this committed and supportive relationship will continue to be the most vital source of the "common ground." For future summer seminars, discussions have turned toward pedagogy: toward providing teachers with models to help them adapt texts for their students and to assist them in helping students relate to a text. Pedagogy cannot be separated from the literary content necessary to teach students.

As the project continues to be adapted to meet teachers' needs, the district's curriculum, too, has adjusted. Written into the Houston ISD curriculum (see Appendix B) are a variety of literary selections and strategies necessary to enrich and connect the lives of thinking individuals, but these have to be explicitly modeled for replication to have positive results. By combining the expertise of both the university and the school district, teachers can achieve a balanced seminar of literary merit and professional practice.

With each year, this dynamic project continues to grow to meet the needs of the classroom teachers and the students being served. One cannot say that this project is anything more than a means to expose university and classroom teachers to the wealth of literature from a multitude of cultures that have yet to be explored. For those classrooms in which the ideals of this project are being practiced, the cultural literacy of all involved is being strengthened. And even though the partnerships are important, the closing of the gaps remains vital.

References

The College of Humanities and Fine Arts, University of Houston. (1990). *Texts and Tradition: The Common Ground 1991–1993, A Proposal to the Division of Education, National Endowment for the Humanities.*

Houston Independent School District. (1990). *Project ACCESS: A Planning Guide for English Two.*

Houston Independent School District. (1990). *Project ACCESS: A Planning Guide for English Three.*

Houston Independent School District. (1990). *Project ACCESS: A Planning Guide for English Four.*

Houston Independent School District. (1991). *Houston Independent School District and School Profiles.*

Texas Education Agency. (1988). *English-Language Arts Framework, Kindergarten– Grade 12.*

Texas Education Agency. (1991). *State Board of Education Rules for Curriculum.*

Appendix A

Arteaga Seminar

Texts
1. Frederick Douglass, *Narrative of the Life of Frederick Douglass, An American Slave*
   Sor Juana Ines de la Cruz, *A Woman of Genius: The Intellectual Autobiography of Sor Juana Ines de la Cruz* (trans. Margaret Sayers Peden)
2. Nathaniel Hawthorne, "Young Goodman Brown" and "Rappaccini's Daughter"
   Emily Dickinson, selected poetry
   Walt Whitman, selected poetry
   Juan Nepomuceno Seguin, *Personal Memoirs*
3. John Edgar Wideman, *Damballah*
   Lorna Dee Cervantes, *Emplumada*
4. Ralph Ellison, *Invisible Man*
   Oscar Zeta Acosta, *The Revolt of the Cockroach People*

My seminar will offer a Chicano perspective, literary and historical, on the theme of the forging of an American identity. We will explore the evolution/revelation of values as it can be seen in two linguistic traditions, a Hispanic tradition which co-defines "America" along with the Anglo tradition, which together imagine a new world/nuevo mundo.

Brown-Guillory Seminar

Texts
1. Nathaniel Hawthorne, *The Scarlet Letter*
   Margaret Walker, *Jubilee*
2. Henry Adams, *The Education of Henry Adams*
   W. E. B. Du Bois, *The Souls of Black Folk*
3. Kate Chopin, *The Awakening*
   Zora Neale Hurston, *Their Eyes Were Watching God*
4. Carson McCullers, *The Heart Is a Lonely Hunter*
   Denise Chavez, *The Last of the Menu Girls*
5. Tennessee Williams, *Cat on a Hot Tin Roof*
   Lorraine Hansberry, *A Raisin in the Sun*
   Ntozake Shange, *For Colored Girls Who Have Considered Suicide/When the Rainbow is Enuf*

This seminar will explore the primary source of tension in these texts: the individual's quest to become a part of the community and yet maintain independence. It is my hope that seminar participants will be challenged to encourage their students not only to go in search of the American cultural garden but to see that each individual produced from that garden has distinctiveness as well as a common function of regeneration or sustenance.

Dachslager Seminar

Texts
1. William Shakespeare, *Romeo and Juliet*
   Philip Roth, *Goodbye, Columbus*
2. William Shakespeare, *Hamlet*
   Herman Melville, "Bartleby, the scrivener"
   Edith Wharton, *Ethan Frome*
   J. D. Salinger, *The Catcher in the Rye*
3. William Shakespeare, *Othello*
   Richard Wright, *Native Son*
   Eugene O'Neill, *The Emperor Jones*
   James Baldwin, *Blues for Mister Charlie*
4. William Shakespeare, *The Merchant of Venice*
   Arthur Miller, *The Crucible*

This seminar is an attempt to show literature's preoccupation with that most characteristic fact of our culture: the presence of the outsider and misfit, whether by virtue of emotional and psychological, social and familial, racial or ethnic, or sexual distinctions.

Gingiss Seminar

Texts
1. Frederick Douglass, *Narrative of the Life of Frederick Douglass, An American Slave*
    Nathaniel Hawthorne, *The Scarlet Letter*
2. Rudolfo Anaya, *Bless Me, Ultima*
    Samuel Clemens (Mark Twain), *The Adventures of Huckleberry Finn*
3. Maxine Hong Kingston, *The Woman Warrior*
    Sylvia Plath, *The Bell Jar*
4. David Bradley, *The Chaneysville Incident*
    Raymond Carver, selected stories

This seminar will begin by taking four works by minorities and women and will look at them for both universal concerns and for insights into their respective subcultures. It will next look at the mainstream works as also coming from subcultures, in order to see them in a new way.

Monroe Seminar

Texts
1. Walt Whitman, *Song of Myself*
2. Rudolfo Anaya, *Bless Me, Ultima*
3. Samuel L. Clemens (Mark Twain), *The Adventures of Huckleberry Finn*
4. Kate Chopin, *The Awakening*
5. Willa Cather, *The Professor's House*
6. Ralph Ellison, "King of the Bingo Game"
7. Flannery O'Connor, selected stories
8. Richard Wright, *Black Boy* and *American Hunger*
9. William Kennedy, *Ironweed*

The study and teaching of literature has become more difficult in late twentieth-century America because both majority and minority readers and writers inhabit a common ground of alienation. If alienation is what we share, perhaps we should see our unconnectedness not as a problem to be solved but as a mystery of existence to be accepted and endured—but not necessarily intensified. So in this seminar we will look beyond alienation to community. We will concentrate on ways that stories can facilitate affirmation and community.

Rothman Seminar

Texts
1. *Family roots and establishing new families*
   Mary Rowlandson, *A Narrative of the Captivity, Sufferings, and Removes*
   Phillis Wheatley, *Poems on Various Subjects, Religious and Moral*
2. *The role of society in establishing standards of conduct*
   Frederick Douglass, *Narrative of the Life of Frederick Douglass, An American Slave*
   Henry David Thoreau, *A Week on the Concord and Merrimack Rivers*
3. *Family abuse*
   Henry Roth, *Call It Sleep*
   Alice Walker, *The Color Purple*
4. *Growing up*
   Ernest Hemingway, *In Our Time* and "The Killers"
   Tomás Rivera,—*Y no se lo grago la tierra (And the Earth Did Not Devour Him)*
5. *Facing family crises*
   Rosellen Brown, *Street Games*
   John Edgar Wideman, *Damballah*

The family is a central focus of communality. How we live together largely shapes adolescence and provides for maturity. The principles of life, liberty, and the pursuit of happiness can be embodied in the concept of family; unfortunately, where these principles are violated, society encounters conflict with psychological scars and structural defects.

Weldon Seminar

Texts
1. Nathaniel Hawthorne, *The Scarlet Letter*
   Douglass, *Narrative of the Life of Frederick Douglass, An American Slave*
   W. E. B. Du Bois, *The Souls of Black Folk*
2. Samuel Clemens (Mark Twain), *The Adventures of Huckleberry Finn*
   James Weldon Johnson, *The Autobiography of an Ex-Colored Man*
   Rudolfo Anaya, *Bless Me, Ultima*

3. Kate Chopin, *The Awakening*
   Alice Walker, *The Color Purple*
4. Donald Barthelme, *Paradise*
   Ralph Ellison, "King of the Bingo Game"
   Raymond Carver, "Cathedral"

My seminar will be organized around works in which the central characters see themselves as displaced people, strangers and outcasts in a hostile world, and it will explore the way in which they strive to create meaning for their lives despite, or perhaps because of, their position in society.

Westervelt Seminar

Texts
1. W. E. B. Du Bois, *The Souls of Black Folk* (selections)
   Henry Adams, *The Education of Henry Adams*, Chapters 1–6, 15, 19, 25, 33
2. Louis Chu, *Eat a Bowl of Tea*
   Henry James, *The Europeans*
3. Maxine Hong Kingston, *The Woman Warrior*
   William Faulkner, *The Unvanquished* (selections)
4. Sandra Cisneros, *The House on Mango Street*
   Wallace Stegner, *Recapitulation*
5. Bharati Mukherjee, *Darkness* (selections)
   Thomas Pynchon, *The Crying of Lot 49*

This seminar will pair traditional texts with works by Asian Americans and other minorities to explore the transition from adolescence to young adulthood, especially as that transition causes the young person not only to explore his or her identity but also to question loyalty to the family or the community. These characters share the feeling that they are a part of an old order and a part of something new.

Appendix B

Common Ground has found its way into the curriculum of Houston ISD. Project ACCESS (A Collaborative Curriculum to Enhance Student Success) is an integrated curriculum that is written by teachers who take a one-year leave of absence from the classroom to become full-time writers. Of the three American literature curriculum writers, two had participated in the Common Ground project. Because of the experiences these writers received in the project, they were able to bring more depth and creativity to the writing of a traditional course of study. Literature has been taught traditionally in a chronological manner. These teacher/writers utilized a thematic/genre approach in a relevant manner.

One example of this approach is a unit of study for American literature entitled "The Harlem Renaissance: A Common Ground of the Human Condition." This unit shows how one might use the works of a variety of authors from this period paired with poets selected by students. The overview of this unit states, "During the Harlem Renaissance, a period of the 1920s, poets captured the history of a people and the emotional experiences that draw people together in their humanity. This unit focuses on the poetry of the Harlem Renaissance, which students will later pair with traditional and more contemporary poems as they explore the common ground of human emotions." An author list is attached as a reference in the curriculum.

7

Multicultural Literacy and Literature: The Perspective of School Policy

Gregory A. Morris

The Need for Change

The purpose of my paper is to attempt to establish a perspective on the policies that provide the basis for the current focus on multiracial, multiethnic, and multicultural (Triple M) education in the Pittsburgh Public School District. It is not always clear how or why decisions are made, but a review of the pertinent records and discussion with key policymakers and program developers may provide some clarification. First, I will examine the perspective for Triple M education for schooling and the district in general. Then I will look specifically at Triple M education and its relation to literacy and literature in the school district.

Writing about the historical development of multiethnic education, Banks (1988), a longtime student of this concept, notes that during the turn of the century and the World War I periods, the American schools reflected the prevailing goals of the nation. Schools promoted Americanization and embraced Anglo-conformity goals. They sought to rid ethnic groups of their ethnic traits and to force them to acquire Anglo-Saxon values and behaviors. Banks goes on to cite Ellwood Patterson Cubberley, the famed educational leader, who in 1909 clearly stated a major goal of the common schools:

> Everywhere these people [immigrants] tend to settle in groups or settlements, and to set up their national manners, customs, and observances. Our task is to break up these groups or settlements, to assimilate and amalgamate these people as part of our American race, and to implant in their children, as far as can be done, the Anglo-Saxon conception of righteousness, law and order, and

popular government, and to awaken in them a reverence for our democratic institutions and for those things in our national life which we as a people hold to be of abiding worth. (Banks, 1988, pp. 4–5)

Political forces, however, have since 1909 forced schools to question Cubberley's assumption. Parr (1989) describes a situation now in which the schools no longer fit the cultures they serve: "Schools which have been designed for children from what might once have appeared to be the 'average American family': a family of Western European extraction, with values reflecting Western European traditions, two live-in parents, and a father who headed the household and earned at least a middle-level income...have been slow to change" (p. 1). Banks (1988) notes that such schools exist in the midst of a "new pluralism" triggered by the Black civil rights revolution and a wave of new immigrants. In such a situation, inevitably, conflict often develops between the home and the school and between teachers and students.

Neither the teachers nor the schools have been ready for such changes. "American teachers have not generally been trained to work with children whose backgrounds and socialization differed significantly from this 'mainstream' pattern" (Parr, 1989, p. 1). Furthermore, Banks (1988) says, "the schools have been reluctant to adapt their curriculum and teaching styles to make them more consistent with the needs of ethnic minority students. In many schools that have multiethnic populations, the curriculum, teaching, and motivational techniques remain Anglo-centric" (p. 12). Parr (1989) contends that "although good teachers have found ways to adjust to differences among their students, many continue to feel uncertain as to how to deal with cultural and ethnic diversity within the school. Societal pressures placed upon educators and educational institutions compound this uncertainty" (p. 1).

These are the circumstances which have led to the need for change. Students from cultural heritages and racial and ethnic backgrounds outside the "mainstream" need to be accommodated. Parr (1989) writes, "Though these students are bright and able, their attitudes and behaviors often differ from those that the school expects. If their teachers are uncertain as to how to cope with these attitudes and behaviors, the students, in turn, may resist the values of the school. Inevitably, a student who feels alienated from the school values may drop out of the educational system altogether" (p. 2). Pittsburgh faces this very problem.

The 1980s: Gathering Forces for Change

The Pittsburgh Public Schools constitute a small urban school district consisting of 39,000 students and eighty-five schools (fifty-two elementary, K–5; fourteen middle, 6–8; eleven secondary, 9–12; and eight special). The student population is 54 percent African American, 45 percent white, and 1 percent other, according to the enrollment report (Pittsburgh Public Schools [PPS], 1990). The changeover from white to African American as the majority category of students in the district is one that has come about slowly over the last decade. The school district serves a city of approximately 250,000 residents, even though students come from only 14 percent of the city's households. A nine-member elected school board sets policy which is implemented by the superintendent and his staff. Special departments of the district are designated to carry out specific functions and responsibilities.

A number of major forces have supported the push for improving racial and ethnic equity in Pittsburgh's schools. One such force was the issue of school desegregation. During the 1970s there was much debate as to equity of educational opportunity for all students. Pennsylvania, through its Commission of Human Relations, required that all school districts file plans for reducing racial isolation in its schools. Districts had to work with legal compliance of the commission, on the one hand, and the wishes of parent and community constituents on the other. The tension between the two sides was most difficult to resolve. The Pittsburgh plan endeavored to strike a delicate balance (PPS, 1980).

The school district began the implementation of its desegregation plan in 1980. After prolonged development and review by myriad staff, community, and parent groups and after being accepted by the Pennsylvania Human Relations Commission, this plan was approved by the school directors. The plan decreed that the focus of the mandatory desegregation effort would be at the middle school level. A series of voluntary magnet school options were set forth to effect desegregation at the elementary and secondary levels. Implementation of the plan, however, brought forth new concerns (PPS, 1980).

In a proposal to solicit funding for the multicultural program effort, Parr (1989) highlighted the concerns generated as a result of the implementation of the desegregation plan. He pointed out that Pittsburgh is a city of neighborhoods, many of which are still racially and ethnically isolated. As a result many students do not have their first social interactions outside their racial and ethnic groups until they reach the middle schools where full-scale desegregation begins.

Often, however, middle school students continue to socialize with the peer groups that they established in the elementary school and the neighborhood. Thus, though numbers may indicate that a school is integrated, social interactions within the school may continue to preserve racial isolation. This trend may continue throughout the secondary school years (Parr, 1989, p. 3).

District statistics on suspensions and academic achievement offer indications that a number of students are not making the transition to the newly desegregated school settings (PPS, 1985). African American students are suspended at a rate three to four times that of other students. There is a growing gap in the achievement levels between white and African American students. This gap ranges from 21 to 30 percentiles in reading, language, and mathematics. African American students drop out at a much higher rate than other students. The issue of desegregation, therefore, continues to be one of the prime forces for change.

Another force was active in bringing about a renewed quest for change. During 1986–1987, a self-study of the middle schools was undertaken for the purpose of accreditation. Each middle school faculty was given the charge and a plan of action for conducting the self-study. The faculties worked together for an entire school year. During the year the evaluation team made on-site visitations. Throughout the process, participants raised insightful questions, engaged in candid discussions, and reflected on a variety of issues and outcomes.

One portion of the self-study protocol of the school program was consideration of the multicultural/multiracial dimension. The groups explored the instructional materials being utilized, the typical teaching practices and styles employed, and teachers' knowledge about the diverse backgrounds of their students. They thought about strategies for building self-esteem and helping students understand and appreciate the cultural and ethnic backgrounds of themselves and others. They also examined their levels of expectations for their students. It was found that many teachers did not routinely assign homework because they felt that students would not do the homework or it would be a "hassle" getting it back. Few teachers assigned outside reading because they believed that students would not do the reading. Challenging questions or issues were not usually raised because they would be a struggle for the students and the students would be "turned off." Thus, it became evident that changes needed to be made.

Given the results of that self-study and the district's commitment to the creation of a desegregated school environment, a recommendation was made by Dr. Stoops, representing the Middle States

Accreditation Team. He recommended that multicultural education become a priority for the district, but most especially for the middle school level, where full-scale desegregation was first to occur in the district (1987).

Another force for change was a coalition of four school directors led by an African American, Dr. Jake Milliones. This group advocated the development of policies and procedures that would result in greater equity for all students, but especially for African American students. Dr. Milliones went on to become the president of the school board and was reelected for two additional terms. He became an influential leader during the 1980s.

Increasing basic student achievement in reading, language, and mathematics became a district priority as a result of a comprehensive needs assessment recommended by the superintendent, sanctioned by the school board, and carried out by the University of Pittsburgh. The coalition's efforts led to the study of the racial achievement gap. Consequently, a District Task Force on the Racial Achievement Gap was convened. Participants were selected from parent, business, and community groups, as well as from the ranks of educators in the school district and from local colleges and universities. This task force was given the charge, first, to identify the issues underlying the disparate achievement between African American and other students. Then it was to make recommendations for resolving that achievement gap.

After extended deliberations, the task force identified seven "issue areas" and related sets of recommendations (PPS, 1987). The nature of the issue areas suggested that major changes in curricula, teaching methods, course materials, and staff development had to be undertaken if all students were to have equity of educational opportunities and come to appreciate and understand the diversity of cultural backgrounds that their fellow students represented.

Still another factor for change must be acknowledged. Pittsburgh was fortunate to have an outstanding educational leader during the decade of the 1980s. Dr. Richard C. Wallace joined the school district in 1980 just as it was inaugurating its plan for desegregation. With background in school administration and research and development, he immediately directed that a needs assessment be undertaken for the district. This activity was broad-based, giving the opportunity for input to far-ranging and diverse stakeholders, including parents, community leaders, teachers, and students. The results of this process were shared with the Board and together they shaped an agenda for the 1980s (PPS, "News," 1981).

Heading the list of this new agenda were the priorities to improve student achievement in all areas, but especially in reading, language, and mathematics, and to upgrade and evaluate the performance of instructional and administrative personnel. Moreover, a precedent was established that objective data culled from a range of sources would be the basis for making decisions and that decision making was to become a more open and collaborative process. Dr. Wallace became recognized for his ability to move the agenda. He decided to focus on the two most crucial areas of need. To improve achievement he instituted a multiphase achievement-monitoring procedure known as MAP, Monitoring Achievement in Pittsburgh. To upgrade and evaluate the performance of instructional and administrative personnel, he instituted a program known as PRISM, Pittsburgh Research-Based Instructional Supervision Model. He became a force for change.

One final factor for change must be included. As indicated earlier in the background information on the school district, Pittsburgh has a nine-member elected school board. School directors are elected by districts to serve overlapping three-year terms. This structure provides for the possibility of periodic change. During the 1980s there were a number of changes. Persons campaigning for school director were primarily concerned about the decisions being made about the schools in their communities. Fiscal responsibility and quality education for all students were the goals of their campaigns. New directors, sensitive to the concerns of their constituents, have forced periodic review of the mission, goals, and plans for the district.

It is apparent that there were many forces gathering during the 1980s to bring about change in the district. The issue of school desegregation and its attendant problems, the results of a middle school self-study for accreditation, the efforts of a coalition of school directors, the appointment of a new superintendent who provided strong leadership, and the changing memberships of the school board were the major forces supporting the need for change in the district.

In 1988, the school board, recognizing its role in promoting all students' social skills and in creating school environments more responsive to each student's needs, proceeded to make two key decisions which would begin to address major areas of need (Parr, 1989):

1.   The board decided to engage in an examination of its systemwide policies and practices and of all program development within the district in order to improve the level of racial and ethnic equity in its operations.

2. The board also decided to select a school in which an approach could be defined and established that would embody multicultural and multiracial relations at their best. This approach, once established, would then be further disseminated across the District.

A middle school was selected because:

*   Full-scale integration begins at the middle school level in Pittsburgh as decreed by the plan for desegregation. Middle schools throughout the district therefore have a wide mix of cultures and races and draw from a variety of neighborhoods in the city.
*   A pressing need exists to reduce the likelihood of students becoming alienated from school and dropping out during the difficult transition between middle school and high school.
*   The interdisciplinary model is introduced at the middle school level, making it possible to expose students to a wider variety of group interactions and a more integrated set of learning experiences.
*   In transescence (the period of transition from childhood to full adolescence), students develop a strong interest in and awareness of social relationships, and thus are especially likely to benefit from examining how cultural backgrounds affect the social interactions in their lives. (pp. 6–7)

These decisions came about as the result of the many forces that gathered during the 1980s. They represent a critical turning point for the district.

Multicultural Education at the Middle School Level

A number of implications and significant actions grew out of the board's major decisions on multicultural education. Pittsburgh has had a history of creating demonstration projects to test the various theories and hypotheses that have evolved in connection with program changes. The opening of the Schenley High School Teacher Center, the Brookline Elementary, and Greenway Middle School Teacher Centers, which are models for ongoing staff development, are the most recent examples. The decision was made at the superintendent's cabinet level to establish a demonstration project for the district's multicultural program.

Four distinct outcomes envisioned for this multicultural demonstration project were:

- Establishment of a top-level position, director of multicultural education, to supervise the infusion of multicultural education into all aspects of the district's programs.
- Development of a multicultural school program to be piloted at Prospect Middle School, the middle school designated as the demonstration site.
- Development of a dissemination plan that will extend the multicultural perspectives and strategies developed at Prospect to all district middle schools.
- Creation of a Board of Visitors, composed of nationally recognized scholars, whose expertise will serve as a resource to the district in planning, implementing, and disseminating multicultural approaches to education (Parr, 1989).

Next, a Steering Committee for Multicultural Education was formed from the superintendent's cabinet. This group discussed and devised the overall goals, rationale, and guide questions for the various subcommittees that would be required to complete the task. Finally, a task force for planning the Prospect Middle School Center for Multiracial, Multicultural, and Multiethnic Education was commissioned by the superintendent. The district's goals for multicultural education as written by the steering committee are the following:

Goals
1. To infuse a culturally based perspective in the development of systemwide curriculum policies, priorities, and programs.
2. To improve the climate for learning and increase the academic performance of all students throughout the district.

The charge for the task force can best be summed up by the following statement:

By developing and implementing a multicultural approach to education, the District has an opportunity to test this hypothesis: If the focus of school is altered so that the school environment, both systemwide and at the local building level, is sensitive to developing students' social skills and reflecting the cultures of the entire student body, then changes are likely to occur in students' bonding with school and in their resulting academic performance. (Parr, 1989, p.11)

The districtwide Task Force on Multicultural Education was convened (G. Morris, personal communication, February 28, 1989). Members of the task force represented many and varied roles and areas of responsibility. Fourteen specific subcommittees were formed with specific charges and focus questions. Members of the subcommittees engaged themselves in individual and group study and deliberation. They wrestled with terminology and concepts: What is meant by *multicultural* and *multiracial*? What groups belong where and what should they be named? Is the term of preference *Black, Black American,* or *African American*? What terms are to be avoided because of misinterpretation? Is the focus of multicultural education national or international or global? Should the initial emphasis be on African Americans because they constitute a majority in the district? The timeline for completing assignments and developing recommendations for moving ahead was short, but the initial efforts were completed.

One particular subcommittee, on needs assessment, conducted a most insightful sampling of staffs in all of the district's middle schools (PPS, 1989). Sixty-four percent of the 234 middle school staff persons who were sampled in the needs assessment affirmed their willingness to work in the new center. Further, the respondents strongly affirmed a philosophy that is based upon both academic excellence and cultural pluralism. Finally, the respondents identified the following as their greatest personal staff development needs: "a) education of low achieving students; b) demonstration of high expectations for all students; c) accommodation of diverse learning styles; and d) creation and selection of instructional materials that emphasize multiracial and multicultural education" (p. 2). This feedback from staff underscored their need to be better prepared to cope with a very different student body.

The final reports of each of the planning subcommittees provided many ideas and points of view for the multicultural steering committee, the newly appointed director of multicultural education, the principal of the Prospect Middle School, and the superintendent. This concluded the first phase of planning. The next phase directly involved literacy efforts and multicultural education.

During the early part of the new school year, deliberations were under way as to how to begin the specific exploration and planning for specific curriculum infusion which had been identified as a starting point by the Subcommittee on Professional Development and Curriculum Update Activities. At this juncture, the director of multicultural education determined that a series of subcommittees be formed to carry the planning to the next level of specificity.

One subcommittee was given the responsibility for planning for curriculum infusion. The membership of the Subcommittee for Curriculum Infusion consisted of representatives from the areas of language arts, reading, art and music, and science. In Pittsburgh, all of the preceding content areas are organized under the umbrella of a department known as Curriculum and Program Management. The school-based representatives on this subcommittee, teachers and administrators, are part of the Office of School Management. This structure created some inherent problems when committee members attempted to organize to work on the tasks on their agenda. There was still a concern about where to look for leadership and direction. Subcommittee members tended to align themselves along curriculum content or school-level lines.

The deliberations of the subcommittee were filled with uncertainty during the first several meetings. There were questions about the vision, terminology, and direction. There was even a lack of clarification as to which groups or areas would actually be involved in the infusion effort. As it turned out, the less interested or resistant groups finally bowed out of the deliberations. After protracted discussion and consultation with representatives from a number of offices and departments, the Subcommittee for Curriculum Infusion drafted a vision statement and three major recommendations.

The vision statement advocated that "multicultural, multiethnic, and multiracial education embraces a curriculum that incorporates an equitable balance among the five geo-cultural groups in American society" (Leff & Pace, 1990, p. 5). As a result of consultation with the director of multicultural education, those groups were determined to be African American, Asian American, European American, Hispanic American, and Native American.

The three major recommendations were for the following:

1. A developmental model for curriculum infusion that begins in the sixth grade with the study of self and the family, progresses to the seventh grade with the study of community (Pittsburgh), and culminates in the eighth grade with the study of the nation and the world.
2. The development of a curriculum that includes an interdisciplinary approach to Triple M (multicultural, multiethnic, and multiracial) education, the use of thematic discussion, and the development of interpersonal and intergroup relations.
3. Training for teachers in the areas of cooperative learning, discussion models, planning of interdisciplinary lessons, multimodal instruction, and teaching to various learning styles. (Leff & Pace, 1990)

After the recommendations were made, policy formulation, curriculum development, and instructional activities and practices for Triple M education moved very slowly. A clear mandate to those most able to bring the project to fruition was lacking. For this reason, I would like to discuss the plans and activities which are proceeding and the rationale for those efforts in the area of literacy. It is becoming apparent that the rationale, plans and activities thus far undertaken may indeed become the direction or policy for further developments. Finally, as director of reading and literature, I was able to play a more significant role in the literacy infusion effort.

Multicultural Literacy at the Middle School Level

In the current middle school context classes in reading and language arts constitute the major vehicles for literacy instruction. The major goals of the reading classes noted in the *Middle Schools Reading Handbook* (PPS, 1990) are not only to develop and refine the skills and strategies students need to make meaning of text, but also to help them learn to read to satisfy their own personal needs for ideas, information, and pleasure. Furthermore, students are provided with opportunities to read literature that enhances their perception of themselves and others as valuable human beings and members of a multicultural, multiethnic, and multiracial society.

The major goals for the language arts classes are to develop and refine students' abilities to write and discuss, especially in response to literature. A literature component organized around genre is taught by the language arts teacher (PPS, 1988). Reading and language arts teachers hold membership on interdisciplinary teaching teams; they are in a position to discuss, plan, and assess their literacy efforts with those teachers with whom they share a common group of students. It should be pointed out that the interdisciplinary team is a structure that has been revitalized to bring about more coordinated and integrated instruction at the middle school level. It is the district's contention that the multicultural infusion effort will have a greater impact on students as a result of organizing teachers and students in this manner (Stoops, 1987).

The literature component for the language arts classes is organized around specific genres, and does include text selections of from two of the five geocultural groups recommended and endorsed by the Subcommittee on Curriculum Infusion. At the time of revising the middle school language arts literature component, the director of reading and literature and the director of writing and speaking, who share joint responsibility for this literature component, recognized three driving forces (PPS, 1988). First, there was the need to include selections which were in keeping with the needs and interests of the young adolescent. Second, selections which revolved around African Americans were sorely lacking, so special emphasis was placed on securing text pieces to meet this need. Third, the texts were to be springboards for meaningful reading, writing, and discussion experiences.

It must be pointed out that the curriculum revision efforts in this area were completed prior to the deliberations of the various task force groups charged with developing the directions for the district's Triple M focus. Plans will be formulated to reexamine the current selections and to broaden the range of selections to include offerings from the other geocultural groups.

The revision of the middle school reading program has been a recent effort. The committee was composed of reading teachers, a reading specialist, a learning disabilities teacher, two reading supervisors, and the director of the Division of Reading and Literature. The last three members formed a small planning team. We endeavored to provide the committee with the necessary resources and experiences to make the effort a successful one. We requested that the professional library in our district conduct literature searches for information, texts, and titles. We arranged for members of the committee to work with consultants from local universities, the community, and the National Faculty of Humanities, Arts, and Sciences. We engaged them in discussions of issues and texts.

This committee was driven by a number of factors. The new *Pennsylvania Framework for Reading, Writing, and Talking across the Curriculum* (Botel & Lytel, 1988), a sourcebook for curriculum planning predicated upon the powerful notion of Rosenblatt's transactional theory of reading, influenced our efforts. Rosenblatt (1984) believes that "reading is always a particular event, involving a particular reader, a particular item of the environment—a text—at a particular time, under particular circumstances" (p. 67). We were mindful, too, that "reader and text are mutually essential to the transaction; meaning happens during the transaction between the reader and the text" (p. 62). Finally, we were cognizant of the "predominantly aesthetic stance," where the "span of attention. . .opens out to attend. . .to what we are seeing and feeling and thinking, on what is aroused within us by the very sound of the words, and by what they point to in the human and natural world" (Rosenblatt, 1984, p. 70).

On the other hand, we jostled over the role of the writer's cultural background and the influence that information will have on the reading of the text. We agreed that that kind of background was important. This point became especially lucid when a member of the national faculty shared "Lessons in Living" from *I Know Why the Caged Bird Sings* (1969) by Maya Angelou (G. Morris, personal communication, August 21, 1990). His point was that this particular excerpt would cause the reader to focus on a point of experience that was not the point of Maya Angelou's story. If the reader were not familiar with the entire text, this excerpt might lead him or her astray. We concluded that to help students make meaning from text, we must start with students and where they are with the text and then expand from that point. Students will expand their range and depth of meaning as they share that meaning with increasingly broader audiences and learn more about the cultural background relevant to the text.

We were conscious of the issues raised by scholars such as Banks (1984), who believes that multiethnic education which focuses on race and ethnicity is not enough. Rather, a focus on multicultural education which highlights many cultural groups, such as women, handicapped persons, religious groups, and even regional groups such as Appalachian whites, is also imperative. We were mindful, too, of the concerns raised by scholars such as Ravitch (1990), who cautions us to move carefully as we define what we do and how we achieve equity for the various cultural, ethnic, and racial groups. The issues, concerns, and frustrations raised by Banks and Ravitch led us to consider the approach used by the Portland Public Schools.

The Portland Public Schools (1988), under the direction of Prophet, the superintendent, and Leonard (1990), the director of the multicultural program, commissioned the development of a series of baseline essays and lesson plans for each of their identified geocultural groups. The *African-American Baseline Essays* (Portland Public Schools, 1988) and *African-American Lesson Plans Grades K–5* (Leonard & Baradar, 1988) were the first to be infused into the mainstream curriculum. We heeded Leonard's (1990) advice to look not just to the Eurocentric and Afrocentric, but to a truly multicultural focus.

We searched the literature for the advice of still other experts regarding the importance of using literature to increase cultural awareness. Researchers who provided well-thought-out rationales, strategies, and listings of references appealed to us. Tway (1989) wrote about how literature can meet the needs of students and help them grow in understanding themselves and others. Norton (1990) advised that through carefully selected and shared literature students learn to understand and to appreciate a literary heritage that comes from many diverse backgrounds. Further, she stated that of equal value are the personal gains acquired by students when they read great works from their own cultural backgrounds and those of other cultures.

Harris (1990), in examining the status of the first one hundred years of African American children's literature, contends that an argument can be made that culturally conscious books are essential for African American children specifically and for all children generally. She cites the earlier work of Purves and Beach (1972), who "found that children prefer literary works with subject matter related to their personal experiences, that they engage more with materials related to their personal experiences, and that they seek out works with which they can identify or which contain characters whose experiences reflect their own" (Harris, 1990, p. 552).

Tiedt and Tiedt (1990) provided the last dimension of affirmation with the reminder that reading literature plays a special part in teaching multicultural understanding:

> Good fiction enables the reader to "walk in another person's moccasins," to feel the humiliation or joy by a boy or girl of a different color. Well-written nonfiction provides background information about other countries and cultures. Poetry gives students insights into the thinking of a writer who has a message to share about life. Multicultural literature provides vicarious experiences that lead students to recognize the commonalities they share with others. (p. 190)

This was the advice, caveats, and support from writers, scholars, and practitioners in the field that we heeded as we attempted to generate literature experiences for middle grade readers. We knew from our own past practices that literature experiences can be highly stimulating and meaningful. Our language arts teachers have had success with the literature experiences which they have orchestrated using the *Middle School Language Arts Literature Component for Grades 6-7-8* (PPS, 1988). These experiences have been developed around texts such as *Yellow Bird and Me* (Hansen, 1986), *Life Is Not Fair* (Bargar, 1984), *Words by Heart* (Sebestyen, 1979), *Sing Down the Moon* (O'Dell, 1970), and *The Upstairs Room* (Reiss, 1972). In many instances, the reading and language arts teachers have collaborated to provide students with an extended experience in integrated reading, writing, and discussion.

The reading teachers have developed and implemented *Student Novel Activity Programs (SNAP)* (PPS, 1990) for activities at the beginning of the school year. These units center on novels selected for their multicultural appeal. They included titles such as *Philip Hall Likes Me* (Greene, 1975), *Old Yeller* (Gipson, 1956), and *Call It Courage* (Sperry, 1940). Teachers and students were extremely pleased with the novel reading experience. Units that were to be taught for a week or two grew into expanded literature experiences. Imaginative writing, readers' theater (such as dramatizations of the readings), and art projects expanded the means for sharing responses to the literature. Students of varying levels of reading ability eagerly read and discussed their responses and ideas. The same has been true of focus literature units developed to highlight the contributions of writers from specific geocultural groups. Examples of titles for these units are *M. C. Higgins, the Great* (Hamilton, 1974), "Raymond's Run" (Bambara, 1972), "The Streets of Memphis" (Wright, 1969) and "Thank You, M'am" (Hughes, 1963).

As we explored literature for inclusion and infusion into the reading program, we not only looked for selections representative of the five geocultural groups, but we also searched for literature that included the elderly and the handicapped. A breakdown of gender and the roles played by males and females also guided the search. For the 1991–1992 school year, we adopted an anthology and a classroom selection of paperback titles as the baseline reading materials in all middle grade reading classes (Sulzby et al., 1990). These materials portray various cultural, racial, and ethnic groups.

We continue to search for appropriate titles which relate to the major geocultural groups and themes identified by the Subcommittee on Curriculum Infusion. A draft of a *Multicultural Literature Resource List* (PPS, 1990) has been developed to be used as a source list for literacy and literature efforts. A *Checklist for Evaluating Literature for a Multicultural Curriculum* (PPS, 1990) has also been developed to guide selection efforts. We are piloting a number of novels at the Prospect Multicultural Center in order to expand the list of pertinent titles for which teaching units can be prepared. *Walkabout* (Marshall, 1959) and *Journey Home* (Uchida, 1978) are two of the most recent titles which were piloted with students.

During the piloting we are interested in determining how well the text engaged the students. Are they willing readers? Are they anxious to share their reactions and experiences with others? Does the novel promote "honest" discussion? How does the novel enhance the grade-level theme (self, community, nation, world) and relate to specific geocultural groups? Texts that engage the students and receive positive marks on the checklist will become the focus for a teaching unit. Once teaching units are prepared they will be piloted in many schools and classrooms. Pre- and post-piloting sessions will be conducted with the teachers. Their verbal and written feedback as well as that from students and parents will aid in the revision of these units. The revised units will be submitted for adoption, after which they will become a part of the district's curriculum.

In summary, the infusion of multicultural literature is moving forward. A number of novels and a literature-based reading program have been adopted for use in the middle schools. A checklist for evaluating instructional materials for multiculticural literacy and a multicultural literature resource list have been created to guide the ongoing search for additional materials which can be infused into the curriculum. The establishment of themes for the sixth, seventh, and eighth grade levels and the consensus regarding the geocultural groups help to focus the infusion efforts. Finally, a plan is in place for disseminating materials for infusion throughout the district.

Prospects for Future Change

The prospects for the future of multiculturalism look very promising. A board-level subcommittee on multicultural education and a broad-based steering committee have been created to monitor the progress of the district in carrying out the mandates. This will certainly enhance the effort. At the end of the 1990–1991 school year, the directors approved a policy statement on multicultural education for the district (PPS, 1991).

There remain, however, a number of major questions to be answered. Will all of the curricular areas undergo multicultural infusion? What kinds of changes are needed to bring about greater interdisciplinary collaboration? What additional policies are required to move the multicultural infusion effort forward? What guides or models might the district at least investigate to speed up the infusion process? And most importantly, how will the continuing efforts of multicultural education be focused?

The major goal in the early 1900s was to "rid ethnic groups of their ethnic traits and to force them to acquire Anglo-Saxon values and behaviors" (Banks, 1988, p. 3). It appears that our major task in today's schools is to provide all students with the strategies, attitudes, and knowledge they need to function within their ethnic culture and the mainstream culture, as well as within and across other ethnic cultures. If this is the case, and I believe that this is indeed a major goal, then multicultural infusion, especially in the areas of literacy and literature, will help to achieve that end. I acknowledge the contention of Sims-Bishop (1990) that "literature functions as a major socializing agent. It tells students who and what their society and culture values, what kinds of behaviors are acceptable and appropriate, and what it means to be a decent human being" (p. 561). Nevertheless, the policies which will be needed will be those which focus on the total school environment as the unit of change.

In closing, it must be noted that the district has taken some giant steps in terms of creating certain policies and organizational units which have a certain degree of autonomy to lay the groundwork for change. On the other hand, it is also apparent that there is considerable latitude for the program planners to forge ahead relying upon their expertise and resources to move the agenda as it becomes increasingly better defined. The next year will be a pivotal one for the development and implementation of policy for the Triple M effort as it relates to literacy and literature and all other areas of schooling. The words of two individuals are instructive for planners:

> Make no little plans, they have no magic to stir men's blood and probably themselves will not be realized. Make big plans; aim high in hope and work, remembering that a noble, logical diagram once recorded will not die.
>
> — Daniel H. Burnham

> Only those who have already experienced a revolution within themselves can reach out effectively to help others.
>
> — Malcolm X

References

Angelou, M. (1969). *I know why the caged bird sings*. New York: Random House.

Bambara, T. C. (1972). Raymond's Run. In *Gorilla, my love*. New York: Random House.

Banks, J. (1984). *Teaching strategies for ethnic studies* (3rd ed.). Boston: Allyn & Bacon.

Banks, J. (1988). *Multiethnic education* (2nd ed.). Boston: Allyn & Bacon.

Bargar, G. (1984). *Life is not fair*. New York: Clarion Books.

Botel, M., & Lytel, S. (1988). *Pennsylvania framework for reading, writing, and talking across the curriculum*. Harrisburg, PA: Pennsylvania Department of Education.

Gipson, F. (1956). *Old yeller*. New York: Harper & Row.

Greene, B. (1975). *Philip Hall likes me. I reckon maybe*. New York: Dell Publishing.

Hamilton, V. (1974). *M.C. Higgins, the Great*. New York: Macmillan.

Hansen, J. (1986). *Yellow bird and me*. New York: Houghton Mifflin.

Harris, V. J. (1990). African American children's literature: The first one hundred years. *Journal of Negro Education, 59*, 540–555.

Hughes, L. (1963). Thank you, M'am. In *Something in common and other stories*. New York: Hill & Wang.

Leff, R., & Pace, V. (1990). *Report of the committee on curriculum infusion*. Pittsburgh, PA: Pittsburgh Public Schools. Office of Multiracial, Multicultural, and Multiethnic Education.

Leonard, C. (1990). *Report of the Board of Visitors of the Prospect Center for Multicultural, Multiethnic, and Multiracial Education*. Pittsburgh, PA: Pittsburgh Public Schools, Office of Multiracial, Multicultural, and Multiethnic Education.

Leonard, C., & Baradar, M. (1988). *African-American lesson plans, Grades K–5*. Portland, OR: Portland Public Schools.

Marshall, J. (1959) *Walkabout*. Littleton, MA: Sundance.

Norton, D. E. (1990). Teaching multicultural literature in the reading curriculum. *The Reading Teacher, 44*, 28–40.

O'Dell, S. (1970). *Sing down the moon*. New York: Dell.

Parr, P. (1989). *Multicultural program*. Pittsburgh, PA: Pittsburgh Public Schools, Office of Program Funding.

Pittsburgh Public Schools. (1980). *Amended Pittsburgh desegregation plan*. Pittsburgh, PA: Author.

Pittsburgh Public Schools. (January 8, 1981). "NEWS." Pittsburgh, PA: Author, Division of Information Services.

Pittsburgh Public Schools. (1983). *Textbook adoption policy*. Pittsburgh, PA: Author, Division of Curriculum.

Pittsburgh Public Schools. (1985). *Report of suspensions*. Pittsburgh, PA: Author.

Pittsburgh Public Schools. (1987). *Recommendations of the district's task force on the racial achievement gap*. Pittsburgh, PA: Author.

Pittsburgh Public Schools. (1988). *Middle school language arts literature component for grades 6-7-8*. Pittsburgh, PA: Author, Divisions of Reading and Literature and Writing and Speaking.

Pittsburgh Public Schools. (1989). Summary of findings: The Prospect Middle Center for Multiracial, Multiethnic, Multicultural Education needs assessment. Pittsburgh, PA: Author.

Pittsburgh Public Schools. (1990). *Checklist for evaluating literature for a multicultural curriculum*. Pittsburgh, PA: Author, Division for Curriculum.

Pittsburgh Public Schools. (1990). *Enrollment report*. Pittsburgh, PA: Author, Division of Student Information and Statistics.

Pittsburgh Public Schools. (1990). *Middle schools reading handbook*. Pittsburgh, PA: Author, Division of Reading and Literature.

Pittsburgh Public Schools. (1990). *Multicultural literature resource list*. Pittsburgh, PA: Author, Division of Reading and Literature and Division of Curriculum.

Pittsburgh Public Schools. (1990). *Student novel activity programs (SNAP), grades 6-7-8*. Pittsburgh, PA: Author, Division of Reading and Literature.

Pittsburgh Public Schools. (1991). Policy statement on multicultural education (Board Minutes of July 10, 1991). Pittsburgh, PA: Author.

Portland Public Schools. (1988). *African-American baseline essays*. Portland, OR: Author.

Purves, A., & Beach, R. (1972). *Literature and the reader*. Urbana, IL: National Council of Teachers of English.

Ravitch, D. (1990). Multiculturalism: E pluribus plures. *The American Scholar, 59*, 337–354.

Reiss, J. (1972). *The upstairs room*. New York: Harper & Row.

Rosenblatt, L. M. (1984). Language, literature, and values in language. In S. N. Tchudi (Ed.), *Language, schooling, and society* (pp. 64–80). Upper Montclair, NJ: Boynton/Cook.

Sebestyen, O. (1979). *Words by heart*. Boston: Little Brown.

Sims-Bishop, R. (1990). Walk tall in the world: African American literature for today's children. *Journal of Negro Education, 59*, 556–565.

Sperry, A. (1940). *Call it courage*. New York: Macmillan.

Stoops, J. (1987). *Middle states accreditation report*. Pittsburgh, PA: Pittsburgh Public Schools.

Sulzby, E., Hoffman, J., Mangrum, C., Niles, J., Shanahan, T., Teale, W., Webb, A., Klein, M., & Matteoni, L. (1990). *Crystal Stair*. New York: Macmillan/McGraw-Hill.

Tiedt, P., and Tiedt, I. (1990). *Multicultural teaching* (3rd ed.). Boston: Allyn and Bacon.

Tway, E. (1989). Dimensions of multicultural literature for children. In M. K Rudman (Ed.), *Children's literature: Resource for the classroom* (pp. 109–138). Needham Heights, MA: Christopher-Gordan.

Uchida, Y. (1978). *Journey home*. New York: Macmillan.

Wright, R. (1969). The streets of Memphis. In *Black boy*. New York: Random House.

8

Reading against the Cultural Grain[1]

Phillip C. Gonzales

"This story is dedicated to you the Children of Sanchez," bellowed the producer of the movie based on the Oscar Lewis anthropological description of an abusive husband with an exaggerated machismo who maintains two poor, dysfunctional families in Mexico. The audience of five hundred invited Latino/Hispanic movie-goers gasped and visibly were offended. "Was this what Hollywood producers think of us?" "Is this the way we want to be portrayed?" "What impression will a non-Hispanic audience get from viewing this movie?" "My family is not like the one in Lewis's book nor like the one depicted in the movie." "Ay Diós de mi vida."

Having begun to teach at a time when ethnic awareness was rising and multicultural education as a response was germinating, I realized early that in our haste to validate the Hispanic/Chicano/Mexican American experience in the United States, we had accepted literature containing visuals with white children painted brown, accented dialogue pasted onto caricatures who behaved differently than did my Hispanic associates, and story lines depicting life experiences not resembling those of friends and relatives in my community. Yet I believed that in the schools' literature program lay the answer to resolving the problem of disenfranchisement felt by most minority students. My search for a "better way" continued throughout my professional life. I came to California in 1986 believing that we must do more to help students, especially minority students, feel a part of the greater society and able to profit from a more equitable education. It was about this time that the *California English-Language Arts Framework*[2] was developed and the California Literature Project began.

The *California English-Language Arts Framework*, a California Department of Education philosophical document, encouraged student response to literature as the instructional focus of K–12 English-language arts programs. The *Framework* called for district teachers to select unabridged core literature to be studied in depth at each grade by ALL students. It asked that recreational literature be made available for students to read at their leisure. And it recommended that selections be assigned to students to extend the study of a core text or fulfill a student's desire or need for additional readings.

To help implement the intentions of the *California English-Language Arts Framework*, the California legislature established the California Literature Project (CLP) to help train and retrain teachers to provide instruction consistent with the *Framework*. The CLP program which I now codirect with Mel Grubb at California State University, Dominguez Hills,[3] trains teachers to help students make sense of and construct personal meanings in response to ideas in written literary texts. It encourages teachers to promote collaboration among students and thus lessen competition. Teachers learn to function as coaches and guides for exploration, helping students to operate as active generators of meaning as well as negotiators and exhibitors of personal and group interpretations of text. Teachers in this program integrate the language arts of reading, listening, writing, and speaking and help students draw upon them authentically as they interact with ideas in the text and explore their validity in the world beyond the classroom. Skills in this curriculum serve the meaning(s) of ideas emphasized in lessons and are not isolated for independent study. The most dramatic change called for by the *Framework* and implemented by teachers involves making this dynamic curriculum available to all students regardless of socioeconomic class, ethnicity or primary language, perceived giftedness, or prior educational history.

The tasks faced by school districts as they implement this curriculum are both exciting and challenging. Nowhere are decisions more important than in the selection of literature, the centerpiece of the curriculum. The need for literature that represents divergent worldviews, life experiences, and personal histories has long been discussed by educators. This was felt necessary not just because the students living close to our campus and increasingly throughout California are primarily nonwhite, nonnative English speaking, and often immigrant populations, but because the greater American society is becoming increasingly more diverse and the people in the world in which we live are in closer and more constant contact than ever before. Fortunately, the quality and quantity of ethnic literature has been increasing and now is becoming more readily available. Although there is common agreement that in this literature everyone, particularly minority students, needs successful role models to emulate, cultural perspectives to match their own, and points of view that validate their way of making sense of their world, African American, Hispanic, Native American, and other minority students too often find little to identify with in many of the literary selections used in traditional English-language arts instruction. This chapter examines the uses and misuses of ethnic literature with the minority student populations it is purported to affirm.

Criteria Used in Selecting Ethnic Literature: "We need ethnic literature that is authentic."

Most school districts have adopted criteria which they use in the selection of ethnic literature. Collectively, their criteria ask that characters in stories be authentic: that is, that they be culturally identifiable because of their behavior and use of language. Visuals are expected to depict physical traits assumed true of members of that group. Finally, the criteria usually ask that values, beliefs, traditions, fears, and myths as well as biases be true to the cultural norm of the group. Some criteria even ask that the author be of the same group that is ethnically portrayed. When the language is other than English, the criteria frequently specify that the literature not be a translation.

When literature strays too far from the identifiable cultural pattern, the story is assumed to be too ethnically homogenized to be truly authentic. African American characters living in suburbs, assuming mainstream values, and speaking textbook English are viewed as inauthentic. Hispanics who belong to Kiwanis Clubs, play golf, or listen to jazz are considered not typical. Conversely, college professors are typically depicted as white-haired gentlemen wearing tweed jackets and speaking a Bostonian dialect, and women wearing white lab coats are immediately thought to be nurses. Literature depicting individuals in nonculturally identifiable behavior or nonstereotypic situations is dismissed as inaccurate and thus inauthentic.

An obvious "catch 22" is evident. Authors and publishers are damned if they do and damned if they don't. Is it possible to portray ethnic and cultural groups authentically without perpetuating stereotypes? Must we in order to assert authenticity characterize Hispanics as guitar players, African Americans as poor and struggling, Catholics as members of large families, and Native Americans as craftspeople? Can students read literature about divergent life experiences without overgeneralizing and incorrectly typecasting members of that cultural group? Is it possible for students to learn to live with diversity without others telling them what or how to think about it? Is authenticity a false goal?

"You don't play a guitar?"

"You people have always had it rough."

"I bet you come from a large family."

"No, my mother does not weave rugs."

Ethnic Literature as Definition of Group Membership:
"Read what this piece of literature says
about you and your minority group."

The dangers of relying on typecasting of characters are obvious. Native Americans in many literature selections are typically characterized as passive, in harmony with the environment, and living traditionally in rural settings sometime prior to the twentieth century. Hispanic males are described as macho and females as subservient. Hispanics all speak Spanish or a mix of English and Spanish, have relatives in Mexico, Puerto Rico, or Cuba, and live in neighborhoods in large numbers as extended families. Asian characters are hardworking and tolerant of much pain and suffering. African Americans live in inner-city ghettos with "no way out," are poor, speak a dialect of English, and sing spirituals when they are sad. Whites are educated, in traditional intact families, and live happily in suburban areas. An implicit "This is the collective 'you' " is communicated. Yet the reality may be quite different. Few Middle Easterners are nomadic today; few American Irishmen have ever been to Ireland or speak with a brogue; and some African Americans are Republicans. When an individual does not see himself or herself in the characters depicted in stories, especially those purported to reflect cultural group membership, an unconscious cultural challenge is received: "Why are you not like the group to which you belong?" An African American fourth grade student in a class I was observing recently was asked by his teacher his term of choice in describing himself: *African American, black, Negro,* or *colored.* The student looked perplexed by this question and responded: "I don't know; I am into comic books." This nonconforming student, like others not fitting stereotypic notions of group membership, is often marginalized, thought not to fit the cultural norm, and can be seen as rebellious and therefore subject to ridicule or social exclusion by peers or by the school culture in general. Because this experience is defining for many, it is less than affirming for most. This influence is subtle and often nonconscious, yet over time and with multiple exposure to a singular direction of bias, it can be potent.

Some possible cultural messages are as follows:

In *The Legend of El Dorado* (1991),[4] the king receives gold and jewels from his people to pay ransom to a lake serpent who has captured the queen and her daughter, the princess. This legend is Argentine and reinforces, perhaps unknowingly, the caste system that exists in much of Latin America—the wealthy oligarchy can extract tributes from their lesser-status countrymen. The females are victims in this story and are definitely not in control of their destiny.

In *Abiyoyo* (1986),[5] a magician and trickster saves his town from the monster Abiyoyo by singing, dancing, and using magic. In this African tale, the townspeople are incapable of fending off a threat to their village and have to rely on someone using trickery to do it for them.

After the Indian boy in *Arrow to the Sun* (1974),[6] is mocked by other Pueblo youth for having been raised in a single-parent family, he sets out to prove himself. This story communicates the need to prove oneself beyond that which is expected in two-parent families in order to overcome society's nonacceptance of families led by a single mother.

Narrow Acceptance of Author's Choices: "What is the author saying?"

Before the *Framework*, reading success was defined as information gathering. Text teaching was the prevailing practice. Students read stories or poems and were asked questions about the settings, characters, and situations and/or predetermined messages. Their answers were checked by the teacher, who referred to the text for verification. Author's choices regarding point of view, expression of mood, affirmation or questioning of a moral conviction, and the persuasiveness of the plot, although comprehended, were left unchallenged.

This approach does not acknowledge that when literature is written, authors make decisions regarding how they will portray characters solving problems and overcoming challenges. They exercise control over the manner in which characters are "colored" (the light by which they reveal their traits). An author's words and pictures stimulate interest and lead readers to believe that character portrayal is plausible and characters' points of view are reasonable. Authors communicate their value prejudices[7] through their literature. And they can reinforce or challenge social constructions and rigid social structures. The more skilled the author, the more convincing the message.

Although most authors don't write to convey personal notions about a culture, they frequently employ preconceptions and recognizable patterns to establish believability. Ministers are God-fearing and honest. College professors are reflective. Blonds are not too bright. And southern law enforcement officials are "bubbas."

Authors communicate compulsory roles and behaviors throughout their writings. Through Cinderella-type stories, authors characterize girls as helpless individuals who must be assisted by males in overcoming most obstacles. In traditional stories, authors often suggest that females nurture while males provide reasoned but challenging guidance. Females are shown to be passive, incompetent, and modest. Men, on the other hand, are portrayed as dominant, competent, and self-promotive. Messages about acceptable gender roles in children are communicated as well. Boys engage in rough behavior as kids, as adventurers as adolescents, and as leaders as adults. Girls play house, argue about boyfriends as teenagers, and resign themselves to serving "their men" in society as adults.

In stories about ethnic individuals, authors often depict minorities as victims who must rely on outsiders to help them through crises. They hint of a stratified society in which some "winners" exercise control, have more enlightened thoughts, can be adventuresome and reckless, and deserve reverence and deference—all not because of the strength of their character but because of their position in the community. And, in the same community, the "losers" can be denied privilege, must be subservient to the lords of the manor, and should live a quiet, uneventful life unquestioning of the status quo. This population is punished if it varies from this norm.

Color and physical appearance bias can also be apparent. Evil characters are depicted as shady. Dark, gloomy nights or alleyways suggest danger. A crooked nose signifies an individual who is dishonest. Downcast eyes are signs of guilt. The word *mafia* indicates not just unlawful behavior but Italian-looking individuals committing crimes. Questioning by minority individuals is described as "uppity." Diminutives such as *boy* or *Juanito* and apparent foreign names such as

Mohammed and Maria are used to characterize nonmainstreamed presence and therefore lessor status. A "tomboy" will grow out of it. A sensitive or assertive Asian will soon learn to conform. This subtle communication is pervasive in our literature.

Authors communicate societal values about language as well. Although individuals who speak a language in addition to English in our world are valued, in our literature, monolingualism is the norm if not the expectation. Bilingual individuals in stories too often are characterized as lacking intellectual capability, are treated as second-class individuals, are comedic, and are seen as deprived as long as they carry the baggage of second language and culture with them. Agricultural workers, whether southern or immigrant along with household domestics, are heard speaking substandard English. Employers speak in their presence as though the workers are not present or will not understand the employer's third-person referent. Broken English is used by authors not to show that English capabilities are emerging but to suggest that such speakers are inadequate communicators. At times, authors have characters mix two languages as they speak not because this occurs normally in communication but because this exemplifies a difference and therefore inferior station. Speakers of a nonmainstreamed dialect are similarly depicted. Dialect is used to suggest status, intellectual capacity, and education. Participation in our society is reserved by too many authors only for those who conform to linguistic, social, and behavioral norms. What a limited definition of democracy this attitude conveys.

There is probably no universal plot to stereotype women and minorities. Yet in pursuing authenticity, the literature may do just this. Authors seldom have individuals of mixed color fall in love and live happily ever after—yet they sometimes do. They seldom allow individuals from different cultural groups to meet and become friends without struggle—yet this occurs. When characters come from different socioeconomic classes, the poorer individual is usually cast as ill-mannered and offensive—yet this is usually not the case. We realize that unconscious and damning messages regarding norming behavior, values and beliefs are transmitted through literature, particularly when there is uniformity in the direction of thinking and interpretation in the writings by many authors. Although espoused indirectly through children's literature, these unconscious messages do have an effect. The persuasiveness of a singular or monolithic portrayal in argument of gender and ethnic roles and attitudes can affect a child's perception of self, his or her view of and relationship with his or her family, and his or her feelings toward participation in mainstreamed culture. We know from acculturation studies of immigrants that first-generation offspring separate from their parents linguistically and culturally yet do not fully participate in mainstreamed society. Second-generation offspring are likely to become disenfranchised from their family culture, yet they only participate marginally in mainstreamed society. We can only speculate about how much of this is attributable to constant and consistent images of acceptable appearance, behavior, and language presented through literature read in school.

The culture of these children does not resemble that which they read about in books, yet it is different from that of their parents. It is no wonder that so many minority children seek group affiliations outside mainstreamed norms for validation of their personal worth and for affirmation of their personal cultures. I believe we need to examine the cultural messages present in the literature children read at school and the ways teachers traditionally have used this literature to find out why this scenario has been established and how we can overcome its negative effects.

"I didn't realize that you spoke with an accent until after our phone conversation when we met face to face."

"Boys will be boys."

"That is not the way real people I know behave."

"Do you have four pieces of identification?"

The Right to Accept or Reject Author's Choices: "What do I believe about what was written?"

The *California English-Language Arts Framework* calls for a meaning-centered language arts curriculum. The student's prior experiences, cultural schemas, and personal worldviews are revealed, valued, and incorporated into literature-based lessons. Successful reading has occurred when readers have "constructed" an understanding of a selection after reflection, collaboration with peers, and verification of the validity of the messages through comparisons to the world of the student. Mature readers readily question the behavior of story characters, the choices the author wrote in for them, and the point of view expressed in the literature. It is common for these readers to annotate their thoughts in the margins of books, poems, or plays. They often discard or disregard stories which they find too offensive or too unbelievable.

Unfortunately, younger readers either are seldom encouraged to challenge what authors have written or they do not know that this behavior is acceptable. These immature readers leave stories with unconscious messages still ringing in their minds regarding acceptable behavior, world perspectives, notions about right and wrong, and the "politically correct" attitudes they should assume. We realize that literature affirms or challenges the moral convictions we all have about life. Left unexamined, readers can become confused as well as victims of literary cultural influences. The "Leave it to Beaver" social situations found in much of our literature too often do not resemble the harsh realities faced by many of our students today. Many of the children in parts of Los Angeles face the potential of drive-by shootings as they walk home, wrestle with the dilemma of selecting either to shoplift food or have their families go hungry, and see police officers as repressors rather than community helpers. Yet all students to some extent are like characters in stories, and at the same time they are different. How do we deal with this?

In California, about 50 percent of our school-age children grow up in one-parent families. Most of these children are healthy, their families are functional, and the parent well adjusted. Yet the portrayal of family units by literature for the most part suggests that only two-parent families can be functional and well adjusted.[8] Stepmothers are for the most part depicted as evil and abusive. Single fathers raising children are viewed as unusual if not abnormal. And authors write about gang-related or other antisocial behavior as having its origins in nontraditional family units.[9]

In Los Angeles County, 59 percent of the school-age population is Hispanic. The culture of the Hispanic may range from traditional to mainstreamed. When "Hispanic literature" is brought into the classroom, educators should raise the question of the match of literature with the cultures of the students. Los Angeles has Hispanic populations whose origins are from many parts of the world. Many are Mexican Americans, some are "Chicanos," others are Central Americans, a few have cultural origins in Spain or South America, and quite a number have influences from indigenous native cultures that are not Hispanic. Hispanic cultures and experiences are not monolithic. Worldviews vary, life experiences differ, behaviors run the gamut, and languages range from monolingual to multilingual. A student told "This is your literature" may find little with which to identify in the selection. A Hispanic raised in northern New Mexico may identify more closely with

Huckleberry Finn (1884) than with "Pocho," a fictional character from California. A rural upbringing in northern California does not prepare a Hispanic child to make sense of The Inquisition Spanish Catholic mentality surrounding *Don Quixote* (1615), nor does it ensure appreciation of Gary Soto's poetry about life in an agricultural labor camp. Yet most educators believe that students grow in their understanding of the world as they read an increasingly wider range of literature.

Likewise, most African Americans in California live in families with middle-class incomes and have never been to the South. Most non–African Americans I know identify with Malcolm X. More Native Americans live in cities than on reservations. Third-generation Japanese Americans may be more similar to their Jewish American friends than to members of a Japanese family sent to California for five years so that the father can help manage a Japanese-owned firm. We are finding that individuals from various ethnicities living in the same Los Angeles neighborhood may have more in common with each other than they may with their ethnic counterparts living in other parts of the country. Similarly, the role of females in California society is changing and may differ in many ways from that in other parts of the country.

We owe it to all of our students to help them to become critical readers, able to compare what an author has decided to write about in a story, poem, or play with what they themselves might have done, thought, or felt about similar situations, and to accept, reject, or conditionally approve or disapprove the author's messages as "truth." Not allowing students to do so potentially harms those whose circumstances or hopes for their future do not match that of the author.

> "What do you mean, 'Describe how it felt to sneak into the United States to do farm work.' I was born in Chicago."

> "I agree with Malcolm X." "But, you are white!"

> "The way I see it is..."

Activites Which Promote Critical Reading against the Grain:
"I can disagree."

California State University, Dominguez Hills, is situated in Los Angeles County, and thus serves an area with a linguistically, ethnically, and culturally diverse population also characterized by high unemployment rates and low income levels. Over 50 percent of the students in the area do not complete high school, many attend school but do not participate, and too many experience a literature-based English education that is similar to the problems I have described above. In the California Literature Project at California State University, Dominguez Hills, we have developed a program to help urban teachers provide English-language arts instruction that is literature based and affirms the individual cultures of students, validates their personal experiences and perspectives, encourages personal parallel stories to be told and accepted, indicates challenge of cultural statements in literature, and moves education away from seeking the right answer and the correct perspective to constructing an understanding which is both collaborative and personal. In short, we help teachers to teach children to read against the grain. Since no literature reflects the entire life experiences and personal interpretations of any one student, we believe that all students but particularly the ethnic and linguistic minority students, need to learn to read literature in the manner described below.

Reading against the grain involves more than just understanding that authors make decisions about the message they have selected to share and the slant or bent they use in communicating it. It involves helping readers become familiar with the cultural biases authors are communicating and to compare them with the idiosyncratic culture students possess. This analysis includes helping students come to understand and appreciate their own personal choices regarding right and wrong and the circumstances under which decisions might reflect such choices, behaviors and when and where they are acceptable, and the uses of various forms of language.

In the California Literature Project at CSU, Dominguez Hills, we believe that students have both a right and a responsibility to examine all literature through idiosyncratic cultural filters. Personal interpretations supported by student-generated and text-related evidence, judgments regarding the casting of individuals in the literature, conclusions regarding the reasonableness of the author's hidden messages, and the decision to closely examine the author's use of persuasive techniques are all thrusts in the training we provide teachers. We encourage students to reflect on the myriad options and their consequences that are faced by the characters in the literature they are reading. We want students to test their thoughts, to hear the insights of others, and perhaps to come collaboratively to new understandings.

A typical lesson would begin with students tapping their prior experiences and personal perspectives related to a selection and sharing these in small groups. As they read the literature students would write personal reflective responses to the story, find parallels in their lives, record questions and challenges raised by the selection, and meet frequently in small groups to share perceptions of the piece of literature. During these face-to-face discussions contrasting views would be examined. In addition, the class would meet as a large group to receive teacher guidance regarding techniques for identifying the author's bias and perspectives that influence meaning. Finally, students would be guided to take the literature's "big ideas" and apply them to their personal worlds.

Although we can't change the way an author has written a piece of literature, we can suggest strategies teachers can use in guiding students as they read. There are numerous simple-to-use classroom strategies that encourage students to "read against the grain." All of these activities are open-ended in ways that allow student-generated thought to be expressed, tested, and changed or retained if necessary and reasonable. They include the following:

1. Journal entries allow students to record first or reflected thoughts. Although the entries are not judged for correctness, it is expected that they be supported either from evidence presented in the literature or from a student's personal knowledge of related circumstances and judgments of them. Two column journal entries may include what the author is saying (what I believe), what the story is about (parallels in my world), statements from the story (do I agree/disagree), what——character did (what I would have done).

2. Choice-consequence trees allow students to see that other choices expressed by characters would have resulted in different outcomes. Through this procedure, students map out those choices-consequences exhibited in the story. Then they speculate about alternative choices characters could have selected and the potential consequences or outcomes that would reasonably be expected.

3. Discussions of the author's message encourage students to explore literature beyond the obvious by asking questions regarding the subtle and usually unconscious cultural messages in the literature: What occurred in the story? Why did it occur? What does it mean? What I believe.

4. Analysis of the author's techniques by more capable and more mature readers answers the question "What did the author do to make me believe as I did?" In this close examination, students look at how authors persuaded them to think as they did using the plot, language, and other devices to convince them of their point of view.

5. Rewriting the story with a different ending, time setting, cultural perspective, or point of view helps students explore alternatives and generate a new or altered way of developing the story: How would or could I have written this story?
6. Rank ordering—listing beliefs, situations, items, and so on from the story in order of preference—allows students to share how they value the ideas, objects, behaviors, and attitudes from the story.
7. With contrived situations—similar to the literary theme study but developed by students—students write about situations related to but not exactly like those presented in the selection. Older and more capable students determine the tone, direction, and bias to be taken in writing about the new situation.

The California Literature Project at CSU, Dominguez Hills, is also beginning to involve parents in the education of their children. We believe that it is important for the entire family, the culturally significant others, to examine the author's unconscious messages as the school's core literature is discussed. Students are assigned homework that requires them to go back into their community and back to their families to rethink, evaluate, and perhaps reinterpret the ideas, biases, and messages communicated by authors through their literature, and to thus become a voice for their culture, family, and community. Using the following discourse types, students can come to realize what they think about various subjects, topics, and concepts, as well as begin to explore how authors manipulate their media to control the messages communicated. The discourse types our teachers ask students to employ include the following:

1. Autobiographical incidents—identifying an event in the student's life that resembles that which is depicted in a story. In this self-disclosure, the student shares a story about a personal experience. The narration includes an examination of the meaning this incident held for the student author and his or her feelings about it then and today. Back in the classroom, each autobiographical incident shared is considered as valid as that read about in the literature.
2. Firsthand biography—the student reveals another individual's personal experience. Although like an autobiographical incident, this type focuses on another person and the relationship the student writer has with that person. The student author explores another's story, examines and interprets that person's actions, motives, and beliefs, and relates the significance of the second person to his or her own life. This sharing of another's experiences—

both related and similar to the literature—validates the unique life experiences and worldviews of family and community.

3.   Speculation about effects and causes—student authors conjecture about what may cause or result from a situation, event, or trend. Students learn to predict "what ifs" and elaborate on the plausibility of their speculations. This type of persuasive writing can be used in exploring multiple perspectives, considering many possibilities, and making plausible predictions—and the techniques that make their reasoning convincing. Because there are no right or wrong speculations, this allows for divergent explanations.

4.   Report of information—emphasizes the gathering, organizing, and reporting of useful information in a clear manner. Students are asked to gather information from their community related to cultural themes studied in school. This primary research asks students to collect data from a variety of sources in a variety of ways: interviews, priority listings, and others using likert scales, semantic differentials, and so on. These surveys or polls can be summarized, organized to illustrate a point of view, and shared with classmates at school.

5.   Problem-solution—taking dilemmas faced in a story, students with their families define a problem, propose a solution(s), and work on persuading the class of its (their) feasibility by drawing on real-life experiences and the prevailing wisdom of the students' family and community.

6.   Evaluation—involves arriving at a judgment about the worth of a subject (story, decision, a character) and using established or asserted criteria to support judgment with evidence. Students with their parents or siblings together develop the argument that reasonably and persuasively supports their conclusion.

7.   Interpretation—involves staking a claim about an event, character, or resolution of a problem in a story and supporting it with evidence from that story or from experiences and information beyond the story. Through this type of thinking, student authors explore the conclusions they draw from the literature they have studied, attempt to persuade an audience of their reasonableness by carefully selecting evidence to support it, and experiment with language to effectively communicate their interpretation.

8.   Story—a believable but not necessarily true narrative that may be based on a family story or known occurrence. The student authors explore the "what ifs" as they make sense of how a dilemma, problem, or challenge posed by a piece of literature plays out in their world. This writing may be of a parallel experience to that

read in the classroom literature. This imaginative writing may be a departure from the classroom story at a crucial scene in the narrative, or it may be a similar story to that read in the classroom but one which was written with a different bias, point of view, or message.

9.   Observational writing—focuses on recording or re-creating remembered experiences. Here the student author is in a role of observing and not participating. The author may write an essay, poem, log, journal entry, or letter that records conclusions drawn, speculations, or reflections based on extended observations. This type of writing is more distant and impersonal than autobiographical or biographical types of discourse.

Reading against the grain involves actively constructing a sense of an author's message, comprehending the story, reflecting on it, checking its validity against what the reader already knows to be true or believes from his or her own experience, accepting or rejecting the specific responses by story characters to situations they encounter, and finding parallels or divergent ways of responding in the reader's world. It means that readers understand that all writers convey their biases, their worldviews, through the life experiences they choose to write about. Unchallenged, these perspectives present the reader with a single point of view. Left unchallenged, the "correctness" of this position unconsciously influences readers, their view of themselves, and the validity of their idiosyncratic cultures—and communicates indirectly a message that the reader is on target or off base. We owe it to our students to help them learn to read against the cultural grain, as Forrest Carter in *The Education of Little Tree* (1976) said the grandfather did when he read *Macbeth* and attempted to discuss it with his family:

When Granma read about Macbeth, I could see the castle and the witches taking shape in the shadows, alive on the cabin walls, and I'd edge closer to Granpa's rocker. He'd stop rocking when Granma got to the stabbings and the blood and all. Granpa said none of it would come about if Lady Macbeth had minded doing what a woman was supposed to do and kept her nose out of the business that rightly ought to have been done by Mr. Macbeth, and besides, she wasn't much of a lady, and he couldn't figure out why she was called such, anyhow. Granpa said all this in the heat of the first reading. Later on, after he had mulled it over in his mind, he commented that something was undoubtedly wrong with the woman (he refused to call her Lady). He said, however, he had seen a doe deer one time, that was in heat and couldn't find a buck, go slap-dab mad, running into trees and finally drowning herself in the creek. He said there was no way of knowing, because Mr. Shakespeare didn't indicate as such, but it all could be laid at the door of Mr. Macbeth—and indications was along that line—as the man seemed to have trouble doing just about anything.[10]

Notes

1. Inspired by Bill Corcoran, Queensland College, Australia, and talk presented at the California Literature Project at California State University, Dominguez Hills (CSUDH), during summer 1991.

2. *California English-Language Arts Framework* (Sacramento: California State Department of Education, 1987).

3. The teacher certification program at CSUDH symbiotically works hand in hand with the California Literature Project (CLP). Many CLP-trained classroom teachers have taught courses in our preservice certification program, often serving as master teachers for our students, and CSUDH English and education faculty work with the CLP staff in retraining several hundred experienced teachers yearly.

4. Beatriz Vidal, author and illustrator (adapted by Nancy Van Laan), *The Legend of El Dorado* (New York: Knopf, 1991).

5. Pete Seeger, *Abiyoyo* (New York: Macmillan, 1986).

6. Gerald McDermott, *Arrow to the Sun* (New York: Viking, 1974).

7. These are shown by decisions regarding manner of dress, language variety, behavior under specific circumstances, and choices about how to handle situations. There is no universal right or wrong value prejudice, only choices made by individuals.

8. Even former Vice President Dan Quayle seemed to believe this. He criticized a fictional unwed TV sitcom character, Murphy Brown, for choosing to have a child out of wedlock. This for him signaled a breakdown of "family values" that was responsible for many of our unresolved national concerns.

9. After the Los Angeles riots of 1992, President Bush, ignoring other social causes, agreed with this point of view when he blamed single-parent families for the looting and arson that occurred.

10. Forrest Carter, *The Education of Little Tree* (Albuquerque: University of New Mexico Press, 1976), p. 15.

9

Some Notes on the Canon and Multiculturalism

Catharine R. Stimpson

In this section, entitled "Making Space," the papers, explicitly or implicitly, share a set of attractive beliefs: in multicultural education, in students as participants in transactive readings, in stronger connections among the disciplines and among educational communities (primary schools, middle schools, secondary schools, postsecondary institutions), and in the difficult possibilities of institutional and social change. The papers are *tonally* different. Sutherland is visionary and optimistic, for example, and Purves is toughly realistic. Together, however, the papers provide a range of attitudes, which we need if we are to create a literate, multicultural society.

I have organized my comment on these papers around a theme that appears in each of them, but most fully in Purves's—the theme of the canon. I hesitated before making this choice for two reasons: (1) I feared that I might seem insular, too embroiled in postsecondary education and literary criticism; (2) even more, I feared that I would have to ignore questions that the papers acknowledge but do not foreground. One example: the citizens of the post-Gutenberg society do experience "information overload." How can a multicultural curriculum add to our knowledge of the world, each other, and ourselves without intensifying this strain? Another example: how does a multicultural curriculum, classroom, and society respect freedom of speech? How, in brief, do we speak, not only good, but also ill of each other? Still another example: can we have the courage of complexity? Can we avoid oversimplified labels? As Purves points out, not all Europeans were Anglo-Saxons. Can we avoid easy, even glib references to "Eurocentric," "Afrocentric," or "phallocentric"? Still another example: when do we stop speaking of differences? This question is really two. First, when is a group difference insufficiently significant to become a basis of social policy and general study? Next, what are our unities? The bright flags of a common identity?

Nevertheless, I chose the canon for four, perhaps equally obvious, reasons:

1. At its most spacious, a canon formally represents the "best self" a culture or genre has to offer. A canon is the formal sitting room, not the family room, in the house of culture. Whatever the particular content of a canon, it makes a statement about the values of the culture that has created it. Inter alia, a multicultural canon would symbolize respect for cultural differences and, perhaps, for the attics and basements of the houses of culture in our historic districts.
2. A canon also formally displays the memory of a culture or of a genre. The history of canon formation shows how necessary and treacherous the processes of memory are.
3. For these two reasons, a canon provides a basis for a curriculum, a link between the regulations of a culture and its classrooms.
4. The words *the canon* have become fighting words in contemporary U. S. culture. Like Purves, I fear that "canon wars" may tear the schools further apart. Unlike Purves, I believe that the "canon wars" have had some "impact" on contemporary culture and education. For they are a significant terrain on which we are contesting the meaning of being a multicultural society. I use the present tense deliberately, for we are in the thick of things.

Now, my comments. As Purves reminds us, the urge to categorize literary and artistic works is old. The use of the word *canon* for a selective list of such works is comparatively new. Indeed, it began in 1768 (Zetzel, 1983, p. 103). In the same year, the first numbers of the first edition of the *Encyclopedia Britannica* were published. My harnassing of the canon and the encyclopedia together beneath the yoke of chronology might initially seem perverse. Is a canon not exclusive? An encyclopedia not inclusive? Are canon formers not picky? Encyclopedists not wide-ranging?

My gambit is meant to exemplify a truism that, like virtue, often gets mislaid. A literary canon, whatever the name, gets formed in the manufactories and networks of history. Literary scholarship can and does trace these processes.[1] A canon is the consequence of turbulent, impure historical dramas. When the last act seems to be over, a canon stands forth as "the canon." Each drama has three sets of actors: texts (visual, oral, musical, written), institutions, and audiences. Because all of these actors change over time, the drama of the canon must be performed again and again.

To take each set in turn:

New texts will keep on being written. Dante follows Homer; Shakespeare, Dante; Milton, Shakespeare. Matthew Arnold can mine them all as he quarries for his touchstones in "The Study of Poetry" (1880). An element of suspense in the plot of the canon is which texts will survive, and then, which of the survivors will be taken in marriage by that sturdy partner, the school curriculum. In "The Study of Poetry," Arnold said that good literature survives and maintains its "currency and supremacy" because it is necessary for life. It appeals to "the instinct of self-preservation in humanity."[2] Less grandly than Arnold, I suggest that the texts we want to remember have these qualities. Physically, they have survived. Next, they have, like Plato or the Bible, been immensely, demonstrably influential. Next, they are rereadable and rewritable— within and across cultures. They have significance both to the members of an author's own community *and* to members of other communities. Finally, they show "especially concentrated forms of universal features of language," for example, "the tendency of figurative language. . .to subvert straightforward grammatical or logical meaning" (Miller, 1989, p. 110). If all of these are criteria for a canonical work, multiculturalism expands a canon.

The second set of actors is the constellation of institutions and groups that renovate, keep, guard, and transmit a culture. Sometimes these institutions cohere, sometimes collide. Institutions and groups are their culture in a double sense of the word. They shape their culture; it shapes them. In other words, institutions have the same relationship to their period as waves do to water. Recently, the *New York Times* told a pleasant story about the move of the *New Yorker* from one space to another. The Smithsonian Institution was to transfer two offices to Washington, D.C., and preserve them. "The New Yorker magazine produced much of the 20th-century canon, but these offices. . .are almost 19th century," a museum official said happily (Carmody, 1991, p. 135). Correctly, the official describes an *institution,* not atomistic individuals, as a powerful canon-forger. A second institution, the museum, then canonizes the canonizer. A multicultural critic might ask what the *New Yorker* did not publish.

The contemporary quarrel about the canon, the canonized, and the canonizable began in the late 1960s. It now goes on within certain institutions—the professoriate, more intellectual publications, museums, funding agencies, and, in the last few years, the mass media. It means something about our culture that the quarrel began because our demography began to change. It became more diverse. So did our society as a whole. My hunch is that the writers of this section are as tired as I am of having to note this obvious, overwhelming truth. The defenses against it are currently strong enough to constitute a brand of social pathology. The quarrel over the canon turned grim and snarly because the newcomers to powerful cultural institutions have often had a triple allegiance: first, to the institution; second, to cultural reform; and third, to a cultural family of origin (a race, a sex, a postcolonial nation) as a vital source of reforming work and energies.

Some neoconservative voices in the canon wars have then argued—with varying degrees of fear, trembling, rage, and tact—that such cultural families of origin are largely without intrinsic cultural merit. The bimbos and barbarians are, a priori, acanonical. Obviously, then, the voices continue, any place the bimbos and barbarians might claim in a canon or curriculum is unearned and unmerited. An example is the Great Books of the Western World series, which the Encyclopedia Brittanica publishes, another conjunction of canon and encyclopedia. To their credit, the Great Books include science and mathematics. Moreover, the Great Books are important books. I want people to read Homer and Dostoevsky, blurbed as "a truly great Russian author," Herodotus and Engels, Plato and Hegel, Hippocrates and Freud. The charge that we canon-changers are canon-stompers is a canard meant to turn reformers back into barbarians.

Still, the Great Books are canonical, aggressively and adamantly so. They include no "minority" writer. Not until 1990 do they anoint a woman writer. This Great Books canon is the construct of one subspecies of academics in the United States in the twentieth century. They believe that they have located transcendental, universal cultural values. They make, however, two serious errors. First, they are obtuse about multiculturalism, aggressively and adamantly so. The history of the West is a multicultural history. I think, for example, of the relations among Judaism, Christianity (in all its variety), and Islam. These academics, however, equate multiculturalism with the decline of the West and seek "to restore" its putatively going-going-going-gone greatness. Second, they have a self-contradictory attitude toward the mass culture of the twentieth century. They draw a sharp binary distinction between "high" *and* "mass" culture, between the enduring work of "the greatest minds" and "great men" *and* the quicky trash of "supermarket 'literature' " and "shallow, televised answers."[3] And yet, Great Books is really Great Books Inc. As a corporate entity, it manipulates these distinctions for commercial gain. It *hustles* the best to the sad hearts in the supermarket. It markets what it calls "endlessly rereadable books...the perpetual best-sellers." Its unique selling proposition is the promise that great books are instrumental. Once bought and read, they will improve self-esteem, career, and family life.

At once despising and exploiting mass culture, Great Books Inc. cannot help with the most serious of questions about literacy and literature today. What is the relationship among mass culture and the written text? Why do music and TV represent pleasure while "good books" represent stern duty? Are popular music and TV informing us about our differences in a multicultural society and helping us to live with them handsomely? Or are popular music and TV homogenizing forces, great big mashers-and-blenders? If so, do they provide a genuine or a temporary, spurious unity?

The third set of actors in the drama of the canon consists of readers, the eager or indifferent recipients of institutional judgments. These readers help to decide whether a canonical text will leave the library shelves—as text or audiocassette. Readers vote with their collective and individual sensibilities. The promise of multiculturalism is that it will decrease the alienation of many readers from literature and increase the powers of literature and textuality.

One of my sharp regrets about the quarrel about the canon is this. In part, the quarrel is a deeply serious argument about Western culture as a reservoir of ethical and aesthetic values. In part, however, the quarrel is a shadow, a deflection of attention away from even harder issues. One such issue is literacy. Without a literate audience that wants to read texts from several cultures in past and present, literature is an endangered species. "What is a canon?" and "What is the canon?" are good questions. "What is literacy?" and "Who are the literate?" are better. As the writers of the papers in this section know, the answers to the first questions depend now upon our answers to the second.

Notes

1. I think, for example, of the work of Barbara Herrnstein Smith, John Guillory, Joan DeJean, or Paul Lauter; of the September 1983 "Canons" issue of *Critical Inquiry*; or of Frederick Crews's mordant analysis of the shaping of William Faulkner's reputation.

2. The title, *Criticism: Twenty Major Statements*, promises that the volume will include canonical statements. The volume's obvious pedagogical intent, that is, the presence of "Questions for Discussion" at the end, shows a conflation of canon and curriculum.

3. All quotes from a Great Books brochure copyrighted 1987.

References

Arnold, M. (1880). The study of poetry. In C. Kaplan (Ed.), *Criticism: Twenty major statements.* San Francisco: Chandler.

Carmody, D. (1991, February 19). There at the New Yorker, with Thurber. *New York Times,* p. 135.

Crews, F. (1991, March 7). The strange fate of William Faulkner. *New York Review of Books,* pp. 47–52.

Miller, J. H. (1989). Theory of the present time. In R. Cohen (Ed.), *The future of literary theory* (p. 110). New York and London: Routledge.

Zetzel, J. E. G. (1983). Recreating the canon. *Critical Inquiry, 10,* 103.

Part III

Making Space for Difference: Perspectives on Teaching

10

Multicultural Literacy and Literature: The Teacher's Perspective

Violet J. Harris

The language arts coordinator of a local middle school approached administrators of a literacy research center at my university about conducting a research project. The coordinator wanted to determine why African American students scored considerably lower than European American students. After several talks with the coordinator, researchers at the center decided to conduct a two-year collaborative study. The first year involved observing and interviewing teachers, students, and administrators and assessing curricular materials. The second year of the project began with university researchers offering a literacy course for teachers at the middle school. Upon completion of the course, teachers and researchers collaborated on projects for the last half of the second year.

I was paired with Mrs. Howard, a sixth-grade teacher and a graduate student at the university. She posed a question to me after she discovered that my area of speciality was children's literature and that I had a special interest in multicultural literature. Her question related to the absence of coursework, classes, or workshops devoted specifically to apprising pre- and in-service teachers of multicultural literature. She asked her question in a plaintive tone: "Why didn't I ever learn about these books in my education?" Unmistakably at the center of Mrs. Howard's question were feelings of frustration, anger, and hurt. She wanted information about the literature and desired to share the literature with her students immediately. She stated that multicultural literature, especially African American, would provide her students with opportunities to read books which related to their lives.

I gathered several boxes of multiethnic literature, that is, literature written by and about African, Asian, Latino/a, and Native Americans.

I selected books on the basis of genre, reading interests of middle school students, and suggestions from Mrs. Howard. Among the books selected were *Hoops* (Myers, 1983), *Felita* (Mohr, 1979), *Tales From Gold Mountain* (Yee, 1990), and *Nathaniel Talking* (Greenfield, 1988). The books were arranged by genre throughout Mrs. Howard's classroom. Students were instructed to browse, ask questions about the books, and list ten books that they would want to read or have read to them. Later in the year, Mrs. Howard and I alternated reading the books to the students. Throughout the readings they were encouraged to ask questions, discuss, and write about the literature. As a result of the project, Mrs. Howard's conception of multicultural literacy and literature has changed permanently, and her beliefs about schooling have changed as well.

On the surface it seems that Mrs. Howard's decision was spontaneous; it was not. Mrs. Howard had engaged in a number of processes prior to her meeting with me which provided the catalyst for her decision to include multicultural literature in her literacy curriculum. She knew, for example, that African American children in her school tended to score well below European American students. She believed that the differential achievement did not result from inherent mental differences. She believed that changes in curricular materials and her instructional techniques might improve students' academic performances. Most importantly, she made a decision to find information which would, according to her, enable her to improve her students' literacy performance, enhance their self-esteem, and motivate them to read.

There are many Mrs. Howards in schools across the country. They are women, and occasionally men, who find themselves working with students who rarely find affirmation of their cultures in schooling. These teachers possess an intuitive belief that a more diverse curriculum might motivate their students. Many of these teachers do not have a name for the more inclusive curricula they desire. Some recognize and use various names but are not familiar with underlying ideologies. A few can articulate the philosophy, approach taken, and goals for their particular method for including multiculturalism in literacy curricula.

The purpose of this overview is to describe some of the components of the processes which enable teachers to implement multicultural literacy curricula. The components are not necessarily developmental, nor are they hierarchical. They include (1) understanding definitions and conceptions of multicultural literacy; (2) identifying philosophy and approaches; (3) becoming knowledgeable; (4) making curricular decisions; and (5) becoming aware of opposition to multiculturalism.

Definitions and Conceptions

Definitions and conceptions of *multiculturalism* vary. For some, the term parallels others, such as *multicultural diversity, cultural diversity, multiethnic diversity,* and *cultural pluralism.* For others, the term represents one stage in the development of antiracist curriculum and pedagogy (Asante, 1991; Banks, 1991; King, 1991; Sleeter & Grant, 1988). A few associate multiculturalism with metaphors such as a salad bowl, "glorious mosaic," or tapestry. Central to each definition and conception is the belief that several varied cultures exist within the country. Some of the cultures cited are African, Native, Latino/a, Asian, gay and lesbian, working class, and minority religious groups such as the Amish. Those who believe in the melting pot, an assimilationist view, argue that something called the "American mainstream" or "Americana national culture" exists into which each individual labeled a minority, a participant in a subculture, or nonmainstream, should try to blend. In other words, schools are fine as they are; it is the individual who needs to adjust. This middle-class or mainstream culture promotes patriotism, Judaic-Christian ethics, patriarchy, capitalism, notions of manifest destiny, meritocracy (strictures limit access to cultural knowledge for many individuals, which prevent the existence of a true meritocracy), and the Puritan work ethic.

In contrast, those who view the United States as a salad bowl recognize that individual cultures contribute to the making of the American culture. American culture is in a continuous state of flux because elements from the various cultures (language, values, arts, and so on) filter into the nation's store of ideas, values, and institutions. In addition, participants accommodate themselves to the status quo while retaining some aspects of their primary culture. In this view, schools have to adjust and reform in some ways, but fundamentally, they serve their purposes well.

A third, more radical view posits that parallel cultures exist along with the dominating American culture with its hegemonic institutions and institutionalized strictures. Specific to this view are certain beliefs. No culture or its members are inherently superior to others on the basis of the members' physical characteristics. Culture and all of its artifacts and institutions exist to socialize individuals to conform to and believe in the ideology of the dominating culture. Further, the power of the dominating culture is maintained because of stratification and differential access to institutions and cultural knowledge. Many of the parallel cultures make enormous contributions to the dominating culture which are appropriated, omitted, ignored, or valued negatively.

Consequently, for those adhering to these views, schooling must advance beyond multiculturalism, which is viewed as a necessary step but not the final step, to a stage whereby fundamental changes in society are engendered.

Citizens need awareness and knowledge of these varied cultures for essential reasons. At the very least, members of the various cultures encounter each other in schools, businesses, churches, sporting events, and any number of other venues. Some minimal level of understanding and cooperation has to prevail if the society is to continue to function. Citizens derive some benefit from their newly acquired knowledge. Most essentially, their knowledge base is expanded; they can begin to perceive the shared attributes all cultures share; and they can broaden cross-cultural interactions that advance the quality of life for all. Finally, the realization that individual cultures contribute in some way to an ongoing American culture can possibly lead to increased national unity and a lessening of competition for limited resources and privileges. Perhaps it is easier to visualize the contributions of the various cultures in nonthreatening contexts such as the spread of ethnic restaurants, music, sports, and dance. It is far more difficult to imagine contributions to the intellectual and spiritual development of the country and the ways in which negative power affects those who are marginalized.

Definitions and conceptions of multiculturalism are further complicated by the number of groups categorized under the label *multicultural*. For example, in previous years, diversity meant focusing on issues of race (Banks, 1981). Currently, depending on one's ideological stance, the category now includes issues of race, gender, ethnicity, language, religion, and "ableism." A few critical theorists include concerns with "thinism," heterosexualism, and environmentalism (Ellsworth, 1989). It would seem that the emerging trend is to include any aspect of difference under the rubric of multicultural. The expansion of the category raises the possibility that the trivialization of multiculturalism will occur. For instance, issues of race merit significant and continuing examination because of de facto and de jure policies which institutionalized stratification, racism, and discrimination. But to argue that issues of fat versus thin are equal or comparable gives reason for concern. Those individuals ostracized or discriminated against because they are fat would argue that thinism is just as oppressive as any other "ism." Yet they are not equal.

Many teachers believe that including any aspect of difference lessens the seriousness of the issue. For example, a student related that the leader of a prejudice reduction workshop trivialized the workshop by including discrimination against people with big feet as something to be avoided! Further, many teachers will not feel comfortable with some or all of the categories and must decide how expansive or restrictive their definitions and conceptions of multiculturalism are. Teachers' understanding of definitions and conceptions might well be considered as part of a continuous process influenced by changing conditions and knowledge. A possible next step would involve teacher determination of philosophy and approach(es).

Philosophy and Approaches

Several philosophies exist which offer the ideological underpinnings for approaches to multiculturalism. The range includes assimilation to maintenance of cultural identity to social reconstructionism. Banks (1991) identifies four approaches most often adopted by teachers since the 1960s. The underlying philosophy of the first approach, the contributions approach, seems to be one which values and maintains current traditions and whose adherents see little need for major change. It is a conservative philosophy which guards and sanctions tradition. The method entails including the contributions of heroes and heroines in a curriculum which otherwise remains unchanged. For example, a teacher might add Sojourner Truth, Sitting Bull, or Billy Wong to a social studies curriculum or a unit on biography without examining the political or social significance of the individuals. Banks characterizes this approach as the easiest to implement. The second approach Banks labels as additive. This approach emphasizes mainstream perspectives. In this approach, "concepts, themes, and perspectives are added to the curriculum without changing its basic structure, purpose, and characteristics" (pp. 23–24). For instance, a teacher might add *M. C. Higgins, the Great* (Hamilton, 1974) to a unit of "coming of age" novels. The third approach, transformation, involves changes in the structure of curriculum "to enable students to view concepts, issues, and themes from the perspective of diverse ethnic and cultural groups" (p. 26). Students might decide to focus on the development of labor unions and their status today. Some might investigate which industries have the best unions in terms of ensuring workers the best benefits. Others might discover the differences between trade unions and general unions. Still others might choose to interview local labor leaders. The fourth approach, the social action approach, emphasizes students making "decisions on important social issues" and taking "actions to help solve them" (p. 26). After reading *A Yellow Raft in Blue Water* (Dorris, 1987), a student might decide to collect books and other learning materials to send to a reservation school or send letters to a congressional representative urging an increase in the amount of money allocated to reservation schools.

In a similar manner, Sleeter and Grant (1988) delineate five approaches to multiculturalism. The first approach, teaching the exceptional and culturally deprived, "focus[es] on adapting instruction to student differences for the purpose of helping the students more effectively succeed in the mainstream" (p. 28). This would be the assimilationist model. Schools do not have to change, but students have to conform to the curriculum. For example, schools might institute compensatory programs that remediate student deficiencies in basic skills but do not necessarily alter curricular or teaching methods. The second, the human relations approach, concentrates on engendering "love, respect, and more effective communication" in order to develop more cordial relations among people; it is a socio-psychological approach. One method for doing so is to create clubs within the school that interest a range of students with a shared interest, such as a musical group. Ideally, through this shared interest would come love and respect. The next approach would be the single studies approach, focusing on one issue such as ethnicity, race, gender, or class with the central purpose of "raising consciousness and mobilizing for action." Quite simply, a school might create a course on African American history. One could characterize it as a sociopolitical model. Sleeter and Grant characterize the last two approaches as more assertive. They include the multicultural education approach, which "links race, language, culture, gender, handicap, and, to a lesser extent, social class, working toward making the entire school celebrate human diversity and equal opportunity." In this instance, a school would move beyond celebrations that emphasize food, festivals, and costumes. Instead, a school would offer curricula which integrate the various groups throughout all aspects; the teaching faculty and the student body would reflect the diversity; and everyone would have to develop more tolerant attitudes. The last approach, education that is multicultural and social reconstructionist, "extends the multicultural education approach into the realm of social action and focuses at least as much on challenging social stratification as on celebrating human diversity and equal opportunity" (p. 28). For example, after reading an article on latchkey children in a social studies class, high school students decide to canvass their neighborhoods to determine to what extent the problem exists in their community. After collecting data, they approach teachers, parents, and administrators to discuss the idea of establishing some kind of after-school recreation program.

Sleeter and Grant's approach differs from that of Banks in one essential way: they emphasize affective changes. First, their approach attempts to create positive, loving, respectful feelings. This goal seems difficult to achieve given the myriad beliefs and attitudes that combine to determine if individuals will like or even tolerate each other. Second, their approach seeks to develop individuals who value and celebrate multiculturalism.

Other approaches are possible which are not linked specifically to multicultural perspectives but which offer parallel methods of analysis. Three major ones are feminist/womanist theory, literary theories such as semiotics and deconstructionism, and critical theory. These movements provide ideologies and guidance for curricular and social change. However, most curricula reflect the models delineated by Banks and Sleeter and Grant. Another critical component in establishing multicultural curricula involves teachers acquiring knowledge about various cultures.

Becoming Knowledgeable: Teacher Education

Teacher training programs, in general, do not emphasize training teachers to meet the needs of multicultural populations (Banks, 1981, 1991; Gay, 1988). Acknowledgement of this situation occurred when the National Council for the Accreditation of Teacher Education revised its accreditation standards in 1979 to require that teacher training programs include a multicultural education component (Sleeter & Grant, 1988). However, research indicates that most teachers in the schools do not include multicultural education components (Sleeter & Grant, 1988). When teachers include a multicultural component, it tends to appear in those schools with large populations of students of color. An underlying assumption seems to be that European American students do not need or desire multicultural education. Yet changing racial and ethnic demographics in urban, public schools—they are increasingly populated by students of color—highlight the need for multicultural training for teachers. Recent census data document the growth in population of nonwhites. Between 30 and 40 percent of the population is classified as African American, American Indian, Eskimo or Aleut, Asian or Pacific Islander, Hispanic origin, or other race (United States Census Bureau, 1991). By the year 2020, it is estimated that students of color will constitute 46 percent of the student population (Banks, 1991). Currently, the majority of California's elementary school students are students of color.

Gay (1988) identifies another problem crucial to teacher education. She contends that one first step in teacher education was the eradication of an ideological misconception held by many, the belief that creating pluralistic curricula for diverse learners would result in the creation of mediocre academic standards. She argues that many teachers perceived educational equity and excellence as "mutually exclusive and inherently contradictory" (p. 327). Further, she states that teachers would have to distinguish between "instructional input factors and outcome expectations" (p. 327).

These observations would suggest that teachers involved in literacy and literature should have courses, workshops, in-service training, and independent study which would enable them to acquire knowledge about the cultures of the various groups listed under multicultural categories, including some information about their history, literature, science, art, music, and other cultural artifacts. For example, the Kamahameha school in Hawaii has improved the opportunities for numerous children to learn to read by developing teaching techniques which emphasize the linguistic and social interaction styles which the children use in their homes and communities. More practically, a teacher's knowledge of her Vietnamese students' history could prevent her from sharing a picture book likely to incur parental wrath. The book entitled *Tuan* (Boholm-Olsson, 1986) is a story set in the north of Vietnam. The specific knowledge needed is the fact that the most recent immigrants come from the former nation, South Vietnam. This is not to suggest that teachers engage in self-censorship, but rather to suggest that teachers apprise themselves of events, ideas, or objects which are subject to dispute whenever possible. In addition, teachers would have to obtain knowledge of the specific patterns of interactions among the various groups, including any culturally specific learning styles and general knowledge about human cognition and language acquisition and development. One would not have to acquire this vast array of knowledge immediately, but it would become a part of an ongoing process for teachers.

In terms of literacy and literature curricula, teachers would have to garner access to information about familial and community conceptions of, experiences with, and purposes for literacy and literature, both historically and currently. Teachers would need to acquire familiarity with major authors, the themes they address in their works, and the authenticity of the content included in the works. One of the best examples of a text viewed as inauthentic is *Hatter Fox*, which librarian and critic Doris Seale characterizes as perpetuating images of Native Americans as self-destructive incompetents who cannot survive modern society without the help of paternalistic European Americans (Seale, 1989). Moreover, because many writers of color see their work as fulfilling aesthetic and sociopolitical functions, teachers should apprise themselves of what those might be. For instance, illustrator Tom Feelings (1985) discusses his work in terms of a metaphor related to jazz. He describes his experiences and those of ordinary African Americans and his philosophy as "the ability to improvise within a restricted form, an artistic way of surviving, a celebration of survival in spite of oppression" (pp. 76–77).

Many would argue that this kind of information is not necessary for making literary judgment and that it has no place in the analysis of literature (Mingle, 1984). However, a few would argue that such information is critical to understanding the perspectives of writers and illustrators and the themes and images depicted in their work. Moreover, Kelly (1985) and Taxel (1986, 1988) argue that literature for children always involves extra-literary evaluative criteria because adults use literature to ensure that children acquire appropriate values and perspectives. Some extra-literary evaluation criteria include those that relate to whether or not "proper" notions of patriotism, family, morals, and politics are expressed within the work. For example, Kelly (1985) examines texts which purport to evaluate literature primarily on the basis of form and content. In each statement of purpose or somewhere within the text, the authors mention assessing works in terms of moral values emphasized and perceptible didactic value. Literature for children simply does not exist solely to entertain or provide aesthetic enjoyment. It must also teach the alphabet, demonstrate how children should behave in the dentist's office or avoid potential molesters, and teach the proc er respect for family, country, and God. Examples of literature designed to imbue specific ideologies are the various Horatio Alger stories of the past and, more recently, the Berenstein Bears series. Recent court challenges involving the content of some basal reading series support Kelly's and Taxel's arguments. For example, Harcourt, Brace, Jovanovich's basal reading series, *Impressions*, generated considerable opposition and some court challenges (Davis, 1992). Parents complained that some of the stories encouraged a belief in the occult, portrayed America unfavorably, and contained a general tone of pessimism.

Another aspect of teacher training is the identification of resources such as summer institutes, conferences, organizations, librarians, scholars, texts, and teachers who specialize in or possess knowledge about multicultural literacy and literature. For instance, a perusal of texts for language arts, reading, and literature methods courses reveals that very few integrate information about multiculturalism or accommodating the needs of diverse learners. A typical method of inclusion is to focus on multiculturalism in one chapter, usually at the end of the book. Literature texts deviate somewhat because the work of authors and illustrators appears throughout as a result of the emphasis on genre and major contributors. Resources exist, but the central task involves creating linkages with teachers and the sources. For example, how many know of two organizations, the Association for the Study of Afro-American Life and History and the Children's Interracial Books Council, that create curriculum guides related to ethnic studies or multicultural studies? This means that those who possess the information must share that information in a variety of places, churches, club meetings, and so on and must continuously update their knowledge by attending conferences and book talks and by subscribing to a variety of journals and newsletters. After teachers have acquired some knowledge of the various groups, then another step would entail deciding which new knowledge to include in curricula.

Curricular Decisions

At least three types of curricular decisions are required which focus on content, pedagogy, and educational outcomes. Inherent in the decisions is the need to articulate or acknowledge the underlying purposes for multicultural literacy and literature. Teachers should contemplate several questions, principal among them: Will the new curricula assimilate students, reform current curricula, or radically alter curricula and schooling in order to help students achieve academic excellence? The answers will, in part, shape the type of curriculum which emerges. Additionally, teachers will have to decide if literacy among females, people of color, the handicapped, or religious minorities manifests itself in ways which parallel or differ significantly from literacy in "mainstream" populations.

On the surface, "whole-language" instruction, with its emphasis on teacher autonomy, situated assessment, meaningful and whole texts, and inclusion of the child's ways of interacting, talking, and thinking, would seem to offer the ideal curriculum for multicultural literacy (Goodman, 1989). Yet, as Delpit (1986, 1988) argues, the philosophy and approach might not necessarily work within a multicultural context. It would seem prudent to argue, instead, that teachers need experience with creating a variety of learning contexts which accommodate the needs of diverse learners. For instance, a teacher in New York City schools, Dawn Martine Harris, is able to meet the literacy needs of her students through an eclectic approach grounded in her knowledge of language acquisition and development, reading and writing processes among children, African American history and culture, children's literature, pedagogical techniques (individual, small- and whole-group instruction), parental and/or familial involvement, and the genuine sense of caring she has for her students. One measure of her success (as evident on a videotape produced by the Center for the Study of Reading) is the community of readers and writers that emerges in her classroom early in the academic year. Another indicator of achievement is the fact that her students tend to score at or above national norms on standardized tests. Ms. Harris is an exceptional teacher, but her success is not due to something she was born with or because she is lucky. She realized that teaching her students would require a variety of ways of knowing and doing.

Harris draws upon her students' natural pleasure in talking and working and playing in groups. For example, she begins the day with the "morning message." The students discuss how the day will possibly proceed or make comments about something that happened to them. After discussion and agreement, Harris writes the students' comments on the board. They read the message in unison several times with Harris soliciting discussion. Her students write in journals and create their own stories using a modified process writing approach. They recite poetry. When they line up at the door to leave, the students face a flip chart which has a poem written on it; they often recite the poem as they line up. Most importantly, Harris shares her reading and writing experiences with the students. Through these and other activities, the students learn that literacy serves various functions and that it is valued.

Another issue for consideration is the debate on culturally specific learning styles. Some argue that pedagogical techniques currently in use are in direct contrast to the interactive learning or cognitive styles associated with diverse populations, especially children of color (Shade, 1989). They argue that many children of color cannot perform well in learning contexts which emphasize individualism, competitiveness, and noncooperative behavior. The learning environments must emphasize directly opposite behavior. The most appropriate learning environment, according to Shade (1989), nurtures respect and a sense of belonging through a warm, inviting environment, develops motivation rather than concentrating on discipline, emphasizes the process as well as the product, contains a teacher who is authoritarian yet warm and encouraging, and uses small groups and cooperative learning (pp. 331–333). Notably, Shade's ideal classroom resembles the classroom format recommended for all children.

The creation of multicultural literature curricula involves some of the same concerns. Children's literature has served functions other than aesthetic ones since the eighteenth century (Kelly, 1974). Other functions include inculcating specific values such as commitment to the community's moral standards, instilling nationalistic sentiments, forging a common cultural heritage, and educating and entertaining children. Arguments to include multicultural literature in curricula follow a well-established pattern of using literature for extra-literary purposes. A classroom which uses literature for extra-literary purposes does not fit any particular pattern or adhere to any particular ideology. One cannot say that a teacher who uses a "whole-language approach" will never use literature for extra-literary purposes. Similarly, one cannot say that a teacher who uses a basal approach will negatively exploit literature for extra-literary purposes. Some research, however, indicates that those wishing to incorporate multicultural literature will encounter difficulties (Larrick, 1965; Sims, 1985, Sims-Bishop, 1990a, 1990b). The number of books available varies considerably. For example, books about children of color represent less than 5 percent of the nearly five thousand children's books published yearly. Many books do not remain in publication for significant periods of time. For example, many of the early books of Lucille Clifton, Pirie Thomas, and Eloise Greenfield are out of print. Even a noted author such as Virginia Hamilton will have works in limbo as publishers exchange paperback rights. Cheryl and Wade Hudson (1991), publishers and owners of "Just Us Books," detail some of the reasons advanced for the limited availability of books related to multiculturalism. Parents and teachers report difficulty finding the books in local bookstores. A few publishers state that they receive fewer manuscripts from people of color. In contrast, many publishers of color report that a number of market factors prevent them from making their products available (Igus, 1990). For instance, small publishers argue that general bookstores prefer not to interact with small presses; bookstores prefer to offer blockbusters or certain best-sellers such as the Waldo books; major distributors prefer large presses; and small presses cannot compete with the advertising budgets of larger presses, many of which are now subsidiaries of multinational corporations. However, a market, largely untapped, exists for multicultural literature. Again, it's a matter of linking teachers with resources.

Fortunately for teachers, a number of excellent writers and illustrators continue to produce exceptional work, such as Laurence Yep, Jamake Highwater, Virginia Hamilton, and Walter Dean Myers. New illustrators and authors have emerged as well, such as Sheila Hamanaka, Rita Williams-Garcia, and Angela Johnson. These authors and illustrators examine a number of themes and historical occurrences. Occasionally, the content of the works differs from that typically found in children's literature. Herein lies a problem for teachers: which depiction is more authentic? For example, many school texts do not fully describe the pain, anger, and discriminatory acts perpetuated against Japanese Americans prior to World War II. In contrast, Sheila Hamanaka's *The Journey* (1989) does. An ideal learning situation could evolve from the use of Hamanaka's book with other tradebooks about the treatment accorded Japanese Americans.

Because the experiences of people of color range from brutal to painful to enjoyable, inclusion of the more brutal experiences is likely to result in well-intentioned or intentional censorship. For example, the use of derogatory names for people of color has been routine, yet some publishers are unwilling to include them in school texts even when placed in correct historical context.

The type of curricular decisions made will depend, to a great extent, on the goals of multicultural literacy explicated by teachers. Banks (1991) identifies seven common goals associated with multicultural curricula: (1) develop decision-making and social action skills; (2) analyze events from diverse perspectives; (3) develop cross-cultural competencies; (4) provide cultural and ethnic alternatives; (5) reduce ethnic encapsulation; (6) expand conceptions of what it means to be human; and (7) help students master essential reading, writing, and computational skills (pp. 24–28). Given Banks's seven goals, teachers might feel overwhelmed with all that needs to be accomplished. They can reduce some of the magnitude of the task by deciding to begin by reading and gradually sharing that knowledge, as well as any other materials, with students. They can engage in self-reflective journal writing to record and monitor their responses. They can enroll in courses or join an organization which promotes the celebration of diversity. Spears-Bunton (1990) presents an excellent discussion of one European American teacher's attempts to diversify her high school English curriculum. The journey was not without moments of frustration, anger, and hopelessness.

One potential pedagogical concern not addressed is what happens when diverse populations meet and engage in discussion with majority populations. Occasionally anger erupts, which teachers will have to find some way of dissipating or resolving if continuous, meaningful inter-actions are to occur. Similarly, Spears-Bunton (1990) chronicles the procedures one teacher used to decrease ethnic tensions in a racially diverse classroom and how one powerful book convinced a few students who believed in racist ideology to change their perspectives. The teacher did not lose hope. She consistently sought out Spears-Bunton's expertise and camaraderie. The teacher encouraged students to talk, listen, and try to understand others' views. She continued to share literature and was fortunate enough to assign *The House of Dies Drear* (Hamilton, 1968). This book enabled the students to discover the humanity they share in those unlike themselves. The teacher had no magic formula; she simply continued in the belief that what she was doing was correct.

These tasks might seem insurmountable, but they offer teachers opportunities to read, think, write, and engage in critical discussions about literature and its role in society. The possibilities of engendering discussions which lead to students thinking, talking, and writing critically provides an answer for those who argue that diversifying the curriculum will lead to mediocrity in schooling. The following demonstrates how a junior high or high school teacher might structure an activity. She or he can initiate a discussion about the images that come to mind when one thinks of Asians or Pacific Islanders. After discussing these images, the students might explain how they acquired them. Next, the teacher can question students about the contributions of Asians and Pacific Islanders to American culture. Then, she or he can share the picture from *The Chinese Americans* (Meltzer, 1980) which shows the laying of the golden spike for the transcontinental railroad. The caption of the picture asks, what's wrong? What is wrong is that there are no Asians in the picture. Significant discussion about the role of Asians in the building of the transcontinental railroad should ensue. After discussion, the teacher can distribute a copy of the book to each student. In subsequent class meetings the students can share journal entries, collect articles about Asians in periodicals, and invite members of Asian and Pacific Islander groups to class to discuss issues. Clearly, the students will have engaged in thoughtful, meaningful learning.

Response of Critics

A certain amount of nativist sentiment has pervaded education in the United States. Some members of the scholarly community and the popular press have argued against the proliferation of multicultural curricula. For example, *Newsweek* magazine (December 24, 1990) signaled the opposition in a series of articles which excoriated what it termed as either the "new enlightenment" or the "new McCarthyism." In a series of quotations and interviews, the reporters presented a view of multiculturalism as being detrimental to the development of a common cultural heritage and scholarly excellence. Other popular periodicals, such as the *New York Times* (December 8, 1990), present views of multiculturalism as representative of the balkanization of American education. Such opposition has engendered a pejorative term for those who seek to infuse scholarly discussions with issues of race, gender, and class. The term is *PC* or *politically correct*. Opponents fear the results of modifying canons and equate expansion for diversity with mediocrity.

Other discussions of opposition are found in the works of D'Souza (1991), Ravitch (1990), and McCarthy (1988). D'Souza perceives of the call for diversity as a threat to the very foundation of what constitutes that cultural knowledge which will form the basis for schooling, as well as a lessening of academic integrity and excellence. Ravitch sees the appropriate opposition as that directed against what she labels "particularistic pluralism," which encourages collective guilt, sense of rage and victimization and does not promote reconciliation. The type of multiculturalism or pluralism she supports would be that which promotes a sense of common sets of political and moral values and a sense of nationhood. Ravitch, while acknowledging stratification and institutionalized racism, questions whether the effects of both continue to determine wholly the academic achievement and self-esteem of individuals.

In contrast, McCarthy views multicultural education as a liberal stopgap designed to ameliorate the effects of racism, sexism, and class bias. He argues that the major problem with multicultural education is its inability or the inability of its proponents to consider the necessity for total, radical reorganization of schooling. He does, however, suggest that multicultural education serves an important interim function until radical reorganization of schools can occur.

The preceding discussion highlights a few of the issues teachers will have to consider if multiculturalism is to become an integral and permanent component of schooling. Despite the opposition to multiculturalism, it offers some hope that children can see themselves affirmed in their school texts and the daily activities of the school. Children can broaden their understanding of their families, communities, nations, and ultimately the world. Rather than mold students to fit the needs of industry or serve as gatekeepers, schools might become institutions in which learning for the sake of learning is one of the primary goals. Stratification and institutionalized racism and discrimination might become less influential as individuals realize that the existence of the nation is dependent, in part, on how well its members can peacefully coexist.

Teachers can initiate some of the aforementioned changes in a number of ways. First, through self-examination, they can determine to what extent they hinder or help students, what kinds of attitudes they convey to students like and unlike themselves; they can begin to understand various power relationships in the classroom and how that power provides access to cultural knowledge; and they can determine if they can commit to notions of multiculturalism or not. If they can commit to multiculturalism, then the next steps are to acquire knowledge and begin including that new knowledge in the curricula. Then they can institute the procedures suggested by Banks and others.

References

Asante, M. (1991). The Afrocentric idea in education. *Journal of Negro Education, 60,* 170–180.

Banks, J. (1981). *Multiethnic education.* Boston: Allyn & Bacon.

Banks, J. (1991). *Teaching strategies for ethnic studies* (5th ed.). Boston: Allyn & Bacon.

Davis, M. (1992). Censorship Update. *Reading Today, 10*(2), 2.

Delpit, L. (1986). Skills and other dilemmas of a progressive Black educator. *Harvard Education Review, 56,* 378–385.

Delpit, L. (1988). The silenced dialogue: Power and pedagogy in educating other people's children. *Harvard Education Review, 58,* 280–298.

D'Souza, D. (1991). Illiberal education. *The Atlantic, 267,* 51–58, 62–65, 67, 70–74, 76–79.

Ellsworth, E. (1989). Why doesn't this feel empowering? Working through the repressive myths of critical pedagogy. *Harvard Education Review, 59,* 297–324.

Feeling, T. (1985). Illustration is my form, the Black experience my story and content. *The Advocate, 4,* 73–82.

Gay, G. (1988). Designing relevant curriculum for diverse learners. *Education and Urban Society, 20,* 327–340.

Goodman, K. (1989). *Report on the basal reader.* Urbana, IL: National Council of Teachers of English.

Hudson, C., & Hudson, W. (1991). *Dialogue: The publisher's perspective.* Paper presented at the Multicolored Mirror: Cultural Substance in Literature for Children and Young Adults. Conference at the annual meeting of the Cooperative Children's Book Center, Madison, WI.

Igus, T. (1990). Publishing books for Black kids. *ABBWA Journal, 4,* 13–18.

Kelly, R. (1984). Literature and cultural values in the evaluation of books for children. *The Advocate, 4,* 84–100.

King, J. (1991). Dysconscious racism: Ideology, identity, and the miseducation of teachers. *Journal of Negro Education, 60,* 133–146.

Larrick, N. (1965). The all-white world of children's books. *Saturday Review, 48,* 63–65, 84–85.

McCarthy, C. (1988). Rethinking liberal and radical perspectives on racial inequality in schooling: Making the case for nonsynchrony. *Harvard Education Review, 58,* 265–279.

Mingle, P. (1984). Some thoughts on judging children's literature. *Top of the News, 40,* 423–426.

Ravitch, D. (1990). Diversity and democracy. *American Educator, 14,* 16–20, 46–48.

Seale, D. (1989). Indians without hope, Indians without options—The problematic theme of *Hatter Fox. Interracial Books for Children Bulletin, 15*(3), 7–10, 22.

Shade, B. (1989). *Culture, style, and the educative process.* Springfield, IL: Charles C. Thomas.

Sleeter, C., & Grant, C. (1988). *Making choices for multicultural education.* Columbus, OH: Merrill.

Sims, R. (1985). Children's books about Blacks: A mid-eighties status report. *Children's Literature Review, 8,* 9–13.

Sims-Bishop, R. (1990a). Windows, mirrors, and sliding glass doors. *Perspectives, 6,* ix–xi.

Sims-Bishop (1990b). Walk tall in the world: African American literature for today's children. *Journal of Negro Education, 59,* 556–565.

Spears-Bunton, L. (1990). Welcome to my house: African American and European American students' responses to Virginia Hamilton's *House of Dies Drear. Journal of Negro Education, 59,* 566–577.

Taxel, J. (1986). The Black experience in children's fiction: Controversies surrounding award winning books. *Curriculum Theorizing, 16,* 217–281.

Taxel, J. (1988). Children's literature: Ideology and response. *Curriculum Theorizing, 18,* 217–230.

United States Census Bureau. (May 16, 1991). Press release # CB91-177. Census counts of the population aged 18 and over for regions, divisions, and states.

Children's Books Cited

Boholm-Olsson, E. (1986). *Tuan*. New York: R & S Books.

Dorris, M. (1987). *A yellow raft in blue water*. New York: Henry Holt.

Greenfield, E. (1988). *Nathaniel talking*. New York: Black Butterfly Children's Books.

Hamanaka, S. (1989). *The journey*. New York: Franklin Watts.

Hamilton, V. (1968). *The House of Dies Drear*. New York: Collier.

Hamilton, V. (1974). *M. C. Higgins, the Great*. New York: Macmillan.

Meltzer, M. (1980). *The Chinese Americans*. New York: Thomas Crowell.

Mohr, N. (1979). *Felita*. New York: Dial/Young Readers.

Myers, W. (1983). *Hoops*. New York: Delacorte.

Yee, P. (1990). *Tales from Gold Mountain*. New York: Macmillan.

11

Questions of Pedagogy and Multiculturalism

Alpana Sharma Knippling

I

I wish to begin not by an answer to how one goes about teaching "multicultural literature" in a North American college in the 1990s but by the articulation of a crisis whose nature defines the very conditions under which one might go about teaching "multicultural literature."[1] There are several aspects of this crisis, which I pose as a crisis of multiculturalism, that may be usefully elaborated here.

First, one cannot extricate the site of the university from its determining ideological functions. For it is undeniable that the university constitutes an ideological apparatus by virtue of generating centralized systems of knowledge that cannot be separated from their operations of power.[2] The entire spectrum of academic practices, from the hiring of teachers to their work of teaching, flourishes not in any seemingly disengaged and apolitical context but in this overdetermined ideological space. Indeed, it is in this space that one needs to understand the current demand for multiculturalism in the American undergraduate and graduate curriculum today. There is, in other words, a larger interest that is being served in the name of multiculturalism that is best reflected in the massive surge of hiring of minority applicants in English departments across the country. It is no coincidence, after all, that at this very time more than one educational state institution has been reprimanded for its low levels of minority membership and that, in certain institutions, hiring freezes are lifted if the job candidate is a minority member. What is being secured by this celebration and inclusion of the margin might be nothing more or less than the center's opportunity to increase state fundings and student enrollment. The recently hired minority teacher may well have no further significant part to play in actual institutional decisions involving curricular revision or graduate program redefinition, and, correspondingly, the extent to which these revisions and redefinitions actually produce a multicultural commitment becomes questionable. By having been included, the margin might, thus, also be effectively silenced.

I do not mean, by this formulation, to evoke images of conniving academic administrators and plaintive junior and minority professors. Far from being self-willing, autonomous agents, we in the university exist in the nexus of numerous determining and hierarchical structures, sheltered by the discourse of a liberal benevolence which, through its benevolence, has either already accounted for our possible resistance to it or already homogenized our difference from it. Indeed, it is precisely because the "real" culprit cannot be located in the academy, let alone named, that the question—For whom is multiculturalism an issue?—continues to be deferred and dispersed to other sites of responsibility.

Exacerbating this present situation of hiring is the imagined homogeneity of what is in fact a heterogeneous, multiracial minority group. The group's actual heterogeneity manifests itself when there is an institutional demand for, say, a Chicano specialist at a particular time rather than a postcolonialist. Disturbingly enough, the shifting value that is placed on racial and cultural identity produces its own set of crises for minorities. A recent statistic demonstrates that even in certain institutions *with* some minimal record of minority hiring there are twice as many Asian professors as black ("Minority Update," 1990).

The second aspect of the crisis of multiculturalism directly involves our own discipline, English, and, within it, the urgent question of curricular revision. The discipline of English stages the crisis of multi-culturalism in several impassioned debates about canon reformation and curricular revision and has led to the publication of alternative anthologies of literature, ones that might productively deprivilege canonical texts of classical literature. The *Heath Anthology of American Literature* (Lauter et al., 1990) might well be our most ambitious example of such an alternative text. The *Heath* anthology is, however, problematic in its conception because it seems to commit the same error of privileging certain texts as, say, the more traditional Norton anthology. Because these texts have been hitherto marginal does not in itself make them suddenly valuable; similarly, because canonical texts have thus far been privileged does not necessarily render them at once defunct. What need addressing are the very processes of selection that dictate the privileging and deprivileging of particular literary texts and the agencies of that selection at particular times: are these mysterious and selective processes and their agencies themselves susceptible to definition, let alone revision? A similar error occurs with the conception of a less recent edition of essays entitled *The Graywolf Annual Five: Multi-Cultural Literacy* (Simonson & Walker, 1988). An overt reaction to E. D. Hirsch's *Cultural Literacy*, it not only fails to question its own necessarily exclusionist process of selection, but it also dangerously repeats Hirsch's own assumption that by presenting a glossary of multicultural words, entire cultures may be suggested and represented; some may view this representation as itself biased and suspect. Admittedly, the *Heath* anthology gives us other literatures. It also, however, gives us merely *more* literatures, more literary texts prepackaged for consumption in the undergraduate curriculum. In this way, it does not sufficiently radicalize its own premise. Hence, on the subject of curricular change, the danger of ghettoization is imminent because we are not at liberty to assume that, because multicultural literatures have been included in the canon, the field of English has automatically been reconstituted for our undergraduate and graduate students. On the contrary, such an inclusion might suggest an effective strategy of containment through isolation, in the event that multicultural literatures are not made to interact productively with either traditional literature or a set of reading practices that has silenced it thus far. By locating and defining the "problem," one may again be likely to dismiss it.

Current attempts to revise the undergraduate English syllabus have, at not a few institutions, accompanied other attempts: to redefine graduate programs in English as programs in cultural studies. Since this redefinition occurs coterminously with the present currency of the term *multiculturalism*, one may well inquire into their interrelationship. Immediately, one sees that, albeit unintentionally, the discourse of multiculturalism itself tends to disguise the current stratifications of dominant or "high" culture and marginal or "mass" culture that one may more usefully study under the rubric of cultural studies. Helplessly trammeled with both the embarrassing, because tokenist, language of affirmative action and the ubiquitous ideology of the melting pot, the discourse of multiculturalism runs the risk of implying a nonhierarchical engagement with a study of multiplicity of cultures (best typified in comparative literature approaches to English). Such a nonhierarchical, "comp-lit" engagement with the study of *all* cultures, an engagement, further, which the term *multi*cultural itself implies, is delusory because cultures are, in fact, systematically stratified and hierarchicized in both the academy and in common life. This systematic ordering of cultures and cultural texts in stratified and hierarchicized ways is evident in the deployment of *multiculturalism* in the literary academy, where the term consistently signifies the study of *other* (minority) cultures. But the *multi* of *multiculturalism* works to disguise such systematic ordering, allowing a rhetorical slippage which produces the semblance and maintenance of a nonhierarchical engagement with *all* cultures.

A course in Indian literatures in English, which I taught early in 1991, enacts the particular ironic predicament implicit in the formulation *multi*cultural literature. This course fulfilled the university's multicultural requirement for humanities undergraduates. Yet one student's course evaluation presented her point that she was initially surprised to learn that we were going to read only Indian literatures in English in a multicultural course. She had imagined the course to cover many national literatures, such as Nordic and Latin American. Through the course of the term, however, she was pleased to learn that Indian literature itself was multicultural (Hindu, Muslim, and so on). My student was not wrong in taking to heart the *multi*cultural nature of such a university requirement. But her dilemma (misreading?) usefully foregrounds the following questions: Why should a course in Indian literatures in English be considered multicultural? Then again, why shouldn't it be considered multicultural?

Perhaps definers of multiculturalism may productively rely on a redefinition of *literature* as *culture*. This redefinition reflects more than a shift in vocabulary, as Jean Ferguson Carr comments in *Academe*: "[The shift] marks a rethinking of what is experienced as cultural materials. . . . It also marks the movement away from the study of an 'object' to the study of a practice. . .of criticism" (1990, p. 28). Carr's tracing of a movement away from the study of an object to the study of a set of critical practices that themselves, in fact, create objects of study is especially useful for the multicultural teacher. A study of marginal texts is necessarily enmeshed in the study of a dominant culture's critical practice, a practice that has historically flourished by dint of having created "objects of investigation" that systematically either control or silence cultural otherness; and such a study can only be possible when one disallows the traditional discourse and history of "literature" to dictate one's own critical methodology. For instance, a postcolonial subject (such as myself) may find it especially debilitating to think of or teach postcolonial literatures from the point of view of a New Critic or a liberal humanist; to do so would mean repeating the very patterns of power and knowledge that have themselves historically excluded the postcolonial subject from their operations.

A third and final aspect of the crisis facing a teacher of multicultural literatures involves what actually transpires in the classroom when American readers encounter a multicultural text (which is typically, though not always, nonmainstream and/or non-Western; see note 1). This aspect needs touching upon here; I will elaborate upon it in the second section of this paper. What seems to be a minimal level of academic discussion in departments focusing almost exclusively on research should be, for the teacher of multicultural literatures, of primary pedagogical concern. If what can bring members of an increasingly divisive discipline together is the simple fact that they are all, after all, teachers, then the pedagogical question of what one does in the classroom has never been more appropriate to raise. It is, in this context, regrettable that certain "high" theory makes occasional reference to pedagogy and teachers, not as entities invested with actual material weight, but as rhetorical devices and strategies.[3]

In the classroom, the multicultural teacher is unavoidably positioned by students, by class discussion, by her syllabus, and by the set of assumptions governing the core curriculum of the undergraduate and graduate programs, as generating the necessary "truths" of her race and culture. More often than not, these "truths" are not viewed as products of either larger contestatory or larger discursive formations; they are precritically and rigidly received as absolute statements of cultural difference and otherness delivered, as it were, from the horse's mouth. The multicultural teacher becomes an encyclopedia of fossilized information. The apparently unpronounceable names of characters in an alien cultural text become the site for insurmountable reading difficulties with the text itself.[4] Consequently, the potential mastery of these unpronounceable names bespeaks a certain mastery of the alien culture itself. Contradictory relationships of estrangement (difference) and familiarity (superiority) are struck by the reader with the text. In brief, the multicultural teacher's pedagogical strategy depends on his or her ability to understand both the constraints governing his or her position in the classroom and the overdetermined nature of a multicultural text as it is read in the classroom.

I mention these three difficult aspects not to deliberately obfuscate and merely theorize but to suggest that what a multicultural teacher does in the classroom is fundamentally dependent on the structures of the university, the status of literature in English departments, and the interactions of an American reader, a racially other teacher, and an alien cultural text.

II

Over the last three years, I have taught the following postcolonial texts by writers of African and Indian descent:[5] Ngugi wa Thiong'o's

Petals of Blood, Chinua Achebe's *Things Fall Apart*, Ben Okri's *Stars of the New Curfew*, Ken Saro-Wiwa's *Sozaboy*, Nadine Gordimer's *July's People*, R. K. Narayan's *The Guide*, *The English Teacher*, and *The Painter of Signs*, Raja Rao's *Kanthapura*, Anita Desai's *Baumgartner's Bombay*, and Salman Rushdie's *Midnight's Children* and *Shame*.[6] These texts are written originally in the English language; that is the most obvious indication to the reader that they are products of British colonialism. This fact should also suggest that they may not be read as purely Indian or purely African texts; the status of the English language denies them any absolute Indian or absolute African nationalist discourse. Two strategies of reading and teaching these generally postcolonial texts are as follows: to read them in conjunction with what produced them—the colonial text—which would be a way of actually integrating them into the undergraduate curriculum while retaining traces of their resistance to it; and to teach the so-called canonical text (for my purposes, this is the nineteenth- and early twentieth-century British text) as itself bound up with the cultural representation and self-representation of a colonial empire.

Encouraging students to read postcolonial texts as both similar to and different from colonial texts means that the former function in not simply oppositional ways. Insofar as they are written in English, they are complicit with a particular "rational" Western discourse and tradition; insofar as they are Indian or African, they participate in the realm of cultural difference and refuse absolute codification in the mainstream syllabus. Emphasizing colonial texts as themselves defined by the other—the colonized subject—means that we shift students' attention to the other; it becomes a question of how colonized cultures have determined, to a radical extent, the colonizer and the history of imperialism.

Already, I hear the insistent question: "All this is very well, but how do you get students to actually *see* all this?" In a classroom structured for discussion rather than lecture, what becomes crucial is not the articulation of right answers but right questions. In an upper-division English class in which I had students read Indian literature in English, for instance, we started out with copies of two *Encyclopaedia Brittanica* entries: one on the British colonial administrator and writer Thomas Babington Macaulay, and the other on the subcontinent of India. Why, I asked students, was the same amount of space devoted to both entries?[7] In a lower-division introductory literature class, it did not take much prodding to get students to admit that the English of an early Indian writer in English compared unfavorably to Forster's. In each class, students were usefully linking literature to questions of histories, dominant and marginal cultures, and the politics of imperialist and academic practices.

These and other strategies notwithstanding, I find teaching postcolonial texts a somewhat disconcerting experience, for at least two reasons. First, because they have been produced as a response to a fairly consensually felt gap in the undergraduate humanities curriculum, they have been determined by the nature of this gap. They become, in other words, both the product and the victim of centuries of nondisseminated knowledge about other cultures, for students cannot even invent ways in which these texts might make meaningful sense to them. For instance, in the introductory literature class, which traditionally introduced students to a closed, normative field of Western classics, my intention in globalizing the syllabus by teaching non-Western novels was to disperse the novel into the place where any of its previous master definitions could be consistently called to question. Far from being crudely brash and naively conceived, such an intention requires the greatest vigilance: my intention was not to substitute the Western, canonical text with the non-Western, noncanonical text; it was to take students away from the field in which dominant definitions of the novel have already been anchored, to the place where definitions of the novel may actually be produced. Such a move empowers students as the agents of their culture. It also calls their attention to the very processes and problems that accompany the definition of any object or field of study, in this case, the novel: What is excluded so that a certain inclusive definition of the novel may emerge? Does a reading of excluded material highlight the inadequacies of any attempt to standardize definitions of the novel? Can there ever be an all-inclusive definition of the novel?

A reading of Raja Rao's *Kanthapura*, coming after a reading of Charlotte Brontë's *Jane Eyre*, let loose not a few ripples in class discussion. In *Kanthapura* (first published in 1938), the Indian writer, Rao, experiments with the English language in order to produce a nativized Indian English that will, according to him, "some day prove to be as distinctive and colorful as the Irish or the American" (1967, p. vii).[8] The novel itself is concerned with a fictive South Indian village's gradual involvement in Gandhi's "Quit India" movement against British occupation. In many ways, *Kanthapura* is as fictitious as *Jane Eyre*: it is a narrative that utilizes a stylized language rhetorically geared toward a particular audience. Indeed, with *Kanthapura*, this utilization is further complicated by Rao's awareness that his audience is more Western than Indian. Hence, his attempts to nativize the English language are complicated by his inclusion of a 59-page glossary in which he, in effect, *de*nativizes his Indian content by providing literal translations and explanations of the Indian religious and social culture that is represented in the text itself.

A reading of the novel in conjunction with its glossary (which cannot, of course, define either the actual or the entire Indian culture) and its strange English (which is so stylized and Indianized as to seem utterly alien) confounded my primarily all-white students. The students who, in our initial discussions of non-Western cultures, complained that those cultures were summarily treated in their "Intro to Western Civ" course, and who also quickly figured out why ("history," one of them sagely pronounced, "is written by those in the majority, those in power"), were the same students who eventually thought *Jane Eyre* was more "real" and immediate to them than *Kanthapura*. *Kanthapura*, according to them, belonged in the realm of anthropology and history as a relic that needs, not reading, but deciphering. It was, of course, my task to point out to them that as products of both the "Intro to Western Civ" course and mainstream American culture, they were already set up to read the text as culturally alien. By undertaking this reading, they were, in fact, reproducing dominant and canonical definitions of the novel. In addition, I asked them to consider the ways in which Jane Eyre articulated her sense of self in relation to the dreaded prospect of going to India with St. John as his missionary wife; to go to India was, for Jane, the ultimate unbearable test of her frail nature and physique. It is no mistake that most British imperialist discourses, such as those informing *Jane Eyre*, articulated themselves in relation to the "Orient" in precisely this trial-by-fire way.

This anecdotal classroom experience should, however, indicate a legitimate concern: if, in the name of multiculturalism, a text has been evoked to cover the gaps in the humanities and the English curriculum, how then may the relation between that gap and that text be a useful, not a debilitating, one?

A second reason for my disconcerting experience in the classroom has to do with the obvious need for curricular change. To what extent must the curriculum be revised so that students may be contextually prepared for readings in multicultural literatures? Just as important is the question, who will be the agents and custodians of such revisions? Last semester, I taught an upper-division English class which had been created not only to fulfill certain credit requirements for English majors but also to afford English seniors the opportunity to undertake advanced research projects along theoretically informed lines. We read both British colonial and Indian and African postcolonial novels, my intention being to expose them to an already political space in which a writer's very use of English constitutes either the condition for or the absence of an articulation of his or her national identity. But we were seldom able to rise above the (imagined) literal difficulty of certain apparently inaccessible cultural concepts and words. If my students had been resistant to that which they did not understand, then I could have made of their resistance something useful. My sophomore students, the readers of *Kanthapura*, had presented such a resistance, which I combatted by pointing out to them the perhaps unconscious defining factors of the "Intro to Western civ" course and mainstream American culture. In that particular situation, too, I was better able to pull *Kanthapura* into their range, encouraging them to read both with and against the grain of mainstream literature. But with my English seniors, it was not the text at hand but my own cultural identity that fell under students' scrutiny, for most of these seniors had developed a profound belief in not only the mastery of literary skills but, more importantly, the authority of the teacher. Hence, they assumed that the translation of foreign words would automatically lead to a complete understanding of foreign culture; being of Indian origin, I was placed in the position of a translator, transmitting the truths of Indian culture to them, and, before long, my students were producing pious analyses of a postcolonial people as "oppressed masses throwing off the yoke of colonialism only to find themselves in poverty." Admittedly, I was primarily to blame for this erroneous circumstance. It is a student's first instinct to ferret out what he or she thinks is the teacher's intention in teaching a particular text; better teachers are perhaps those who thwart such expectations, placing the responsibility of his or her own reading upon the student. If I were to teach the same course again, I would problematize not only the multicultural text but my own cultural identity in the classroom, by placing myself simultaneously in the Indian and the American context as neither purely Indian nor purely American; as a teacher, too, I would productively frustrate their misplaced attempt to decode alien cultural codes in order to demonstrate to them the risk-ridden nature of entering another culture, let alone mastering it. The legitimate concern remains, however, about a curriculum which has not yet theoretically and practically integrated multicultural literatures, so that students have hardly any idea why such a literature exists and how it might be useful to them. Their temptation, more often than not, is to decode this literature in a vacuum and so further ghettoize it.

III

This paper has touched upon what may seem to be the more unsettling aspects of the status of multicultural literatures in the university only because it is at the very moment of these literatures' insertion and institutionalization that the greatest care must be taken. Somewhere in this paper, however, there does lie a blueprint for productive strategies to teach multicultural literatures, the most effective one being a multicultural teacher's willingness to work both with and against the grain of mainstream British and American texts, even as he or she makes as a valid issue in her class the condition of his or her own cultural identity. Most importantly, the teaching of multicultural literatures may benefit from such current work in some American cultural studies programs as Jean Ferguson Carr's (Carr, 1990). In teaching her undergraduate students *McGuffey's Sixth Eclectic Reader,* a nineteenth-century American school text which productively evades both canonization and codification in that its reading sidesteps the entire notion of quick consumption or mastery, she alerted them to their own contradictory cultural makeup:

> In this anthology's silences and evasions about slavery and the Civil War, its bracketing off of women writers to realms of the domestic and lyrical poetry, and its curious fascination with the rise and fall of peoples (Romans and Native Americans), students can begin to discern cultural blindnesses and habits of mind—to discuss a text not just in terms of what it proposes, but in what it ignores, what it subordinates, what it incorporates, and what it only suggests. (p. 28)

We need to add to Carr's project an examination not only of the imbrications of students, texts, and reading and teaching practices in questions of culture but also of the interplay of racially other teachers, American students, and culturally alien texts, which are perhaps even stranger than *McGuffey's Reader.*

But in order to teach multicultural literatures, we must first emphasize their foregrounding and representation of the questions of culture. Literature constitutes an object of study that is already fixed in place, but our aim should be to investigate how objects of study are contructed so that we do not repeat the earlier silencing or controlling of otherness by dominant practices. We have to focus on culture, both inside and outside the university, as the agency that instructs, shapes, and pressures us. We have to recognize that while an entire traditional European influx of immigrants has by now drastically dwindled in the United States (from 69 percent of all immigrants in 1965 to 16 percent since that year), a non-European, nontraditional body of people has already arrived. Witness the demographic growth in metropolitan centers of African Americans, Chicanos, Asian Americans (of Chinese, Filipino, Japanese, Indian, Korean, Vietnamese, and Hmong descent), and, to a lesser but even more crucial extent, Native Americans. We have to take a fresh look at our multicultural culture without taking recourse to the old American ideology of the melting pot.

Notes

1. Although I will not hereafter italicize the term *multicultural literature,* I mean at this early point to call the reader's attention to the fact that the construct *multicultural literature* is, in fact, a construct and a difficult one, for many of the reasons I list in this section. Further, traditionally, literature has not been termed "multicultural"; hence, one is at liberty to presume that "multicultural literature" is considered to be any literature that is marginal, non-Western, postcolonial, "Third World," noncanonical, and/or nontraditional. It is to highlight this oddity that I distinguish the term thus.

2. It is now commonplace among several cultural analyses to position the school as the site for a particular ideological apparatus in Louis Althusser's terms. See Althusser, 1971, p. 127–185. Concurrently, too, however, a certain resistance to Althusser's rather deterministic reading of ideology has produced several pedagogical debates. See, for instance, Margaret Carr, 1988, pp. 213–221.

3. I have in mind Gayatri Spivak's strategic use of the word *teacher* to invent an identity that will be less contestatory than the cultural identity of the Asian/Bengali intellectual in Anglo-America. See Spivak, 1990, pp. 219–244. Elsewhere, Spivak makes reference to the classroom as the stage for intervention. In neither place is it clear what exactly the teacher does in the classroom; he or she survives there as a trope that is evoked and manipulated rhetorically.

4. Today, it is common to hear complaints about "high" cultural texts presenting the same inaccessibility in reading, the general articulation being that students, particularly undergraduate students, have increasingly lost touch with the linguistic expertise and complexity commonly associated with texts by, say, Shakespeare or Dickens. What needs to be recognized, however, is the impossibility of fixing upon a literary standard that will hold true for all readers and that will transcend considerations of race, class, ethnicity, and gender. An Indian reader will tend to overlook the aesthetic delight of lyrical descriptions of Wordsworth's daffodils if daffodils are nonexistent in her or his native landscape; a Chinese reader may read a particular estranging significance into the color red in Hawthorne's *The Scarlet Letter.*

5. In all my references to teaching, I mean undergraduate teaching.

6. Constraints of space prevent me from developing here the problems implicit in the radical differences between native and expatriate African and

Indian writers or, for that matter, between postcolonial Africa and postcolonial India; these problems, however, constitute a large part of class dicussion. Moreover, African American texts such as Alice Walker's *The Color Purple*, Zora Neale Hurston's *Their Eyes Were Watching God*, and Toni Morrison's *Beloved, Sula*, and *The Bluest Eye*, and Chinese American novels such as Maxine Kingston's *The Woman Warrior* have become staples in many undergraduate curricula; Latin American texts such as Gabriel García Márquez's *Love in the Time of Cholera* and *One Hundred Years of Solitude* and Mario Vargas Llosa's *Aunt Julia and the Scriptwriter* have also gained access to the college classroom. Fruitful to teach, novels such as these, however, are not in themselves resistant to appropriation by a dominant humanistic tradition which, by canonizing them, may also slot and hence dismiss them. The most useful way to teach such marginal, multicultural texts is, as I suggest in the essay, to constantly make them work against the grain of dominant literature. As Spivak puts it, "The critical process—through repeated comparisons with what is non-canonical—must accompany the canon" (1989, p. 49).

7. At the heart of this exercise lurks treachery. The entries came from the Encyclopaedia Brittanica Ready Reference; in the Encyclopaedia Brittanica Knowledge in Depth, much more space was devoted to the geography, history, and culture of the Indian subcontinent. Arguably, however, a reader "ready referencing" would come away with as much information about Macaulay as about India, and the question of how knowledge is packaged with cultural bias survives.

8. Originally published by George Allen and Unwin, Ltd., London, *Kanthapura* was next reprinted by Oxford University Press, Bombay, in 1947. It is common for many non-Western novels written in English to first gain popularity in the West before they are reprinted at home and read by an educated native elite. The point needs to be made that *Kanthapura* is not the best example of a non-Western text, but then no non-Western novel written in English is. It is an unfortunate paradox that the material most accessible in the American classroom is the material that is least non-Western.

References

Althusser, Louis. (1971). Ideology and ideological state apparatuses (notes towards an investigation). In *Lenin and philosophy and other essays* (pp. 127–185). New York: Monthly Review Press.

Brontë, Charlotte. (1847; 1988). *Jane Eyre*. New York: Bantam.

Carr, Jean Ferguson. (1990, November–December). Cultural studies and curricular change. *Academe*, 25–28.

Carr, Margaret. (1988, Spring). Teaching and/as reproduction. *Yale Journal of Criticism 1*, 213–221.

Lauter, Paul, et al. (Eds.). *The Heath anthology of American literature.* 2 vols. Lexington, MA: D. C. Heath.

Minority update. (1990, September 26). *The Chronicle of Higher Education,* P. A18.

Rao, Raja. (1938; 1967). *Kanthapura.* New York: New Directions.

Simonson, R., & Walker, S. (Eds.). (1988). *The Graywolf annual five: Multicultural literacy.* Saint Paul: Graywolf Press.

Spivak, Gayatri Chakravorty. (1989, September). Forum: Who needs the great works? *Harper's,* 41–52.

Spivak, Gayatri Chakravorty. (1990). Poststructuralism, marginality, postcoloniality and value. In Peter Collier & Helga Geyer-Ryan (Eds.), *Literary theory today* (pp. 219–244). Ithaca: Cornell University Press.

12

Multicultural Literacy in a Middle School Writing Workshop

Hasna Muhammad

Multicultural attitudes and teaching methods are emerging as effective ways—if not the only ways—to educate students in our pluralistic American society. Literature is being used as a tool to promote multicultural concepts. It connects readers with diverse cultures; it spurs reactions to culturally based issues; it provides a vast resource of perspectives from which to view the world. As a product of culture that can serve as an example and as a bridge between one culture and another, literature can expose the humanness in all of us and lessen the importance of cultural boundaries.

From giving seasonal attention to biographies of famous members of a particular culture to involving students directly in cultural issues, multicultural literature can either decorate or permeate cultural boundaries within our classrooms. Token inclusion of multicultural literature may reinforce the imbalance and misrepresentation of diverse cultures that already exist in some classrooms. The shortest month of the year, for example, is not the only time to pull African American history from the shelves. Even when multicultural literature is deeply infused into a language arts curriculum, the level of inclusion may be too shallow to make a difference in the lives of our students. The cultural sensitivity and the pluralistic attitudes we hope to foster in our students often do not last beyond the classroom.

But how closely does the literature connect with and affect students' attitudes toward culture? I have seen students in my classroom read and discuss Mildred Taylor's *Roll of Thunder, Hear My Cry* (1976) and still call each other "niggers." They still laugh when they hear a classmate speaking his or her native language. And ethnic features are still the butt of ridicule and embarrassment. Thus accommodating culturally diverse literature in our classrooms contributes to multicultural literacy but requires more than working with a global list of books. The literature must be used to support a multidimensional environment that reflects and inspires pluralistic attitudes toward acceptance, tolerance, and coexistence in and out of the classroom. It must not be merely accommodated, but rather engaged as a significant aspect in multicultural education.

The Workshop

I teach in a middle school that houses three magnet programs—a global studies magnet, a law-related education magnet, and a management business awareness magnet. We teachers planned the curricula to expose students to multiculturalism, citizenship, and to career goals with hopes of fostering tolerance, government involvement, and prosperity. I facilitate one of three whole-language reading and writing workshops for both the global studies and law-related education magnets. My students spend all of their time at the various levels of the reading and writing processes. The design of the workshop encourages multiple writing purposes, tasks, materials, and resources. The workshop also accommodates interdisciplinary projects whereby students complete specific writing assignments from other subject areas in the workshop. Students have written papers explaining how scientists have affected the law as a science assignment. They have recreated slave narratives to fulfill a social studies assignment. They have also written poetry for greeting cards that are sold through the management business awareness magnet.

In my literature-based workshop, literature is not limited to printed materials. For my global studies students specifically, it is usually the story that we use to focus on cultural diversity. We include oral literature and the traditions inherent in the art of storytelling around the world. An investigation of folktales set in different places has revealed a similarity between a variety of characters with common traits. West African Anansi the Spider is West Indian Anansi the Spider is Br'er Rabbit from the southeastern part of the United States.

Visual forms of literature are included in an attempt to add cultural diversity in my classroom. Films and dramatic presentations allow students to experience a story in a format that is very much a part of our visually stimulated culture. *Back to the Future Part III* is an amusing example of how time affects culture. *Dances with Wolves* provides an image of Native Americans that many students may not have seen.

In a similar way, we approach music as a literary form of expression. The development of African American music, for example, can be directly connected to the cultural development of African Americans in the United States. The lyrics of oppression, rebellion, love, and inspiration have no cultural boundaries.

The comparison and contrast of a culture's use of a literary form also further the inclusion of literature as a means of cultural diversity. The rolling nature of a nineteenth-century Russian short story, for example, can be compared to the concise nature of a Japanese short story from the same time period. Nathaniel Hawthorne's work was shaped by an American culture quite different from the one that shaped Mark Twain's or Toni Morrison's.

The abundance of written literature in the workshop is read and discussed because it is literature, not because it happens to represent a certain culture. Students make analogies and analyses of cultural concepts based on the books that they read. For example, students might read *Journey to Topaz* by Yoshiko Uchida (1971) and respond to the fact that there were Japanese internment camps in the United States. They might read *Chain of Fire* by Beverly Naidoo (1989) as an example of South African literature. That book can also be used in social studies and math classes to exemplify forms of government and economic policies. *Friedrich* by Hans Peter Richter (1970), *The Upstairs Room* by Johanna Reiss (1972), and *Snow Treasure* by Marie McSwigan (1986) might be read to study the Jewish Holocaust from different points of view.

My subjective view of the workshop is that it accommodates multicultural ideals. We affirm the individual's right to be different, confront discriminatory remarks and sexist behavior in the classroom, and allow these topics to fuel our writing. We encounter concepts—be they scientific, judicial, or social—and translate them into various forms of language. The workshop is prepared for diversity. It is primed to infuse the conscious, permeating level of multiculturalism that I hope to provide for all of my students.

A Multicultural Project

I designed a project that would put students in touch with interesting facts about the cultures of their choice. I didn't want the same stiff reports that students can crank out in half an hour. I wasn't interested in the transcription of an encyclopedia. Instead, I wanted my students to read stories, books, magazines, and poems about the culture they were studying. I wanted them to watch a movie, listen to the music, taste the foods, and learn at least one phrase in the native language of the culture. I urged them to go to travel agencies for pictures and to interview people for stories. Use as many resources as possible, I told them. Literature was to be approached as one of the many aspects of culture, as well as a source of information. Exposure to the literature of other cultures was intended to add a dimension to their written responses that I hoped would reflect insight into the lives of the people the students chose to study. Through the observation of the aspects of culture and the comparison of literature, I expected the students to learn that people are similar as well as different.

We formed study groups, made a flowchart of possible cultures to study, and discussed the components of culture. The students opted to study European, Asian, and Latin American cultures. One student wanted to study Africa as one culture and was unable to choose just one culture from the continent she thought was a country. No one chose any African, American, or Native American cultures to study. Together we defined culture as a conglomerate of qualities. Aspects of our culture, we said, can be found in food, literature, language, religion, art, music, dance, artifacts, traditions and habits, entertainment, technology, geography, people, and more. Each group chose one culture to study, and each group member took the responsibility for studying one aspect of that culture. We decided that the literature, the food, and the language would be studied as a group.

Multicultural Teaching, by Pamela Tiedt and Iris Tiedt, has an extensive bibliography of multicultural literature categorized by culture, country, and genre. To obtain additional resources for the project, I used this list to select nonfiction, folktales, and novels from the shelves of the local library and to bring them to my classroom. I made my choices based on the titles and the publication dates of the books. I tried not to use anything that was published before 1980 in an effort to remain as current as possible for my picky adolescent readers and writers. I was pleased to see that the bibliography contained books already on my shelf. I recognized the literature that represents my own culture but was unfamiliar, for the most part, with the literature from other cultures—especially those not represented in my classroom. I "advertised" the books I brought in, and highlighted the culture the book represented. If I could, I added historical information that coincided with the story line. Students flipped through the books and asked a few questions, but no one asked to borrow any of the books to read for themselves. The global list of books became a global pile of books.

During their research, most of the students' reading stayed within the realm of standard references, and the writing remained stiff.

Students rewrote encyclopedia entries and wrote information concerning the past history of the culture. Responses to student-made Irish soda bread and Jamaican fritters were underdeveloped. Our conversations, usually student directed, became teacher-directed lectures. They contributed less and less to the discussions, and I found myself doing most of the talking. The instructional exchanges ceased to engage any of us, so we stopped working to assess the assignment.

Through discussion I found that the assignment was too ambitious and too singularly teacher directed to succeed within the confines of class time and without the cooperation of additional colleagues—social studies teachers especially. I learned that some students are greatly misinformed about aspects of history. Some students thought Vietnam was only the name of a war, not a country. One student asked who the King of New York was. Some Jamaican students didn't know where the British West Indies were. Most didn't know the difference between race and nationality. Students asked questions that echoed stereotypical views. "Why do Puerto Ricans talk so fast?" "Why do black people eat so much chicken?" "Why do Jamaicans have accents?" "Why are Russians so ugly?" "Are all Colombians drug dealers?" I also realized that the students were unable to grasp what culture is. Perhaps it was the word, the concept, that lead them to misconceptions of culture being something separate from their daily lives. They seemed to think that culture is old-fashioned, polished, and lofty, something one might perceive as elitist, foreign, or uncomfortable. "What does culture have to do with my life?" a student asked me.

Though we had discussed the differences in religious beliefs, though I read African folktales and Native American poetry to the students, though we listened to reggae music, found countries on the map, and read newspaper articles about Chinese schoolchildren, I still had to stop the classroom activity and address the fact that one student was making fun of another student's accent. With all the literary examples in the classroom, in the lesson, in their writing, I still had to show the students that there are alternate ways of viewing people with different hair, lighter eyes, thicker lips, and different circumstances than their own. These questions and gross misunderstandings led me to believe that my students had been unaffected by the multiculturally literate environment I thought I was providing. What does culture have to do with their lives? How can a global list of books connect with the lives of my students? How can they tolerate someone else's culture if they don't recognize their own? I postponed all work on the project and began to concentrate on the students' concepts of their own cultures. I removed my goals for this mammoth project from the agenda and started again.

When I had asked everyone to identify his or her culture earlier in the assignment, some were able to label their cultures: Brazilian, Jamaican, Jewish. Not all of the African American students included their African heritage. They were more prone to explain how they were "half Indian" because their great, great grandmother was Native American. Those who were able to state that their mother came from Poland, their father came from down South, or that their grandma came from Panama at least had a place to start. Some had a religion or in some instances a language that could easily be written about in terms of culture. There were other students who didn't know their cultures, and even others who felt as if they had none. There was no one place they could point to, no one thing they felt they could identify as their culture. "I don't have a culture," some told me. In order to find out about their cultures, I suggested that students talk with family members. Unfortunately, not all had family members who could clearly define their culture.

"What is culture?" I asked—again. No one knew exactly. It is our language, our traditions, our environment, our food, our literature. Remember? It's the way we live our lives, what we do, who we are, how we show that we exist. What they learn in social studies is culture, I told them. The information that they find in the encyclopedia is the history of people's cultures. What they write in the workshop, I continued, is our story. Our stories are records of our lives that reflect our cultures. I challenged them to believe that they too had cultures equal to those represented in history books and other forms of literature, and that they too could document and preserve their cultures.

I tried to get the students to explore who they are by pointing out what aspects of their lives contribute to their individual cultures as well as our collective culture. I used personal narratives to exemplify how seemingly insignificant aspects of our lives can be written and shared as literature. Eating with the family, learning to ride a bike, or watching snow fall are experiences my students can draw upon to write. As their own primary resources, students need not look far for topics. Memoirs, autobiographies, and other forms of personal narratives serve as guiding lights in the students' personal writing endeavors. From journal entries to autobiographical short stories, the various forms of personal narratives lend themselves to the maturation that occurs during adolescent and teen years. They provide a close, safe place for students to discover and to react to the culturally diverse world around them.

I was able to use the literature from an additional perspective. The personal narratives not only exemplified the qualities of good writing, but they also reflected the aspects of culture that were represented in the text. *The House on Mango Street* by Sandra Cisneros (1989) exposes her Mexican culture in ordinary, daily places like her hair, her lunch bag, the origin of a name. *Childtimes* by Eloise Greenfield (1979) connects three generations of African American women and puts family stories in a position to reflect culture. Cynthia Rylant's *Waiting to Waltz* (1984) and Jean Little's *Hey World, Here I Am!* (1986) hold the voices of childhood in poetry. They give childlike visions and reactions to the cultures they reflect. *Man on Earth* by John Reader (1988) is an advanced "portrait of human culture in a multitude of environments." The stories in these narratives reflect pieces of daily life. They become the voices of our relatives, our friends, ourselves. The places that are described are the places that we recognize. When we discussed the stories, we couldn't avoid our own stories. Our habits and surroundings and the details of our daily lives were worth reliving. They were worth talking and writing about.

Some students were unable to write. One came up to me privately and asked me not to ask her about her family. Another blatantly refused. "My father curses at me in Italian. I hate my father. That's all I know about my culture." Usually vocal and mobile, Roger became quiet and still. "My life is confusing. It's all tangled up. I can't write about it." Cole, another student, told his stories. He didn't have the discipline to write them down. He didn't come to school often enough to practice the habit of writing. Yet he was a storyteller. He knew his family. He reenacted how his mother spoke to him, and retold the wise words of his grandmother. "If you lie, you cut your days short." He told stories about his family like a true griot, and I told him that. I also told him how much storytelling is a part of his African American culture. We all contributed proverbial adages and found that although our heritages varied, we had all been passed similar values in different ways, and sometimes in different languages.

A Jamaican student who was barely literate by the standards of the American educational system provided us with a view of Jamaican culture by writing about his life in Jamaica. Another student remembered what it was like to go through customs when she first came to this country. Another wrote about her grandmother's house "Down South." Her grandmother sent poetry to our workshop which was included in our cultural anthology, *Unanimous, Anonymous*. One young lady wrote pages about her family life in welfare hotels with her mother's abusive boyfriends. I talked with her about her life and her work, but I never asked her to share. She did not know that her way of life is part of the culture of this country. Not having a father in the home has become a part of our culture. Homelessness has become a part of our culture.

As a result of the modifications in this project, we have begun to recognize the elements of culture in our lives. Each of us comes from somewhere; we all speak languages; we have different habits, different stories to write. We have recognized our grandmothers and our step families, our relatives and homelands in books and in our stories. Yes, this project yielded a level of success. Unfortunately, however, some students were not comfortable enough to research their cultures in depth. A few did not even bother to try. Students continue to use racial features, nationality, and language as the basis for insults. They use them softly. They catch each other calling names and mimic my dislike to their classmates. When I confront them with their choice of words, they deny making the statements, smile, then apologize. That too is success. The students are at least aware that their remarks are inappropriate.

When we research other cultures, I will return to the library for literature from a global book list. This time I will accommodate the culturally diverse literature in a way that affects the students' lives as well as their literacy skills. The literature will continue to serve as an example of what and how writers write and link one aspect of culture to another. We will pay attention to literary technique and cultural tradition, then compare what we find in the lives of one group to the lives of another. When students recognize their own cultures in the aspects of other cultures, they may be able to accommodate diversity on some level. When individual aspects of culture are identified, they can be used to reflect similarities and differences in human nature throughout the world. Diversity in literature and life can be used to connect and to guide literary thoughts toward qualities of acceptance, tolerance, and coexistence. "Having a culture is nice," a student wrote. "It lets you know you are somebody."

Bibliography

References

Deyhle, Donna. (1987). Learning failure: Tests as gatekeepers and the culturally different child. In Henry Trueba (Ed.), *Success or failure?* (pp. 85–107). Merrimac, MA: Newberry Books.

Ferdman, B. M. (1990). Literacy and cultural identity. *Harvard Educational Review, 60,* 181–216.

Galeano, Eduardo. (1988). In defense of the word: Leaving Buenos Aires, June 1976. In R. Simonson & S. Walker (Eds.), *Multicultural literacy* (pp. 113–125). Saint Paul: Graywolf Press.

Hirsch, E. D., Jr. (1988). *Cultural literacy: What every American needs to know.* New York: Vintage.

Rasinski, Timothy V., & Padak, Nancy D. (1990, October). Multicultural learning through children's literature. *Language Arts,* pp. 576–580.

Tiedt, Pamela, & Tiedt, Iris. (1990). *Multicultural teaching.* Boston, MA: Allyn & Bacon.

Literature

Cisneros, Sandra. (1989). *The house on Mango Street.* New York: Vintage.

Goss, Linda, & Barnes, M. (Eds.). (1989). *Talk that talk.* New York: Simon & Schuster.

Greenfield, Eloise. (1979). *Childtimes: A three-generation memoir.* New York: HarperCollins.

Little, Jean. (1986). *Hey world, here I am!* New York: Harper & Row.

McSwigan, Marie. (1986). *Snow treasure.* New York: Scholastic.

Naidoo, Beverly. (1989). *Chain of fire.* New York: Lippincott.

Nhuong, Huynh Quang. (1982). *The land I lost: Adventures of a boy in Viet Nam.* New York: HarperCollins.

Reader, John. (1988). *Man on earth.* New York: Harper & Row.

Reiss, Johanna. (1972). *The upstairs room.* New York: Crowell.

Richter, Hans Peter. (1970). *Friedrich.* New York: Holt, Rinehart, & Winston.

Rylant, Cynthia. (1984). *Waiting to waltz.* New York: Macmillian.

Taylor, Mildred. (1976). *Roll of thunder, hear my cry.* New York: Dial.

Uchida, Yoshiko. (1971). *Journey to Topaz.* New York: Scribner.

Yolen, Jane. (1986). *Favorite folktales around the world.* New York: Pantheon Books.

13

Literature about Asians and Asian Americans: Implications for Elementary Classrooms

Junko Yokota

In the United States today, the number of Asian Americans is growing at a faster pace than that of any other cultural group. According to the 1990 U.S. Census, the growth rate between 1980 and 1989 was 136 percent, largely due to Asian immigrants who arrived during the decade. Such a growth rate affects the U.S. school-age population in significant ways. Today, 1,267,000 students in American schools, or 3.1 percent of the total school-age population, are of Asian American heritage. What this means for the use of literature in literacy learning and teaching is the focus of this chapter.

Literature occupies a special place in the education of our children. Fiction, especially, has the potential to affect children's learning and development in significant ways. Fiction that is culturally rooted can make strong and lasting impressions. Consider the bonding readers feel with characters as they step inside their lives and begin to understand why those characters think, act, and speak as they do. Such experiences help readers empathize with the people and situations they read about, and in so doing form attitudes through which they view the world around them. In short, reading about people's lives helps us understand the world in which we live. Reading about various cultures helps us understand our culturally pluralistic world.

The specifics of how such literature can affect readers' lives depend on a number of factors. What is available for children to read? What do they select to read? What is being read to them? What opportunities for responding to literature are there in the classroom? How do children respond? What can teachers do? In this chapter, I address such issues as they pertain to literature by and about Asians and Asian Americans.

My personal perspectives on Asian and Asian American literature stem from several aspects of my background. I spent the first eighteen years of my life in my home country of Japan, and am therefore a first-generation Asian American. As an elementary classroom teacher for eight years, I relied on literature for its potential to convey images of Asian and Asian American people. As an elementary librarian, I became especially conscious of the need to be selective in adding to the collection in order to ensure cultural accuracy in portrayals of Asians and Asian Americans. Now, in my role in teaching children's literature at a university, I realize the importance of helping future and current teachers become aware of their role in selecting and using books that are culturally responsible.

I begin this chapter by providing a brief historical perspective on Asian and Asian American literature for children. Next, I raise for consideration issues regarding the selection and use of Asian and Asian American literature in elementary classrooms. Following this discussion, I put forth recommendations about what teachers can do to make Asian and Asian American literature an integral part of their students' experiences in the classroom. The final section of the chapter contains an annotated bibliography of recommended books.

Asian American Literature for Children: A Brief Historical Perspective

Despite the many years that Asians have been in America, the history of Asian American literature is relatively short and has a disproportionately small number of books, considering our large Asian American population. Until recent years, Asian Americans were not writing books for children, and, in general, stories about these cultural groups were not being published. What was published during the 1960s and prior to the mid-1970s often portrayed Asian Americans with stereotyped images. Illustrations commonly included "Fu Manchu mustaches, short straight cereal-bowl haircuts, buck teeth, myopic vision, and clothing that was cruelly and offensively indicative of ancient ways" (Chu & Schuler, 1992).

By the end of the 1980s, more minority authors began writing of their experiences. This fact, along with the increased sensitivity to include a diverse perspective, made way for the inclusion of multiple life-styles and individual experiences within each cultural group (Miller-Lachman, 1992). Authors such as Laurence Yep wrote of their personal experiences and feelings as Chinese Americans. Yoshiko Uchida wrote of her experiences as a Japanese American who lived in the relocation camps during her childhood. Allen Say reflected on his homeland of

Japan, but also on being Asian American. Ed Young's work reflected his Chinese heritage.

Today, there are several small-press publishers who have made a strong commitment to providing children's literature which illuminates various ethnic experiences. Children's Book Press produces bilingual Asian books in Korean, Vietnamese, Khmer (Cambodia), and Hmong (Laos). In addition, it publishes folktales and original Asian American stories. Kane/Miller Publishers has made a commitment to provide books which depict the uniqueness of various cultures, and some of its titles are published bilingually. Miller-Lachman (1992) points to the lack of minority editors in major publishing houses as part of the problem in providing multicultural literature from the mainstream publishers.

Today, the outlook for quality Asian American literature is better than it has been. Major publishing houses are encouraging more Asians to write and illustrate stories based on their own experiences. Small-press publishers are contributing culturally authentic materials. However, there are numerous issues still to be considered, as discussed in the next section.

Issues about Asian American Literature for Consideration

An increasing number of books that reflect the Asian American experience are being made available to children, a trend that is to be applauded. But, as with other trends, there are issues associated with it that must be brought to the fore and discussed. The issues surrounding the publication and use of Asian and Asian American literature in schools involve selecting literature that is of high literary quality, using culturally specific literature, providing a balanced literature collection, and ensuring culturally authentic content.

Quality Literature Reflecting the Asian American Experience. The quantitative lack of Asian American literature has made the selection of such literature for inclusion in recommended reading lists and classroom use difficult. Sometimes books are included that are of mediocre literary quality but that may be some of the few titles available reflecting a particular Asian culture's experiences. First and foremost, it is important to consider all the elements of good literature when selecting Asian American literature and to select books that have literary merit in addition to a depiction of culturally true experiences. (For a discussion of the elements of good literature, see Cullinan, 1989; Huck, Hepler, & Hickman, 1987; Lukens, 1990; Norton, 1991.)

Culturally Specific Literature. Despite the fact that Asian Americans are the most diverse "minority" group in America, they are often clustered into one cultural conglomerate. One instance of such grouping is the notion of "Asian American literature." First, we must distinguish between Asian literature and Asian American literature. Asian literature originates in, or is focused on, the Asian countries. This body of literature may have been translated from the original Asian language, or it may have been written in America but specifically about experiences in Asian countries. On the other hand, Asian American literature originated in America and focuses on the unique ethnic experiences of Asian Americans. Although Asian Americans may continue to uphold their Asian cultural heritage, that heritage often took a different turn when it was mixed with their new American heritage. Two books about the effects of war in Southeast Asia illustrate the differences between Asian and Asian American literature: Minfong Ho's *The Clay Marble* (1991) and Gloria Whelan's *Goodbye, Vietnam* (1992). Despite the parallel nature of these two books, they depict two completely different experiences. *The Clay Marble,* which is set in contemporary Cambodia, is a story of the effect that war had on the lives of families there. It portrays the lives of people who are trying to rebuild a war-torn country. Although many Asian Americans may have experienced such a life prior to coming to America, the story is set in Cambodia. Whelan's *Goodbye, Vietnam,* on the other hand, is an example of Asian American literature. It tells of the experiences of Vietnamese refugees who escape to Hong Kong and of their eventual passage to America. This story reflects some experiences of Asians who have escaped from war-torn countries such as Vietnam and emigrated to the United States.

Some second-, third-, or further-generation Asian Americans have never visited the country of their cultural roots. Although it is important to understand the starting ground of their cultural heritage, it is equally important to understand how that culture has been maintained in this country.

The second point about the need for culturally specific literature is that often many distinct cultures are grouped together as one conglomerate. The 1990 U.S. Census showed that a large number of Asian Americans claimed the following countries as their country of origin: China, the Philippines, Japan, India, Korea, Vietnam, Hawaii, Samoa, and Guam. Each country has a unique culture; yet often they are treated as though they could be grouped as generically "Asian." Some books depict generically Asian experiences in such a way that even Asian country natives are not able to tell if these books are supposed to represent their own country. Lyn Miller-Lachman (1992) divides the Asian literature in the following way: Southern and Central Asia, consisting of Afghanistan, Bangladesh, Bhutan, India, Nepal, Pakistan, and Sri Lanka; East Asia, consisting of China, Hong Kong, Japan, Mongolia, North Korea, South Korea, and Taiwan; and Southeast Asia, consisting of Brunei, Burma, Cambodia, Indonesia, Laos, Malaysia, the Philippines, Thailand, and Vietnam. This allows for some grouping of countries while still recognizing diversity.

Balanced Literature Collection. Within the entire collection of books identified as Asian and Asian American, a high percentage are folktales. In addition, many are historical fiction books. Relatively few books depict a contemporary situation. Today, therefore, there continues to be a need for more books representing the Asian *American* experience. In particular, there is a lack of books which depict Asian or Asian American main characters in contemporary settings.

When viewing literature as a way to understand another culture, one needs a multiple perspective. The following books give a variety of perspectives on Japanese Americans and their Japanese cultural roots. Folktales such as Momoko Ishii's *The Tongue-Cut Sparrow* (1982) give readers an insight into traditional Japanese tales that have been shared by generations. This story tells of a kind old man and his greedy wife. Each pays a visit to the sparrow whose tongue the wife has cut off, and each receives gifts indicative of what he or she deserves. There are cultural references and uses of onomatopoeic words which lend an air of authenticity. Historical fiction pieces such as Yoko Kawashima Watkins's *So Far from the Bamboo Grove* (1986) help readers to understand important periods of Japanese history. The narrator relays the story of what it was like to be a Japanese child living in occupied China and trying to escape the country without being seen by the enemy. But in books like Nomura's *Grandfather's Town* (1991) readers see the Japan of today. In this story, a young boy and his mother go to visit Grandfather in his small-town home, in an attempt to convince him to come and live with them. Their concerns about his ability to care for himself are eased as they join him in his daily activities. The description of these activities, supported by the illustrations, gives readers a glimpse of life in Japan. But although all of these books are part of the literary heritage of Japanese Americans, they are not focused on the unique experience of being Japanese American. Yoshiko Uchida, in contrast, is noted for her contribution in the area of Japanese American experiences in a historical sense, particularly during the period of Japanese American internment during the war. Books such as *Journey to Topaz* (1971) depict this experience in a way that helps young readers begin to understand the complexity of the situation. Contemporary Japanese American experiences can be found in books such as Allen Say's *The Lost Lake* (1989), in which a young boy and his father develop closer relations while on a fishing trip. Books such as these help readers understand that Japanese Americans enjoy much of the same experiences as others in the mainstream population. It is a balance of books from each of these various areas that helps readers gain a sense of the Japanese American culture.

In some books identified by various sources as "Asian American," the only thing Asian American is the inclusion of characters who are identified as being Asian American. When examining the content of the books, one finds no information that helps readers understand more about Asian Americans. Some lists include books that were written or illustrated by Asian Americans, but nothing in them indicates anything Asian American. One such example is Keiko Kasza's *The Wolf's Chicken Stew* (1987), a story about a wolf with a craving for chicken stew. He sees a hen, and in an attempt to fatten the chicken, the wolf bakes a hundred-pound cake, a hundred doughnuts, and a hundred pancakes. A humerous twist ends this story. It is delightful, and it engages both children and adults, but it is simply not Asian or Asian American in content. Keiko Kasza was born and raised in Japan, but because this story has nothing to do with Japan, it does not belong on a multicultural booklist. We need more books that balance the strength of the cultural heritage with contemporary situations.

Culturally Authentic Literature. One problem in Asian American literature today is that of "outsiders" writing about or illustrating experiences without having first-hand knowledge of the culture being portrayed. The result is often a stereotyped image based on generic views of "Asian" culture that mix various elements of different Asian cultures. One such example is found in illustrations depicting characters wearing clothing from a culture different from the culture of the background buildings, and colors which are not at all representative of the culture, with supporting text which tells of an entirely different culture. Books such as these only perpetuate the stereotyped understanding that Asians all belong to one conglomerate group. Nobody who understands Asian cultures will be able to look at such a book and identify its specific culture. If the goal of including Asian American literature is to help Asian American students gain a sense of self-concept regarding their heritage or to help all students understand various cultural distinctions, then neither goal is being met by such literature. Instead, students are being exposed to misinformed images.

Such problems will only be resolved when there is a demand for cultural authenticity in literature for children. Often Asian American literature, as well as other multicultural literature, is evaluated by criteria for good literature applied to literature for children in general. Although it is important to be sure that Asian American literature meets all the criteria generally accepted as qualities of good literature, there is a need to go a step further in evaluating for cultural authenticity.

Cultural authenticity is achieved when there is rich cultural detail reflecting the nuances of the culture in a natural way. This is accomplished by "insiders" who were raised as a member of the cultural group, or by those who through extensive research have acquired a thorough understanding of how a cultural group lives. Yoshiko Uchida is able to tell the stories of growing up Japanese American during World War II because she had first-hand experience living in the Japanese relocation camps of that time period. Laurence Yep tells stories of the struggles between maintaining a strong Chinese heritage and becoming part of the mainstream American heritage because he has lived among people who constantly face those struggles.

Implications for Classroom Teachers and Librarians

The issues previously discussed hold many implications for classroom teachers and librarians. Five issues in particular are important to understand: the role of teachers and librarians in selecting the literature, the influence of cultural values and beliefs, the role of books in influencing cultural perceptions, the need for culturally authentic materials, and the role of teachers and librarians as readers.

The Role of Teachers and Librarians in Selecting the Literature. The classroom teacher plays a critical role in influencing the literary experiences of students. First, teachers select the literature or guide students' selection of the literature. The background knowledge and the attitudes by which teachers and librarians view a culture will be important in this process. Librarians influence teachers as well as students because they decide which books to purchase and recommend books to library patrons. They can also make teachers and students aware of various books, again on the basis of their values and beliefs.

Even though the availability of books determines what is used in classrooms, teachers should be aware of the various countries represented in the United States and make every attempt to locate literature reflecting these various ethnic groups. This is especially important in the classroom. Children rely heavily on what teachers find and place in the classroom as resources.

Despite the need for more Asian American literature, there also needs to be a note of caution and a call to "weed" some books from various collections. Much of the older literature about Asian Americans depicts stereotyped or outdated understandings of Asian Americans. Such books only serve in a historical sense, giving an understanding of how these cultures were viewed during specific time periods in history. However, too often these books are still part of active library circulation, and newer books have not been added because of budgetary constraints. Because the awareness of the need for culturally accurate portrayals was not carefully regarded in the past, this problem needs immediate attention.

The Influence of Cultural Values and Beliefs. The degree of importance placed on culture varies from individual to individual. Some attempt to deny, ignore, or hide their heritage. Others live their heritage in such a way that they cannot imagine a life which is not centered around their cultural heritage. How students cope with these feelings is of importance to teachers. It is also important to understand that fundamental cultural values and beliefs guide the behavior of members of that culture (Ting-Toomey, 1990). The experiences of Asians who have just arrived in the United States will be different from that of subsequent generations who are born and raised in this country and have limited contact with the roots of their cultural heritage. Some have never been to the country of their cultural roots.

The Role of Books in Influencing Cultural Perceptions. Li and Li's (1990) summary of a study conducted on the "perceptions of Asian Americans" shows that many misperceptions and stereotypes still exist, and that the sources of these beliefs are media, films, and books. Therefore, books hold an important position in helping people formulate images of other cultures. This awareness reinforces the repeatedly stated need for culturally authentic books that transmit a culturally true view. In order to avoid the further development of stereotypes, multiple perspectives and multidimensional images of cultural groups are necessary. How we interact with others of differing cultures is determined by what we believe to be true about them (Ting-Toomey, 1990).

The Need for Culturally Authentic Materials. Locating culturally authentic materials is critically important. Because it is impossible to know about all of the world's cultures, reliance on a variety of resources is important. It is also necessary to understand that because people have individual experiences within each culture, each person's perception of a culture may vary somewhat by the specific experiences that person has had within the culture. Therefore, what may seem to reflect an Asian American experience to some may not be indicative of another's experiences. Understanding this will help teachers realize the need for books which show multiple perspectives and multiple experiences within each cultural group.

The Role of Teachers and Librarians as Readers. Peter Li (1992) attributes the success of such books as Maxine Hong Kingston's *Woman Warrior* (1976) and Amy Tan's *The Joy Luck Club* (1989) to the fact that Asian American literature has come into its own at the adult level. He cites the reasons as the artistic merit of these works and their ability to help readers become exposed to Asian and Asian American experiences. Teachers must also become readers of Asian American literature at all levels in order to gain an understanding of the various cultures through literature. This is what we hope will happen with the students we teach; teachers can first model such a vicarious acquisition of a cultural understanding by becoming readers of Asian American literature themselves.

The issues surrounding Asian and Asian American literature for children are numerous. Although some are still under considerable discussion, one thing is certain: as educators, we have a responsibility to provide our students with the best literature available and to raise their awareness as well as our own awareness of the cultural heritage of Asians and Asian Americans.

A Bibliography of Asian and
Asian American Literature for Children

This list emphasizes books which are currently available. Some older titles which may not be generally known are also included. Because a comprehensive list is not within the scope of this chapter, older and classic works that are more widely known have not been included. However, it is possible to cross-reference other titles by noting the names of authors and illustrators who are producing culturally authentic Asian and Asian American books for children. The annotations that follow each title, when enclosed in quotation marks, are taken from each book's Library of Congress Cataloging in Press information on the verso of the title page. The books are alphabetized by author, and the cultural group represented is named following the annotation if it is not apparent from the annotation itself.

Ai-Ling, Louie. (1982). *Yeh-Shen* (Ed Young, Illus.). New York: Philomel. "A young Chinese girl overcomes the wickedness of her stepmother and stepsister to become the bride of a prince."

Alexander, Lloyd. (1991). *The remarkable journey of Prince Jen*. New York: Dutton. "Bearing six unusual gifts, young Prince Jen embarks on a perilous quest and emerges triumphantly into manhood." (Chinese)

Bang, Molly. (1985). *The paper crane*. New York: Greenwillow. "A mysterious man enters a restaurant and pays for his dinner with a paper crane that magically comes alive and dances." (Japanese)

Birdseye, Tom. (1990). *A song of stars* (Ju-Hong Chen. Illus.). New York: Holiday House. "Although banished to opposite sides of the Milky Way, the princess weaver and the herdsman reunite each year on the seventh day of the seventh month."

Blia, Xiong. (1989). *Nine-in-One Grr! Grr! A folktale from the Hmong people of Laos* (Cathy Spagnoli, Adapt.; Nancy Horn, Illus.). San Francisco: Children's Book Press. "When the great god Shao promises Tiger nine cubs each year, Bird comes up with a clever trick to prevent the land from being overrun by tigers."

Blumberg, Rhoda. (1985). *Commodore Perry in the land of the Shogun*. New York: Lothrop, Lee & Shepard. "Details Commodore Matthew Perry's role in opening Japan's closed society to world trade in the 1850s, one of history's most significant diplomatic achievements."

Brown, Tricia. (1987). *Chinese New Year* (Fran Ortiz, Photog.). New York: Holt. "Text and photographs depict the celebration of Chinese New Year by Chinese Americans living in San Francisco's Chinatown."

Brown, Tricia. (1991). *Lee Ann: The story of a Vietnamese American girl* (Ted Thai, Illus.). New York: Putnam. "A young Vietnamese-American girl describes her family and school life, Saturday activities, and celebration of TET, the Vietnamese New Year."

Bryan, Ashley. (1988). *Sh-ko and his eight wicked brothers* (Fumio Yosluimura, Illus.). New York: Atheneum. "When his handsome older brothers set off to woo the beautiful Princess Yakami, ugly Sh-ko must carry their bags, but his luck changes after meeting a rabbit who lost his fur coat."

Cassedy, Sylvia, & Suetake, Kunihiro (trans.). (1992). *Red dragonfly on my shoulder*. New York: HarperCollins. "Thirteen haiku about animals, translated from the Japanese and illustrated with collages and assemblages."

Choi, Sook Nyul. (1991). *Year of impossible goodbyes*. Boston: Houghton Mifflin. "A young Korean girl survives the oppressive Japanese and Russian occupation of North Korea during the 1940s to later escape to freedom in South Korea."

Coerr, Eleanor. (1977). *Sadako and the thousand paper cranes* (Himler, Illus.). New York: Putnam. "Story based on the real life of a real girl who lived in Japan from 1943 to 1955. She died ten years later as a result of radiation from the bomb."

Coutant, Helen. (1974). *First snow* (Vo-Dinh Mai, Illus.). New York: Knopf. "With the help of her grandmother and the first snow she has ever seen, a little Vietnamese girl begins to understand how death can be accepted as a natural part of life."

Demi. (1980). *Liang and the magic painbrush*. New York: Holt. "A poor boy who longs to paint is given a magic brush that brings to life whatever he pictures."

Demi. (1990). *The magic boat*. New York: Holt. "When honest Chang is tricked out of his magic boat, he and his friends venture to win it back from wicked Ying and the greedy Emperor."

Demi. (1991). *Chingis Kahn*. New York: Holt. "A biography of the Mongol leader and military strategist who, at the height of his power, was supreme master of the largest empire ever created in the lifetime of one man."

Demi. (1991). *The artist and the architect*. New York: Holt. "In ancient China a jealous artist plans to eliminate the favorite architect of the Emperor."

Demi. (1991). *The empty pot*. New York: Holt. "When Ping admits that he is the only child in China unable to grow a flower from the seeds distributed by the Emperor, he is rewarded for his honesty."

Demi. (1991). *In the eyes of the cat*. New York: Holt. "A collection of Japanese nature poems organized according to the seasons."

Fritz, Jean. (1982). *Homesick*. New York: Putnam. "The author's fictionalized version, though all the events are true, of her childhood in China in the 1920s."

Fritz, Jean. (1985). *China homecoming.* New York: Putman. "The author returns to China, to relive her memories of her youth and to witness the many historical and social changes that have taken place since she left the country in 1928."

Fritz, Jean. (1988). *China's long march: 6,000 miles of danger.* New York: Putnam. "Describes the events of the 6,000 mile march undertaken by Mao Zedong and his Communist followers as they retreated before the forces of Chiang Kai-shek."

Fujimura, Hisakazu. (1988). *Ho-Lim lim: A rabbit tale from Japan* (Keizaburo Tejima, Illus.). New York: Putnam. "After one last foray far from his home, an aging rabbit decides he prefers to rest in his own garden and let his children and grandchildren bring him good things to eat."

Haugaard, Erik Christian. (1984). *The samurai's tale.* Boston: Houghton Mifflin. "In turbulent sixteenth-century Japan, orphaned Taro is taken in by a general serving the great warlord Takeda Shingen and grows up to become a samurai fighting for the enemies of his dead family."

Haugaard, Erik Christian. (1991). *The boy and the samurai.* Boston: Houghton Mifflin. "Having grown up as an orphan of the streets while sixteenth-century Japan is being ravaged by civil war, Saru seeks to help a Samurai rescue his wife from imprisonment by a warlord so they can all flee to a more peaceful life."

Hayashi, Akiko. (1989). *Aki and the fox.* New York: Doubleday. "Aki and her toy fox Kon make an adventurous journey to Grandma's house so that she can mend Kon's arm."

Ho, Minfong. (1991). *The clay marble.* New York: Farrar Straus Giroux. Twelve-year-old Dara and her family face the effects of war on their lives, trying to struggle as war refugees wanting to start their lives over.

Hoyt-Goldsmith, Diane. (1992). *Hoang Anh: A Vietnamese-American boy* (Lawrence Migdale, Photog.). New York: Holiday House. "A Vietnamese-American describes the daily activities of his family in San Rafael, California, and the traditional culture and customs that shape their lives."

Ishii, Momoko. (1982). *The tongue-cut sparrow* (Suekichi Akaba, Illus., Katherine Paterson, Trans.). New York: Lodestar. "A kind old man and his greedy wife pay separate visits to the tongue-cut sparrow and receive as gifts just what they deserve." (Japanese)

Levinson, Riki. (1988). *Our home is the sea* (Dennis Luzak, Illus.). New York: Dutton. "A Chinese boy hurries home from school to his family's houseboat in Hong Kong harbor. It is the end of the school year, and he is anxious to join his father and grandfather in their family profession, fishing."

Lord, Bette. (1984). *In the year of the boar and Jackie Robinson* (Marc Simot, Illus.). New York: Harper & Row. "In 1947, a Chinese child comes to Brooklyn where she becomes Americanized at school, in her apartment building, and by her love for baseball."

MacMillan, Dianne, & Freeman, Dorothy. (1987). *My best friend Duc Tran: Meeting a Vietnamese American family* (Mary Fane Begin, Illus.). New York: Julian Messner.

Mahy, Margaret. (1990). *The seven Chinese brothers* (Jean Tseng, Illus.). New York: Scholastic. "Seven Chinese brothers elude execution by virtue of their extraordinary individual qualities."

Maruki, Toshi. (1980). *Hiroshima no Pika*. New York: Lothrop, Lee & Shepard. "A retelling of a mother's account of what happened to her family during the Flash that destroyed Hiroshima in 1945."

Mattingley, Christobel. (1985). *The miracle tree* (Marianne Yamaguchi, Illus.). San Diego: Harcourt Brace Jovanovich. "Separated by the explosion of the atomic bomb, a husband, a wife, and mother carry on with their lives in the ruins of Nagasaki and are eventually reunited one Christmas by a very special tree."

Merrill, Jean. (1992). *The girl who loved caterpillars* (Floyd Cooper, Illus.). New York: Philomel. "In this retelling of an anonymous twelfth-century Japanese story, the young woman Izumi resists social and family pressures as she befriends caterpillars and other socially unacceptable creatures."

Morey, Janet, & Dunn, Wendy. (1992). *Famous Asian Americans*. New York: Cobblehill Books/Dutton. "Chronicles the lives and accomplishments of fourteen Asian Americans including Jose Aruego, Michael Chang, An Wang, and Ellison Onizuka."

Morimoto, Junko. (1987). *My Hiroshima*. New York: Viking. A personal account, reflecting on the survival of the bombing of Hiroshima, and what it was like to have been a child in the city during war time.

Nomura, Takaaki. (1991). *Grandfather's town*. Brooklyn, NY: Kane/Miller. "A young Japanese boy, worried that his grandfather is lonely, accompanies him to the public bath."

Paterson, Katherine. (1990). *The tale of the mandarin duck*. New York: Lodestar/Dutton. "A pair of mandarin ducks, separated by a cruel lord who wishes to possess the drake for his colorful beauty, reward a compassionate couple who risk their lives to reunite the ducks."

Rappaport, Doreen. (1991). *The journey of Meng* (Yang Ming-Yi, Illus.). New York: Dial. "A Chinese tale in which a woman goes in search of her husband who has been forced to be a slave for a cruel king."

Sakade, Florence (Ed.). (1990). *Japanese children's favorite stories* (Yoshisuke Kurosalsi, Illus.). Rutland, VT: Charles E. Tuttle. A collection of twenty of Japan's most well known tales, including "Little One-Inch," "The Badger and the Magic Fan," and "Peach Boy."

Say, Allen. (1982). *The bicycle man*. Boston: Parnassus Press/Houghton Mifflin. "The amazing tricks two American soldiers do on a borrowed bicycle are a fitting finale for the school sports day festivities in a small village in occupied Japan."

Say, Allen. (1988). *A river dream*. Boston: Houghton Mifflin. "While sick in bed, a young boy opens a box from his uncle and embarks on a fantastical fishing trip."

Say Allen. (1989). *The lost lake*. Boston: Houghton Mifflin. "A young boy and his father become closer during a camping trip in the mountains."

Say, Allen. (1990). *El Chino*. Boston: Houghton Mifflin. "A biography of Bill Wong, a Chinese American who became a famous bullfighter in Spain."

Say, Allen. (1991). *A tree of cranes*. Boston: Houghton Mifflin. "A Japanese boy learns of Christmas when his mother decorates a pine tree with paper cranes."

Say, Allen. (in press). *Grandfather's journey*. Boston: Houghton Mifflin.

Shute, Linda. (1986). *Momotaro: The peach boy*. New York: Lothrop, Lee & Shepard. "Found floating on the river inside a peach by an old couple, Momotaro grows up and fights the terrible demons who have terrorized the village for years."

Soto, Gary. (1992). *Pacific crossing*. San Diego: Harcourt Brace Jovanovich. "When Lincoln Mendoza and Tony Contreras, barrio brothers, go to Japan for the summer. . . Lincoln discovers what it means to be both Mexican and American and that Mitsuo, his Japanese brother, deserves a place next to Tony as the best kind of buddy a guy can have." (multicultural)

Staples, Suzanne Fisher. (1989). *Shabanu: Daughter of the wind*. New York: Knopf. When 11-year-old Shabanu, the daughter of a nomad in the Cholutan Desert of present-day Pakistan, is pledged in marriage to an older man whose money will bring prestige to the family, she must either accept the decision, as is the custom, or risk the consequence of defying her father's wishes.

Surat, Michele Maria. (1983). *Angel child, dragon child* (Vo-Dinh Mai, Illus.). Raintree. "Ut, a Vietnamese girl attending school in the United States, lonely for her mother left behind in Vietnam, makes a new friend who presents her with a wonderful gift."

Takeshita, Fumiko. (1988). *The park bench* (Mamoru Suzuki, Illus.). Brooklyn, NY: Kane/Miller. "All through the sunny day the white bench in the park provides pleasure for the many people who come by, from the old man taking a walk to the children playing in the park." (Bilingual Japanese/English text)

Turner, Ann. (1990). *Through moon and stars and night skies* (James Graham, Illus.). New York: HarperCollins. "A boy who came from far away to be adopted by a couple in this country remembers how unfamiliar and frightening some of the things were in his new home, before he accepted the love to be found there."

Uchida, Yoshiko, (1971). *Journey to Topaz*. New York: Scribner. "After the Pearl Harbor attack an eleven-year-old Japanese-American girl and her family are forced to go to an aliens' camp in Utah."

Uchida, Yoshiko. (1978). *Journey home*. New York: Atheneum. "After their release from an American concentration camp, a Japanese-American girl and her family try to reconstruct their lives amidst strong anti-Japanese feelings which breed fear, distrust, and violence."

Uchida, Yoshiko. (1981). *A jar of dreams*. New York: Atheneum. "A young girl grows up in a closely-knit Japanese American family in California during the 1930s, a time of great prejudice."

Uchida, Yoshiko. (1983). *The best bad thing*. New York: Atheneum. "At first dismayed at having to spend the last month of her summer vacation helping out in the household of recently widowed Mrs. Hata, Rinko discovers there are pleasant surprises for her, but then bad things start to happen. Sequel to *A Jar of Dreams*."

Uchida, Yoshiko. (1985). *The happiest ending*. New York: Atheneum. "When a twelve-year-old Rinko learns that a neighbor's daughter is coming from Japan to marry a stranger twice her age, she sets out to change this arrangement and gains new insight into love and adult problems."

Uchida, Yoshiko. (1987). *The two foolish cats* (Margot Zemach, Illus.). New York: Margaret K. McElderry. "Two foolish cats go to the old monkey of the mountain to settle their quarrel."

Uchida, Yoshiko. (1991). *The invisible thread*. New York: Julian Messner. "Children's author, Yoshiko Uchida, describes growing up in Berkeley, California, as a Nisei, second-generation Japanese American, and her family's internment in a Utah concentration camp during World War II."

Vuong, Lynette Dyer. (1982). *The brocaded slipper and other Vietnamese tales* (Vo-Dinh Mai, Illus.). New York: HarperCollins. "A collection of five Vietnamese fairy tales, including 'Little Finger of the Watermelon Patch' and 'Lampstand Princess'."

Watkins, Yoko Kawashima. (1986). *So far from the bamboo grove*. New York: Lothrop, Lee & Shepard. "A fictionalized autobiography in which eleven-year-old Yoko escapes from Korea to Japan with her mother and sister at the end of World War II."

Watkins, Yoko Kawashima. (1986). *Tales from the bamboo grove*. New York: Bradbury Press. The narrator relays the story of what it was like to be a Japanese child living in occupied China and trying to escape the country without being seen by the enemy.

Whelan, Gloria. (1992). *Goodbye, Vietnam*. New York: Knopf. "Thirteen-year-old Mai and her family embark on a dangerous sea voyage from Vietnam to Hong Kong to escape the unpredictable and often brutal Vietnamese government."

Yacowitz, Caryn. (1992). *The jade stone*. New York: Holiday House. "When the Great Emperor of all China commands him to carve a Dragon of Wind and Fire in a piece of perfect jade, Chan Lo discovers the stone wants to be something else."

Yee, Paul. (1991). *Roses sing on new snow*. New York: Macmillan. When the governor of South China visits the New World and wants to learn to prepare the delicious dish set before him, Maylin shows how the dish is an example of something based in the traditions of the Old World but transformed to the New World.

Yep, Laurence. (1975). *Dragonwings*. New York: Harper & Row. "In the early twentieth century a young Chinese boy joins his father in San Francisco and helps him realize his dream of making a flying machine."

Yep, Laurence. (1977). *Child of the owl.* New York: Harper & Row. "A twelve-year-old girl who knows little about her Chinese heritage is sent to live with her grandmother in San Francisco's Chinatown."

Yep, Laurence. (1979). *Sea glass.* New York: Harper & Row. "A Chinese-American boy whose father wants him to be good in sports finally asserts his right to be himself."

Yep, Laurence. (1989). *The rainbow people.* New York: Harper & Row. "A collection of twenty Chinese folk tales that were passed on by word of mouth for generation, as told by some oldtimers newly settled in the United States."

Yep, Laurence. (1991). *The lost garden.* Englewood Cliffs, NJ: Julian Messner. "The author describes how he grew up as a Chinese American in San Francisco and how he came to use his writing to celebrate his family and his ethnic heritage."

Yep, Laurence. (1991). *The star fisher.* New York: Morrow. "Fifteen-year-old Joan Lee and her family find the adjustment hard when they move from Ohio to West Virginia in the 1920s."

Young, Ed. (1989). *Lon Po Po.* New York: Putnam. A Chinese "Red Riding Hood" story in which the wolf comes to visit the home of children who are left.

Zhensun, Zheng, & Low, Alice. (1991). *A young painter* (Wang Yani, Illus.). New York: Scholastic. "Examines the life and works of the young Chinese girl who started painting animals at the age of three and in her teens became the youngest artist to have a one-person show at the Smithsonian Institution."

Bibliography

Aoki, E. (1992). Turning the page: Asian Pacific American children's literature. In V. J. Harris (Ed.), *Teaching multicultural literature in grades K–8* (pp. 109–135). Norwood, MA: Christopher-Gordon.

Chu, E., & Schuler, C. V. (1992). United States: Asian Americans. In L. Miller-Lachman (Ed.), *Our family, our friends, our world : An annotated guide to significant multicultural books for children and teenagers* (pp. 93–120). New Providence, NJ: R. R. Bowker.

Cullinan, B. (1989). *Literature and the child,* (2nd ed.). San Diego, CA: Harcourt, Brace Jovanovich.

Greenblatt, M. (1992). *Southern and Central Asia.* In L. Miller-Lachman (Ed.), *Our family, our friends, our world : An annotated guide to significant multicultural books for children and teenagers* (pp. 473–492). New Providence, NJ: R. R. Bowker.

Huck, C., Hepler, S.. & Hickman, J. (1987). *Children's literature in the elementary school* (4th ed.). New York: Holt.

Jenkins, E., & Austin, M. (1987). *Literature for children about Asians and Asian Americans: Analysis and annotated bibliography with additional readings for adults.* Westport, CN: Greenwood.

Kingston, M. H. (1976). *Woman Warrior.* New York: Vintage International.

Lee, G., Lo, S., & Ma, S. (1992). *East Asia.* In L. Miller-Lachman (Ed.), *Our family, our friends, our world : An annotated guide to significant multicultural books for children and teenagers* (pp. 493–527). New Providence, NJ: R. R. Bowker.

Lee, G., Lo, S., & Ma, S. (1992). *Southeast Asia.* In L. Miller-Lachman (Ed.), *Our family, our friends, our world : An annotated guide to significant multicultural books for children and teenagers* (pp. 529–545). New Providence, NJ: R. R. Bowker.

Li, M. H., & Li, P. (Eds.) (1990). *Understanding Asian Americans: A curriculum resource guide.* New York: Neal-Schuman.

Li, P. (1990). In M. H. Li & P. Li. *Understanding Asian Americans: A curriculum resource guide.* New York: Neal-Schuman Publishers.

Lukens, R. (1990). *A critical handbook of children's literature* (4th ed.). Glenview, IL: Scott Foresman/Little, Brown.

Miller-Lachman, L. (Ed.) (1992). *Our family, our friends, our world : An annotated guide to significant multicultural books for children and teenagers.* New Providence, NJ: R. R. Bowker.

Morgan, A. L. (1991). Long ago and far away in Vietnam: Yesterday's folktales for today's children. *The New Advocate, 4*(1), 47–56.

Norton, D. (1991). *Through the eyes of a child: An introduction to children's literature* (3rd ed.). Columbus, OH: Charles Merrill.

Tan, A. (1989). *Joy luck club.* New York: Putnam.

Ting-Toomey, S. (1990). *Stereotypes and misperceptions.* In M. H. Li & P. Li (Eds.), *Understanding Asian Americans: A curriculum resource guide.* New York: Neal-Schuman.

14

Why a Dialogic Pedagogy? Making Space for Possible Worlds[1]

Suzanne M. Miller

Although all of the contributors to this volume agree that open-mindedness about human difference is the proper human disposition, they also suggest that it is not the "natural" one. Typically, any unconsidered human response to people and ideas which are different or "foreign" tends to be negative. The articles from this section, "The Teacher's Perspective," along with many of the papers in this book, thus pose an important question: How, practically, do we help students learn to respect and value sociocultural difference in our richly diverse society and world? More particularly, can we effect such a revolution in consciousness through literature study? Taken together, the essays by Harris, Muhammad, Sharma Knippling, and Yokota point toward a shared answer: we need to diversify the curricular canon and teach about cultures. But just as striking, they all conclude that these alone will not be sufficient goals in our classrooms.

To begin with, curricular change poses unsettling problems. Morris and Sutherland document the basic difficulties for school districts of identifying and selecting representative materials, Muhammad warns about "token inclusion," and Sharma Knippling insists that we question any "exclusionist process of selection." Purves points to the practical problems of limited curricular time and space for studying all possible cultures and subcultures, what Stimpson calls the strain of encyclopedic "information overload." Harris, though, provides a sensible framework for teachers to begin transforming literature programs; she argues that individuals engage in ongoing reflection about what multicultural literacies are, why they are important, and what students in their classroom contexts need.

There is much evidence in these chapters that adding multicultural texts to the curriculum is important, yet will not by itself create respect for cultural difference. As Sharma Knippling illustrates, North American university students often tend to read from a dominant cultural perspective and reject the "alien" text. In the case study of her multiethnic seventh-grade class, Muhammad depicts the inadequacy of attempting to sensitize students to cultural difference simply by adding "a global list of books" to a curriculum. Even carefully chosen, authentic ethnic literature, Gonzales shows, can be misused, possibly creating cultural bias rather than affirmation of difference.

Consequently, in this volume and elsewhere, providing knowledge that puts multicultural literatures in their cultural context has been a suggested pedagogical approach. This is an important strategy, one that Purves and Sharma Knippling examine in their own teaching. Yet to the extent that such information is treated as defining group member-ships, it may encourage stereotyping, much like the "cultural norms" Gonzales points to as possibly limiting ethnic identity (for example, Native Americans all live in harmony with nature in rural settings). But further, Sharma Knippling problematizes the very term *multiculturalism* as "delusory because cultures are, in fact, systematically stratified and hierarchicized," so that students typically study "other (minority) cultures," not all cultures: that is, if multiculturalism is an issue for all of us, if we are making a true "multicultural commitment," she argues, we need to examine the assumptions and practices of the dominant culture, not just include information and texts from "other" cultures.

One of those dominant cultural practices is the traditional way of talking about texts in literature classes, an approach that promotes the dominant cultural interpretation and silences other perspectives. Here is where our attention may fruitfully turn from curricular knowledge content to a pedagogy for a multicultural society. Sharma Knippling steadfastly pursues this issue of "what actually transpires in the classroom when American readers encounter a multicultural text." Gonzales, Purves, and Muhammad also pursue varied productive strategies for students to construct their perspectives of their own and others' cultures through discussion and writing. A recurring theme in this volume is our need to change how teachers interact with students in order to transform typical classroom contexts with a new worldview. I believe it is crucial that we learn how to teach ways of reading and talking about literature which create respect for multiple sociocultural perspectives and provide the means for learning to understand them.

To that end, I want to suggest the promise of what I call a "dialogic pedagogy." Derived from a synthesis of results from my empirical studies of open-forum literature discussions, the fundamental principles of this classroom approach were sounded frequently in the preceding chapters. Its dynamic, transformative aspects derive from reconstruing the purposes for literacy and literature. In this commentary, I first discuss the role of literature in a dialogic pedagogy in contrast to traditional American literature instruction. Then I elaborate the major principles that I have found consistently in innovative classrooms where discussing and writing about texts from multiple perspectives have begun to transform student thinking over time.

The Role of Literature Discussion. Literary theory and numerous empirical studies over the past twenty years have examined how individual readers compose different readings from the same literary text: in creating meaning the reader taps her or his own fund of feelings, beliefs, attitudes, languages, and sociocultural experiences (Applebee, 1977; Beach & Hynds, 1990; Rosenblatt, 1978). Literature invites such personalized reading because it is inherently problematic, with its ambiguous, metaphoric language and gaps in knowledge that require searching for likely connections between events, generating possible links between human intention and action, and testing a personal sense of lifelikeness (Bruner, 1986; Iser, 1978; Langer, 1990). Thus reading literature can stimulate readers' imagination and reflection, as psychologist Jerome Bruner describes it, a "trafficking in human possibilities rather than settled certainties" (1986, p. 26). Literature thereby opens us "to dilemmas, to the hypothetical, to the range of possible worlds that a text can refer to" (p. 159).

Because of the problematic nature of texts and the sociocultural diversities of readers, then, text discussion can be particularly suited to provoke an interplay of differences. Gonzales, Muhammad, and Sharma Knippling in this volume similarly point to the need for a critical dialogue among differences as the starting point of growth in multicultural consciousness. Support for literature discussion as a means of developing sociocultural awareness and critical reflection also comes from the fields of sociolinguistics, sociohistorical psychology, literary criticism, and literacy pedagogy.

In *The Psychology of Art*, Vygotsky (1971) argues that it is imperative to allow for the effects of literature that "shape and excite" the individual reader on an unconscious level, but that the teacher should aim, further, to form reflective consciousness through "intelligent social activity" that extends the "narrow sphere of individual perception" (pp. 79–80). Similarly, Rosenblatt (1978) (and other reader-response literary theorists) contend that students need to articulate their varied responses to texts in "an environment favorable to uninhibited interchange, as the starting point for growth in critical power" (p. 146). When the text becomes a "more general medium of communication among readers," such discussion can reveal values, assumptions, and life experiences based in cultures or subcultures, including questioning of dominant cultural "truths." When alternatives challenge a reader's assumptions and understandings, "he may be stimulated to clarify his own values, his own prior sense of the world and its possibilities" (p. 145). Teachers and theorists, then, argue that text discussion can provide students with the motivating occasion to derive a new critical awareness of the bases for their own and others' sociocultural perspectives.

Authoritarian Classroom Contexts. But over the century empirical evidence suggests that such reflection about different perspectives in discussion rarely occurs in American schools. Even in literature class some teachers persistently use the recitation—asking closed questions and evaluating the correctness of student answers—as the main structure of classroom talk. This pattern is quite consistent with the emphasis on evaluation and testing of discrete facts and skills in our educational system. Studies of literary instruction often describe how students are cut off from their own sociocultural response and thinking by the teacher's insistence on a "correct," culture-bound translation (Marshall, 1987). In such contexts, students consume interpretations, replete with their "cultural blindnesses and habits of mind" (Carr, 1990). It is not surprising, then, that results of recent large-scale testing in the United States suggest that most students have not learned to reflect about their own interpretations of what they read (National Assessment of Educational Progress, 1981; also, Applebee, Langer & Mullis, 1989). International studies suggest, as well, that students learn culturally approved ways of responding to what they read, narrowing their responses to literature as they move through each country's education system, and eventually mirroring their teachers' dominant cultural interpretations (Purves, 1973, 1981; Steffensen, Joag-Des, & Anderson, 1979; Dollerup, 1983–1989).

A Model for a Dialogic Pedagogy from Empirical Studies

Over the past six years, I have investigated what roles the secondary school teacher might play in promoting growth in students' reflection about sociocultural perspectives through text discussions

(Miller, 1988, 1990, 1991a, 1991b, 1992a, 1992b, 1992c, 1992d, 1993, in press). To begin, I observed widely in schools to identify teachers who had successfully introduced open-forum discussion into multicultural classroom groups. These groups included African American, Asian American, and Latino/Latina students—cultural groups sometimes relegated to a "culture of silence" (Freire, 1970) in our predominantly European American society. Such discussion classes were difficult to find. For example, in one school noted for its progressive teaching approaches, only 10 percent of the English teachers held discussions, defined in the studies as putting forth and examining more than one point of view (Bridges, 1979). The classes I did identify as using open-forum discussions were in urban and suburban schools, in both rich and poor communities. The teachers were mostly women with more than fifteen years' experience, both African and European Americans.

In the series of ethnographic studies in five schools, I examined (1) how teachers transformed ways of talking typical in classrooms to promote reflection through text discussion and (2) what new ways of thinking about alternative perspectives developed in these social-cognitive contexts over time.

During the yearlong observations in each of ten case study classes, I audiotaped discussions, transcribed them, and interviewed students and teachers about their perceptions of the purposes for discussion, the roles participants played, and the thinking that occurred. Through recursive analysis of the different data types and participant perspectives, I identified recurring themes and examined their relationships to identify the patterns in each context which prompted and shaped student reflection.

The teachers who successfully transformed the typical classroom context focused on creating conditions that produced motivated discussion about texts. Working within similar sets of principles, these teachers fostered what students called "the right atmosphere for discussion," arousing student response and reflection about differences in four closely connected, mutually reinforcing ways. Successful teachers (1) initiated ways of talking which induced a new stance toward texts; (2) provoked collaborative reflection about alternative responses and interpretations; (3) when necessary, scaffolded learning of heuristic strategies for making and examining meanings; and (4) encouraged student-initiated and sustained inquiry. In what follows I elaborate each condition in turn, drawing on my studies and the chapters in this book for examples of productive strategies.

Making Space for Difference

First of all, teachers who successfully transformed classroom ways of talking did nothing less than create a new classroom epistemology. In their verbal and nonverbal behaviors they created a space where texts were open to multiple interpretations and ways of knowing. In essence, these teachers initiated a new learning community by sending consistent messages that they would not function as the class text authority and by encouraging students to respond to and question the text and each other to make and examine their own meanings.

These new role expectations and purposes were communicated persistently in many ways. Sometimes the teachers signaled a distribution of authority physically—often placing the desks in a circle and sitting there with students. They asked genuine questions about what puzzled them in the text and about how different students responded: for example, asking in a perplexed tone, "I wondered why that last reason was different—What do you think?" or "How do you feel about Holden Caufield so far?" They focused on students' learning to ask questions of texts during reading and journal writing and to take those questions to discussion and further reading and writing. They helped students learn to try out answers that held a text problem open to possibilities by patiently exhibiting and encouraging new behaviors that avoided absolute statements. For instance, they modeled a reflective tentativeness in speech, often beginning with "I'm not sure" or "Maybe" or "Could it be?" They focused attention on students' making and considering meanings by allowing long silences for thinking and not evaluating the "truth" of responses.

In general, these teachers communicated that reading itself was dialogic: that is, students had to question and speak for the text in the words of their own languages in order to understand (Gadamer, 1976; Salvatori, 1986), and not depend on teacher translators. As Sharma Knippling argues, in a classroom structured for discussion the teacher must avoid providing "fossilized information" and provide the means of learning "not the articulation of right answers but right questions." To this end, students learned to annotate the text margins with their own questions and responses, a written dialogue with the author of the text that promotes reading with *and* against the grain, as Gonzales recommends. By capturing responses and questions in response journals, students materialized initial reactions and thinking, making them available for further reflection in discussion and writing. Successful teachers moved students to a space where multicultural interpretations could be produced and examined, where power relations were restructured to unsilence students.

Successful teachers also provided a consistent sense of group purpose through procedural explanations and descriptions that gave students the "feel" for collaborating in discussion. One teacher, for instance, emphasized social-cognitive strategies for listening actively ("Look at the speaker," "Try to understand"). She suggested often that students respond to the previous speaker so that "meanings can build and grow." The class spent time talking about whether their discussions were successful and about what that meant to them. Consistent ground rules and metacommunication of these kinds helped them to construct their discussion goals. Students in that group often told the story of developing respect for difference, "how we learned to listen" because "[we] were trying to understand together."

Many students accustomed to passivity in traditional classrooms dominated by teacher interpretations at first, like Enrique, a Puerto Rican boy, were quiet and just observed to learn "what we were supposed to do." In time, some students took up the invitation to see themselves in new roles—as composers of meaning who actively performed their own understandings. Differences emerged, and meaning itself became problematic. As students tried to understand emerging alternatives, that new attitude contributed to the developing atmosphere of safety, a respect for difference which encouraged others to pose questions and take the risk of casting the text into their own sociocultural terms. Similarly, Hasna Muhammad moved away from teacher-directed activity and found that students' writing and discussing to cast the text into their own stories, habits, and languages created the best multicultural environment, a "safe place for students to discover and to react to the culturally diverse world around them."

In such a new climate for discussion, Enrique said he eventually became "not afraid to talk out" in discussions. Student interviews revealed that an incentive of making sense through talking (Britton, 1970) grew out of students' growing feeling of authority to talk back to texts. With their teachers' assistance, then, students were developing a reflective stance, approaching the text as an artifact to be questioned and transformed by readers interpreting and discussing, as "an occasion for meaning, not a meaning in itself" (Bartholomae & Petrosky, 1986). As in a just society committed to multiculturalism, the different students in the class needed to play a part, have a voice, make meanings, and reflect on diverse understandings.

In contrast, when this crucial first step of creating a new stance toward meanings was undermined, discussion failed. In a few contexts teachers asked for student interpretations of open-ended questions, but then in other ways signaled that the literary text contained a single, authoritative meaning. For instance, in one class, students offered different interpretations of an Aristotle excerpt, but the teacher prodded students toward one interpretation, discouraging differences as failures in thinking rather than promoting them as opportunities for reflection. Eventually the teacher spoke for the author, telling students "what Aristotle is saying." These students became increasingly passive, waiting "to see if we had the right answer." Without an authentic "sense-making" activity there was no motivation for thoughtful engagement, no perplexity, no problem, no "matter at stake" to provoke response and reflection (Dewey, 1933). Only when students felt the interpretive authority that motivated them to break the silence and generate responses from their own sociocultural perspectives did a dialogic "problem-solving environment" (Vygotsky, 1981) begin to emerge.

Provoking Collaborative Reflection about Alternatives

Still, as individual responses materialized in oral language, students were at first surprised by their varied perspectives. Challenged by these multiple ways of understanding, some students dogmatically asserted, as one student put it, "I'm right, I know I'm right." In response, successful teachers prompted collaborative reflection about alternatives by provoking expression and exploration of possibilities and by providing socially useful strategies for responding reflectively to differences.

In particular, successful teachers modeled probing strategies for responding to different perspectives. Frequently they questioned in a puzzled tone, "So are you saying. . ."? or "So why do you say that?" Students tried these useful strategies as conversational responses to others' alternative responses and interpretations. Requesting and providing clarification and explanation were thus learned in their context for immediate use in discussion.

To prompt collaborative reflection, successful teachers often questioned to generate or emphasize student problems and differences. For instance, they sought alternatives to hold open interpretative possibilities—"Any other ideas?" They dramatized existing differences to prompt explanation—"So you say Holden was crazy, or normal, or both—where do you stand?" Successful teachers monitored student nonverbal reactions to encourage questioning of difference: "You look puzzled, Antoine; did you want to ask Anna a question about what she said?" Or when a student asked a question, these teachers made sure the group considered it as an authentic problem worth pursuing together: "Let's go back to Julie's question. 'Why does that last line contradict?' What do you think?" By guiding students to raise their questions about different perspectives orally and consider them together, teachers were urging students to pursue personal understanding in a public dialectic.

In that same spirit, the most successful teachers asked students to bring evidence from their lives into the discussion. Often they asked for personal experience—"Has that ever happened to you?" and sometimes they modeled how their own stories served as justification for meaning—"That reminds me of something that happened in my family." Hearing different sources of support for interpretations, students began to see how sociocultural experiences influenced their views of texts and the world.

To illustrate, in one urban-school discussion sequence two ninth-graders questioned each other to try to make sense of their different interpretations of a character. Ma Li, a newly immigrated Chinese American girl from a professional family, responded with examples of how "I think about myself to solve problems" in life. But for Andre, a popular African American boy from a poor urban neighborhood, thinking about himself was something painful to be avoided because the future was uncertain; he explained, "I don't know, I could be a junkie in ten years." Drawing on personal experiences rooted in socially learned languages (of family, neighborhood, ethnic group), each student's way of speaking and knowing were thrown into relief against the other languages for conceptualizing the world. Ma Li and Andre explained and questioned each other in a serious way, prompting examination of the grounds for assumptions or beliefs and an awareness of the sociocultural bases for their different views. (It should be noted that, for many reasons, this conversation about difference was unlikely to happen on its own in the school hallways.)

Finally, some successful teachers introduced critical perspectives students had not, to provoke a new dialectic or to problematize unexamined assumptions in the text or the discussion. Teachers suggested, for example, that Jane Eyre might be unable to see how her position as a woman diminished her choices in that society, that Conrad's perspective might be limited by racist social norms of his time, or that working harder might not solve the problems of an immigrant family. Such critical perspectives introduced as possibilities sometimes prompted the questioning of the dominant cultural assumptions and values of the text, similar to what Sharma Knippling and Gonzales call "reading against the grain." As Sharma Knippling suggests, teachers must ask not only, "What is proposed and incorporated in this text?" but also, "What is subordinated or ignored?" Pairing canonical and postcolonial texts and prodding for comparisons and contrasts serves as another strategy for problematizing the interaction of dominant and marginal cultures to reveal both their mutual influence and the hidden silencing induced through power relations.

In all, the monitoring stream of the dialogue—the questioning, challenging, evaluative one—was introduced as a strategic response to the stream of generated alternatives. Successful teachers actively guided the talk to create a strong sense of purposeful collaborative activity, at the same time that they provided specific strategies for engaging in reflective dialogue about differences. Thus, as they moved class talk to a space where difference flourished, they helped students learn how to respond so that the tension of difference could produce mutual growth. Provoked socially to respond to questions and differences, students became aware of their interpretation as one among many and, with support, began to learn to articulate the assumptions and attitudes evident in their own and others' perspectives.

Scaffolding Dialogic Routines

A third condition in the successful classes was this: teachers scaffolded learning of heuristic strategies. That is, when students needed assistance, teachers conversationally supported their activity by providing appropriate strategies for elaborating and questioning their responses and meanings. Effective teachers saw their role in scaffolding these heuristics, or often-repeated sequences of questions, as stimulating inquiry by providing useful tools for considering individual reactions, questions, and differences, tools students eventually could use on their own. Overall, the strategies and routines supported the move from initial responses toward more reasoned ones in a dialogic procedure that shuttled between text and self, reaction and reflection, personal response and public responsibilities.

For example, one teacher used a questioning routine to encourage personal connections: she would ask for student response to character action, follow up by asking, "Can you connect that to your experience?" and, then, in response to students' experiences, ask, "So what do you make of the character based on your experiences?" This sequence of questioning helped students consciously draw on personal sociocultural knowledge to inform their text understanding and evaluation.

These repeated intellectual routines shaped context-specific ways of talking and thinking about texts and sociocultural perspectives. In another dialogic heuristic, a teacher used questions to structure movement away from the text by asking students to speak for a part of the text—What do you think that means?" and then ask themselves, "Do you think that is true from your experience?" Or when a student made a claim about the text, the teacher asked, "Could you give an example?" When the student gave an example, the teacher asked conversationally for an explanation, and after that she asked for how it all connected to the question they were pursuing. In this class students learned this way of structuring their arguments to justify their claims, particularly by evaluating the text with their own lives. Gonzales emphasizes a similar heuristic learned through using two-column journal entries with questions asking students to point out story statements and actions and then moving to the students' own experiences as a means of deciding to accept or reject the author's perspectives. Another teacher helped structure students' critique of conflicting meanings for texts and the world by asking in conversations, "Whose perspective is that interpretation from?" followed by, "What group's motives does s/he represent?" then, "What alternatives are ignored?" and, "What are the consequences for others?" This heuristic served as a tactic for examining the politics of difference by questioning social privilege and inquiring into the value of social justice.

In Vygotsky's sense (1978) the teachers were lending their structuring consciousness to support student reflection, a kind of instructional scaffolding (Bruner, 1978; Langer & Applebee, 1986) which supported new ways of thinking about texts and alternative perspectives. Other teachers similarly used sequences of questions as structured dialectics for making and evaluating meanings—to prompt students to find problems in texts, hypothesize explanations, and move from character actions to intentions. Students began to use the specific discussion routines to interpret the text, to understand their own and others' perspectives, and to persuade others in the class. The dialectic movements served as the basis for reflection, helping students to consider their own and others' questions, assumptions, and habits of mind.

Allowing Student-Initiated and Sustained Dialogic Inquiry

Finally, successful teachers patiently monitored changes in students' abilities to use these new ways of thinking. Over time students needed less assistance: after weeks of discussion, students began to raise their own questions and initiate scaffolded strategies and routines to pursue understandings together. This development is consonant with Vygotsky's (1978, 1981) formulation that complex cognitive processes originate in assisted performances through social interactions around purposeful activity. Students internalized help from teachers and students as those strategies and routines solved perceived problems of understanding, and thus became socially useful for interpreting or evaluating meanings in their groups.

For example, after five months of discussion, tenth-graders in a general English class initiated the opening question for the first time and pursued differing perspectives on the advisability of fighting for freedom at all costs in a discussion of Thucydides' dramatization from *The Peloponnesian Wars*. When Terry, an African American girl, responded to another's claim that "just causes win," she called into question this cultural homily with counterexamples from her life in the city to illustrate that "that's a fairy tale." Her argument was structured by the heuristic she had learned in discussion for justifying her claims. In lengthy collaborations (for example, thirty turns of talk) without teacher help, students monitored their understanding of meanings, requesting translation ("So are you saying. . .?") and calling to question ("So why do you say that?") for the purpose of making sense out of alternative versions of reality. The dual streams of critical reflection—generating meanings and questioning and monitoring them—were thus dramatized as different voices in discussion. These negotiations spurred clarifications and justifications as students used their new dialectic routines, moving back and forth between text and self, between their personal responses and the needs of the group to understand and be persuaded. In the end, as one student put it, the teacher was able to "slowly break away," and the students felt amazed by what they had done together. Discussion was never the same in that class.

As students became inclined to take over both parts of the discussion talk, at times sustaining it themselves, they shuttled between generating responses, ideas, and interpretations *and* questioning, testing, and evaluating them. Increasingly they asked substantive and probing questions, provided evidence and evaluation, and collaborated without teacher intervention. Thus, in peer collaboration students' scaffolded each other and began to internalize an interdependent phase of strategy use (Tudge, 1990). Their change was most evident in their developing ability to "participate in qualitatively new collaborative activities" (Moll, 1990) as their group appropriated new ways of thinking with language.

Evidence thus suggests that discussion experiences shaped a new dialogic consciousness in students, characterized by both conscious self-reflexive strategies and the intellectual disposition to use them. In stimulated-recall interviews individual students frequently reported their internal dialogues with the oral discussion texts, where they directed and guided their own thinking with self-conversation, a significant transition to taking control through self-assistance (Gallimore & Tharp, 1990). Their conscious use of scaffolded cognitive strategies was evident as they pointed to, for instance, how they used questions to spur their own and others' thinking. One student reported the strong influence of his new internal dialogue: "After literature discussions I have discussions in my mind, so it is hard to concentrate in gym [physical education] class."

The dialogic strategies can be seen as language tools. They were produced through social activity to mediate texts and readers talking, but gradually formed students' inner activity (Hedegaard, 1990; Leontiev, 1978; Moll, 1990; Vygotsky, 1978). Through dialogic transformations, students internalized the reflective processes which originated in the constructive conflict of difference. The qualitative changes in students' motivation and collaborative thinking activities constitute an internalization of cognitive tools (Moll, 1990; Hedegaard, 1990), evident as students mutually invited and guided each other, no longer in need of teacher help.

Creating Dialogic Consciousness from Multicultural Difference

Taken together, these empirical investigations provide evidence that in contexts open to multiple perspectives, students can learn to respond actively, and reflect critically on different ways of speaking and knowing. In their dialogic pedagogy, teachers initiated new roles, the motivating tasks, the social purposes for talking, and they provided assistance at points of need. In the presence of sociocultural differences, they pressed for explanation, for evidence, for understanding. Over time, their students became aware of the multiple, sometimes conflicting languages (e.g., of classes, races, genders, families, ethnic communities) for understanding (Bakhtin, 1981).

Creating this change is a dynamic process that begins with a classroom culture where difference is valued and develops through the play of tension and release that structures attempts to understand (Gadamer, 1976). Students learned firsthand the pull of other ways of shaping the world. Discussion provided the means of testing ideas from multiple perspectives, by questioning the basis for attitudes, ideas, beliefs, and views. With teacher scaffolding, students learned how to move from unreflective speech to reflect consciously about the world through others' eyes. Such dialogic thinking moved back and forth from self to others and among opposing points of view. The importance of discussing multiple perspectives in multicultural education centers in this developing dialogic consciousness. It is the means of achieving awareness of one's own and others' assumptions and values, of creating a reasoned position beyond sociocentrism.

In interviews these teachers revealed that changes in their approaches to literature instruction began through conversations with other teachers (and then with themselves) about how reader-response and language-use theories could inform teaching and learning in their classes. They "read" each class to find ways to enact their social-cognitive goals. Through their dialogues with students, as they reflected about what was happening, about what students could learn to do through supported conversation, the teachers developed, as well. They developed ways of taking a dialogic stance toward each class, trans-forming each social-cognitive context by responding to what students there needed. When an at-risk class had trouble reading, one teacher read aloud and stopped to model, explain, and engage students in meaning-making and questioning strategies; her college-bound students she found required less support. When the class was largely European American, some teachers introduced critical perspectives that students did not generate on their own to question dominant cultural perspec-tives, to seek out what was excluded or marginalized in texts. For these successful teachers, teaching became an ongoing reflective conversation continually under construction by students and a teacher, "a human drama, not a mechanical device" (Petrosky, 1992, p. 164).

Many have noted that discussion is not ethically neutral, but is associated with moral or social values of justice and respect for persons (Bridges, 1979; Paul, 1984). These changes I have described in the fabric of the social relations in classrooms encouraged social and cognitive values fundamental to a democratic classroom culture, producing the motivation for critical reflection. Students became inclined to raise and pursue questions and to socially justify beliefs as bases for decisions rather than accept dogma, authority and tradition without reflection.

With their teachers' help, students in discussion-centered classes were cognitively transforming themselves, developing the means of understanding diversity rather than insisting on one authoritarian, culture-bound perspective. Through literature discussions in one class, Jack, a European American, described how he and his classmates changed from a "debating" attitude of "disputing" and "talking at" those who differed, to an ability to listen to and "talk with" others. He concluded that alternative perspectives could exist simultaneously: "You don't have to come to 'That's the way it is!' and 'That's the point!' [He pounded the desk.] You can just keep on talking about it, you know.

And there are so many points of view, I don't think anybody ever could totally agree in discussion." As he learned to respect different perspectives, learning from those differences became natural.

Particularly when texts posed problems about difference, students were often challenged to think about culture, race, class, and gender. When one white tenth-grader, Sam, argued that the racism in *To Kill a Mockingbird* no longer existed, his mixed-race classmate Desiree told a different story about her experiences with racism in their school and in the local shopping mall. The teacher asked students to consider why these representations differed and prompted examination of sociopolitical conditions in their largely white community. Later Desiree wrote one of her stories to illustrate local intolerance to difference, and Sam, newly aware, chose to investigate racism in America for his research paper. In this and other classes, students were beginning to struggle with issues of difference and social justice. Although few teachers persistently engaged students in the kind of rigorous sociocultural critique of rhetoric and institutions that Knoblauch and Brannon (1993) call "critical teaching," these teachers were beginning to open conversations, to work out the possibilities and the difficulties of such a pedagogy in the sociopolitical realities of their secondary schools.

As we teachers begin to reflect on how to create new classroom contexts where supported dialogues can develop in discussion, writing, and group activity, we can begin to develop pedagogies and meaningful occasions to transform our students' thinking in these ways. If, instead, multicultural education becomes only new booklists and cultural information, a curricular add-on for "minorities," it may fail to become an integral part of schooling, possibly deleted later under time pressures. The question "Who is multicultural education for?" is a crucial one (Sharma Knippling, this volume). These dialogues in classrooms benefitted all students. Even Nicole, so fearful of losing her thoughts that she never spoke in discussion, described how she was drawn into an ongoing internal dialogue. Friere's pedagogy of knowing subjects achieving significance through dialogue was negotiated in these classrooms: "The pursuit of full humanity, however, cannot be carried out in isolation or individualism, but only in fellowship" (1970, p. 73). Discussion clearly contributed to individual reflection but more than that, it contributed to a sense of the group through interdependent relations, resulting in a valuing of diversity and collaboration that are central to social justice. Many educators focus on our country's need to find similarities as well as differences among our sociocultural groups. Discussion, I want to emphasize, also reveals such "common ground" (Sutherland, this volume). Individuals are rarely monolithic in their cultural makeup. As members of several subcultures in our largely immigrant society, students when discussing felt their "contradictory cultural makeup" (Sharma Knippling, this volume) that ensured diversity even in classes superficially homogeneous. But further, agreements and disagreements in class discussions of texts I observed rarely fell along racial or ethnic lines. As socially justifying beliefs became valued, students began to explore their similarities and differences on this rational basis. Multicultural groups with a common perspective worked together to elaborate their arguments.

Consider the case of Mei Wong. After ten discussions this shy Chinese American first spoke, giving an extended synthesis of the group's interpretation from her point of view. Her classmates, for the first and only time all year, applauded. They understood her courage in trying her voice and appreciated her convincing summary as evidence of their success. In short, students also learned that they did have "bright flags" of commonality (Stimpson, this volume); these "unities," however, were created in talking together, not from lessons told by teachers.

If all students are to become more powerfully literate in our complex, multicultural world, I believe we must begin by creating classroom contexts where motivated discussion, supported by teachers at points of need, provokes the dialectic of critical reflection. The problems of social justice, intercultural and interethnic contacts and peaceful coexistence of peoples are central issues in contemporary societies. Developing theory and practice to guide us in educating our students for life in multicultural nations and a multiethnic world is a social necessity. This description of the guiding principles and the influence of a dialogic pedagogy aims to contribute to this important agenda.

Note

1. This chapter grew out of a paper presented at the Third International Conference of the Association for Collaborative Contributions to Language Learning, Moscow, Russia, December 1991.

Bibliography

Applebee, A. N. (1977). ERIC/RCS report: The elements of response to a literary work: What we have learned. *Research in the Teaching of English, 11*, 255–271.

Applebee, A. N., Langer, J. A., & Mullis, I. V. S. (1989). *Crossroads in American education: A summary of findings from the nation's report card*. Princeton, NJ: National Assessment of Educational Progress, Educational Testing Service.

Bakhtin, M. (1981). *The dialogic imagination* (C. Emerson & M. Helquist, Trans.). Austin, TX: University of Texas Press.

Bartholomae, D., & Petrosky, A. R. (1986). *Facts, artifacts and counterfacts*. Portsmouth, NH: Boynton/Cook.

Beach, R., & Hynds, S. (1990). *Research on the learning and teaching of literature: Selected bibliography*. (Report Series R.1). Albany, NY: Center for the Learning and Teaching of Literature.

Bridges, D. (1979). *Education, democracy and discussion*. Windsor, England: NFER.

Britton, J. (1970). *Language and learning*. Harmondsworth, England: Penguin.

Bruner, J. S. (1978). The role of dialogue in language acquisition. In A. Sinclair, R. J. Jarvelle, & W. J. M. Levelt (Eds.), *A child's conception of language*. New York: Springer-Verlag.

Bruner, J. S. (1985, November). *The language of education*. Paper presented at the annual meeting of the National Council of Teachers of English, Philadelphia, PA.

Bruner, J. (1986). *Actual minds, possible worlds*. Cambridge, MA: Harvard University Press.

Carr, J. F. (1990, November–December). Cultural studies and curricular change. *Acadame*, 25–28.

Dewey, J. (1933). *How we think: A restatement of the relation of reflective thinking to educative process*. Boston, MA: D.C. Heath.

Dollerup, C. (Ed.). (1983–1989). *Folktale: A cross-cultural interdisciplinary study of the experience of literature* (Papers 1–13). Copenhagen: The Center for Translation Studies and Lexicography.

Freire, P. (1970). *Pedagogy of the oppressed* (M. B. Ramos, Trans.). New York: Seabury Press.

Gadamer, H. (1976). *Philosophical hermeneutics* (D. Linge, Ed. & Trans.). Berkeley, CA: University of California Press.

Gallimore, R., & Tharp, R. (1990). Teaching mind in society: Teaching, schooling, and literature discourse. In Luis Moll (Ed.), *Vygotsky and education: Instructional implications and applications of sociohistorical psychology* (pp. 175–205). New York: Cambridge University Press.

Hedegaard, M. (1990). The zone of proximal development as basis for instruction. In Luis Moll (Ed.), *Vygotsky and Education: Instructional implications and applications of sociohistorical psychology* (pp. 349–371). New York: Cambridge University Press.

Iser, W. (1978). *The act of reading.* Baltimore, MD: John Hopkins University Press.

Knoblauch, C. H. & Brannon, L. (1993). *Critical teaching and the idea of literacy.* Portsmouth, NH: Boynton/Cook.

Langer, J. A. (1990). The process of understanding: Reading for literary and informative purposes. *Research in the Teaching of English, 24,* 229-260.

Langer, J. A., & Applebee, A. N. (1986). Reading and writing instruction: Toward a theory of teaching and learning. In E. Z. Rothkopf (Ed.), *Review of Research in Education* (pp. 171-194). Washington, DC: American Educational Research Association.

Leontiev, A. N. (1978). *Activity, consciousness, and personality.* Englewood Cliffs, NJ: Prentice-Hall.

Marshall, J. D. (1987). The effects of writing on students' understanding of literary texts. *Research in the Teaching of English, 21,* 30-63.

Miller, S. M. (1988). *Collaborative learning in secondary school discussion of expository texts.* Unpublished doctoral dissertation, University of Pittsburgh. (University Microfilms No. 89-05,229)

Miller, S. M. (1990, April). *Critical thinking in classroom discussion of texts.* Paper presented at the Annual Meeting of the American Educational Research Association, Boston, MA.

Miller, S. M. (1991a). *Learning literacies/learning to think: Reading, writing and thinking in two high school lives.* Final Report to the Research Foundation of the National Council of Teachers of English.

Miller, S. M. (1991b, April). *Supporting literary understanding: Contexts for critical thought in literature discussion.* Paper presented at the Annual Meeting of the American Educational Research Association, Chicago, IL.

Miller, S. M. (1992a, April). *Creating consciousness: Dialogic thinking in literature and content-area classes.* Paper presented at the Annual Conference of the American Educational Research Association, San Francisco, CA.

Miller, S. M. (1992b, April). *Developing metacognitive strategies: Scaffolding thinking in text discussion.* Paper presented at the Annual Conference of the American Educational Research Association, San Francisco, CA.

Miller, S. M. (1992c). Learning ways of talking: Critical thinking and collaboration in classroom discussion of texts. Manuscript submitted for publication.

Miller, S. M. (1992d). Trying to understand together: Restructuring classroom talk about texts. In J. Collins (Ed.), *Restructuring the English classroom.* Portsmouth, NH: Boynton/Cook.

Miller, S. M. (1993, April). *Constructing texts and contexts in discussion across the curriculum.* Paper presented at the Annual Meeting of the American Educational Research Association, Atlanta, GA.

Miller, S. M. (in press). *Critical and creative thinking: Case studies across the curriculum*. Albany, NY: The National Research Center on Literature Teaching and Learning.

Moll, L. C. (1990). Introduction. In L. C. Moll (Ed.), *Vygotsky and education: Instructional implications and applications of sociohistorical psychology* (pp. 1–27). New York: Cambridge University Press.

National Assessment of Educational Progress. (1981). Reading, thinking and writing: Results from the 1979–80 National Assessment of Reading and Literature, (Report No. 11-1-01). Denver, CO: Education Commission of the States.

Paul, R. (1984). Critical thinking: Fundamental to education for a free society. *Educational Leadership, 42*(1), 4–14.

Petrosky, A. (1992). To teach (literature)? In J. A. Langer (Ed.), *Literature instruction: A focus on student response*. Urbana, Il: National Council of Teachers of English.

Purves, A. C. (1973). *Literature education in ten countries*. New York: John Wiley.

Purves, A. C. (1981). *Reading and literature: American achievement in international perspective*. Urbana, IL: National Council of Teachers of English.

Rosenblatt, L. M. (1978). *The reader, the text, the poem*. Carbondale, IL: Southern Illinois University Press.

Salvatori, M. (1986). The dialogical nature of basic reading and writing. In D. Bartholomae & A. Petrosky (Eds.), *Facts, artifacts and counterfacts*. Portsmouth, NH: Boynton/Cook.

Steffensen, M. S., Joag-Des, C., & Anderson, R. C. (1979). A cross-cultural perspective on reading comprehension. *Reading Research Quarterly, 15*, 10–29.

Tudge, J. (1990). Vygotsky, the zone of proximal development, and peer collaboration: Implications for classroom practice. In L. Moll (Ed.), *Vygotsky and education: Instructional implications and applications of sociohistorical psychology* (pp. 155–172). New York: Cambridge University Press.

Vygotsky, L. S. (1962). *Thought and language*. E. Hanfmann & G. Vakar (Eds. & Trans.). Cambridge, MA: M.I.T. Press.

Vygotsky, L. S. (1971). *The psychology of art*. Cambridge, MA: M.I.T. Press.

Vygotsky, L. S. (1978). *Mind in society*. Cambridge, MA: Harvard University Press.

Vygotsky, L. S. (1981). The genesis of higher mental functions. In J. V. Wertsch (Ed.), *The concept of activity in Soviet psychology* (pp. 144–188). White Plains, NY: Sharpe.

Appendix: Selected Resources for Multicultural Education

Expanded, Researched, and Annotated by Kathleen Sims

This is a list of selected resources for teaching and researching multicultural literature and literacies. This list represents what, at time of publication, we the contributors to this volume have found useful in our pedagogy and scholarship. This is not intended as a comprehensive guide. Neither is it intended as a kind of canon of best resources.

The resources indicated in this list are varied in their meanings, multiple in their agenda, and wide-ranging in their scope. The majority operate on a national or regional scale. And because they reflect the interdisciplinary and multimedia interests of our volume contributors, the resources that are compiled below make available not only written publications but also films and audiocassette recordings.

Included among these resources are museums, libraries and archives, research centers and centers for cultural exchange, academic institutes, professional associations, community organizations, clearinghouses, projects for multicultural interaction and social change, book and film distributors, bookstores, and presses. Wherever an entry is annotated, we call attention to specific books, journals, film projects, and/or newsletters that we have found useful and that we have purchased, subscribed to, or rented by contacting this source.

One particular resource that we would like to call attention to here is the database known as ERIC (acronym for Educational Resources Information Center). Many major public libraries and most university libraries have access to ERIC's databases. A search of this database can uncover discussions of multicultural literature and literacies that are contained in a variety of sources: scholarly and professional journals, periodicals and serial publications, separately published books and bibliographies, and even unpublished essays and manuscripts. ERIC organizes listings based on key words and phrases. It can be helpful for an ERIC search to use large cultural headings (e.g., Native American literature, Puerto Rican literature) followed by an age grouping (e.g., adolescent or young adult) and an indication of the form of references (e.g., annotated bibliographies, poetry). Computer networks and databases, an accelerating presence in our libraries and workplaces, can offer rapid access to mass quantities of literatures and resources.

Other resources are often available more locally than we can list here, but accessible by quick inquiry. City halls will often have on hand listings of neighborhood and community centers, as well as Native American reservations and cultural centers. Local museums and performing arts centers often have affiliated lecturers. Some commercial bookstores carry diverse literatures. Also, colleges and universities often have research centers or affiliated faculty specializing in certain venues of broad-based cultural diversity. It often takes little more than a phone call to access these resources.

As all of the writers in this volume imply, making space for difference must prove to be an ongoing process of collaboration, application, scrutiny, and change. We have compiled these selected resources as a guide to encourage you, our readers, to reflect upon our essays once again and respond to issues of literature and literacy in your homes, communities, school districts, and individual classrooms. We hope that this guide will serve, additionally, as a catalyst for your own discussion and debate; and in doing so we underscore our writers' reminder one last time: that dialogue is crucial if space is to be made for difference. These dialogues on multicultural literature and literacies must continue, must accelerate, and more ambitiously, must engage and encourage voices in both the schools and the communities surrounding and supporting them.

As time passes, of course, the individual resources listed below may change in terms of what information they offer, what goals they intend to accomplish, where they are located, and how they can be reached. Slight changes over time, however, should not outweigh the benefits of this guide. Most important is that you, our readers, can interpret and apply our ideas according to your own particular research and classroom needs. You can begin your own assessment of these resources and begin fashioning your conversations toward confronting and defining difference.

A. Philip Randolph Institute
Suite 300, 1444 I Street, N.W.
Washington D.C. 20005
(202) 533-8000
Foundation will send out publications with information on the life
and political influences of A. Philip Randolph, as well as articles
with important bibliographic information.

Afro-Am Distributing Company
407 East 25th Street, Suite 600
Chicago, Illinois 60616
(312) 791-1611
Acts as a clearinghouse for a number of different publishers. Ask
for their catalogue.

Akwesasne Library and Museum
Rt. 37, RR 1, Box 14C
Hogansburg, New York 13655
(518) 358-2240
Ask for their catalogue of publications.

American Association for Higher Education
Suite 360, 1 Dupont Circle, N.W.
Washington, D.C. 20036
(202) 293-6440
Ask for their catalogue of publications.

American Association of University Women
1111 16th Street, N.W.
Washington, D.C. 20036
(202) 785-7700
Publishes reports on gender and race discrepancies in postsecondary education.

American Council on Education
Suite 800, 1 Dupont Circle, N.W.
Washington, D.C. 20036
(202) 939-9300
Ask for a publications list.

American Educational Research Association
1230 17th Street, N.W.
Washington, D.C. 20036
(202) 223-9485
Ask for Curriculum Development to obtain a publications listing.

American Federation of Teachers
555 New Jersey Avenue, N.W.
Washington, D.C. 20001
(202) 879-4400
Ask for the educational issues department.

American Indian Archeology Institute
Rt. 199, Box 1260
Washington Green, Connecticut 06793-0260
(203) 868-0518
Sponsors programs through its Education Department on Native American stereotypes. Has museum, lecturers, teacher's institutes, and does field archaeological work. Also, a non-lending library is available on-site for visiting scholars and librarians.

American Indian Community House
404 Lafayette Street, 2nd Floor
New York, New York 10003
(212) 598-0100
Has a gallery and theater programs, as well as speakers and local contacts willing to work with teachers.

American Studies Association
2101 South Campus Serge
University of Maryland
College Park, Maryland 20742
(301) 405-1364
Works primarily with secondary and college teachers, hosting workshops at meetings across the country as well as publishing curriculum guides, which can be obtained with an order form. Also does a great deal of international education work and can provide contacts to teachers and classrooms in other countries who are studying America's cultural diversity.

The Anacostia Museum
Smithsonian Institute
2405 Martin Luther King Ave., S.E.
Washington, D.C. 20020
(202) 287-3369
Their mission concerns African American cultures from Maryland to Georgia. A Smithsonian affiliate, they network with all other Smithsonian libraries and exhibits. Their education department sponsors tours, lectures, films, and programs. All resources available by phone and appointment.

Anti-Bias Education Leadership Project
    Department of Education
    5 Westmoreland Place
    Pacific Oaks College
    Pasadena, California 91103
    (818) 397-1306
    Runs workshops periodically and will mail recent scholarship and videos on rethinking curriculi.

The Asia Society
    725 Park Avenue
    New York, New York 10021
    (212) 288-6400
    Ask for education; they have two series (six books each) on Japanese, Korean, Indian, and Vietnamese culture.

Asian American Study Center
    3230 Cambell Hall
    University of California
    Los Angeles, California 90024
    (310) 825-2974
    Sponsors students and community projects with UCLA. Publishes a newsletter and journal available to purchase. Their reading room will work with teachers to recommend literature.

Assault on Illiteracy Program
    231 West 29th Street, Suite 1205
    New York, New York 10001
    (212) 967-4008
    Ask for their publications list.

Associated Publishers
    1407 14th Street, N.W.
    Washington, D.C. 20005
    (202) 265-1441
    Publishes studies from the Association for the Study of Afro-American Life and History.

Association for the Achievement of Cultural Diversity in Higher Education
    Office of Affirmative Action
    State University at Stony Brook
    Stony Brook, New York 11794-02511
    (516) 632-6280
    Ask for Dr. Adams. She has dates and times for association activities and publications.

Association of Black Sociologists
Sociology/Anthropology Department
Douglas Hall, Room 207
2400 6th Street
Washington, D.C. 20059

Association of Departments of English
MLA Office
10 Astor Place
New York, New York 10003-6911
(212) 614-6317
Ask for their MLA resource catalogue.

Attanasio & Associates, Inc.
62-06 77 Place
Middle Village, New York 11379
(718) 565-0343
Offers literature featuring minority and new immigrant populations.
Catalogues available.

Audio-Visual Services
The Pennsylvania State University
Special Services Building
1127 Fox Hill Road
University Park, Pennsylvania 16802
(814) 865-6314
Videos on topics of diverse cultures available for rental or purchase.

Ayer Company Publishers, Inc.
P.O. Box 958
Salem, New Hampshire 03079
(603) 669-5933
Specializes in reprints of difficult-to-locate African American classics.

Before Columbus Foundation
660 13th Street
Suite 203
Oakland, California 94612
(510) 268-9775
Write for subscription to the quarterly *Before Columbus Review*.
Contents include multicultural literature(s) and literacy education.
Selections of the foundation's award winners have been published
by Norton Press and in numerous Before Columbus Foundation
multicultural poetry and fiction anthologies.

Bethune-Dubois Publications
Watergate Building, Suite 330
600 New Hampshire Avenue, N.W.
Washington, D.C. 20037
(202) 338-4096
Produces a journal of recent, vital speeches by prominent African Americans.

Black Books Bulletin
Third World Press
7524 South Cottage Grove Avenue
Chicago, Illinois 60619
(317) 226-4000
Contains book reviews and critical essays. Excellent source for librarians and other buyers of African, African American, and Caribbean literatures. Third World Press, the oldest continuously running African American publishing house, also provides its own catalogues of literary and historical texts.

Black Film Center/Archive
Department of Afro-American Studies
Memorial Hall East
Indiana University
Bloomington, Indiana 47405
(812) 855-6041
Is in the process of establishing a National Black Film Archive center.

Black History Curriculum Guide and Background Materials
Indianapolis Public Schools
Indianapolis, Indiana
(317) 226-4000

Bookslinger
2402 University Avenue West, Suite 507
St. Paul, Minnesota 55114
(800) 659-2802
Distributes literature from 300 prominant publishers of multicultural material. Catalogues are available upon request. Also has separate listings by ethnic groupings called "bibliofiles" for people interested in specific groups. Ask for their guide.

The Caribbean Cultural Center
    408 West 58th Street
    New York, New York 10019
    (212) 307-7420
    Publishes directory to regional dance, theater, and performance
    groups as well as provides texts on Afro-Caribbean and Spanish
    Caribbean culture.

Carter G. Woodson Center
    1401 14th Street, N.W.
    Washington, D.C. 20005
    (202) 667-2822
    Ask for the *Negro Bulletin,* a journal of poetry.

Center for the Study of Black Literature and Culture
    3808 Walnut Street
    University of Pennsylvania
    Philadelphia, Pennsylvania 19104-6136
    (215) 898-5141
    Access to on site library by formal written request to the attention
    of Center Director.

Center for Teaching About China
    US-China Peoples Friendship Association
    National Office
    2025 I Street, Suite 715, N.W.
    Washington, D.C. 20006
    (202) 265-5847
    Call for current programs and cultural events, resource people and
    lecturers.

Chadwyck-Healey, Inc.
    1101 King Street, Suite 380
    Alexandria, Virginia 22314
    (703) 683-4890
    Provides microfilm collections of manuscripts and documents for
    researchers in areas of women's studies and multicultural studies.

Chicano Studies Library Publications Unit
    3404 Dwinelle Hall
    University of California
    Berkeley, California 94720
    (510) 642-3859

Has a database in CD-ROM, which emulates the ERIC system, of Chicano literature available for all age groupings. Listings are produced to suit your requests and are mailed without cost. This is an excellent source of classroom materials. Their staff are incredibly helpful.

Children's Book Press
6400 Hollis Street
Amberview, California 94608
(510) 655-3395
Specializes in publishing oral and written mythology and traditions from Spanish, South American, African and Asian communities.

Claudia's Caravan
P.O. Box 1582
Alemeda, California
(510) 521-7871
Offers multicultural books, records, and games for children up to twelve years of age.

Commonwealth Center for Literary and Cultural Change
219 Minor Hall
University of Virginia
Charlottesville, Virginia 22903
(804) 982-2005
Offers two seminars yearly, sponsors guest lectures, and will mail any of their archive of tapes made from these lectures upon request.

Conference on College Composition and Communication
1111 Kenyon Road
Urbana, Illinois 61801
(217) 328-3870 ext. 203
Will provide field-teaching references to contact given your specific pedagogical and curricular concerns.

Cooperative Children's Book Center
4290 Helen C. White Hall
University of Wisconsin at Madison
600 N. Park Street
Madison, Wisconsin 53706
(608) 263-3720
Publishes an annotated bibliography of books from 1980 to 1990 called *Multicultural Literature for Children and Young Adults*, which pays special attention to the geographical breakdown of the literature it presents.

Crosscurrent Media
346 Ninth Street, 2nd Floor
San Francisco, California 94103
(415) 552-9550
Provides nation's source for film on Asian American life letters. A service of National Asian American Telecommunications Association.

Dearborn Publishing
520 North Dearborn Street
Chicago, Illinois 60610-4354
(312) 836-4400
Catalogue includes literature, some of which is accessible only in these editions, from Longman African/Caribbean Classics series.

DuSable Museum
740 East 56th Place
Chicago, IL 60637
(312) 947-0600
The education department will supply exhibit, workshop and publication information.

Filmmakers Library
124 East 40th Street
New York, New York 10016
(212) 808-4980
Videos from around the world, featuring Asian, Indian, African, and Latin American cultures.

The Folklife Store
305 Harrison Street
Seattle, Washington 98109
(206) 684-7300
Ask for catalogues, books, and recordings source for Northwest music.

Garland Publishing, Inc.
1000 A. Sherman
Hamdon, Connecticut 06514
(800) 627-6273
Send for catalogues on microfilm collections and reference sources on peoples of color in the United States.

Graywolf Press
    2402 University Avenue, Suite 203
    Saint Paul, Minnesota 55114
    (612) 641-0077
    Specializes in publishing modern adult literature from outside the
    United States in translation. Catalogues available.

Heinemann
    361 Hanover Street
    Portsmouth, New Hampshire 03801
    (603) 431-7894
    Ask for African and Caribbean Writers Series catalogue.

Hue-Man Experience Bookstore
    911 Park Avenue, West
    Denver, Colordo 80205
    (800) 346-4036
    Features recent and historical literature which promotes positive
    images of African Americans through fiction, autobiographies, and
    anthologies.

Ind-US Inc.
    P.O. Box 56
    E. Glastonbury, Connecticut 06025
    Publishes recent and contemporary South Asian (Indian) literature
    in English.

Irografts Ltd.
    RR 2
    Ohsweken, Ontario N0A 1M0
    (no phone number available)
    Catalogues of texts and products are available through written
    request.

Iroquois Museum
    P.O. Box 7
    Howes Cave, New York 12092
    (518) 296-8949
    Ask about current programs. Center has excellent connections to
    knowledgeable community members.

Kanien'kehaka Raotitionhkwa Culture Centre
    P.O. Box 1988
    Kahnawake, Quebec J0L 1B0
    (514) 638-0880

Has extremely helpful staff who are available to help those interested in the center with their time, knowledge, and library resources.

Kitchen Table: Women of Color Press
P.O. Box 908
Latham, New York 12110
(518) 434-2057
Publishes radical women of color whose works, for financial reasons, might not be published elsewhere.

Ladyslipper Catalog and Resource Guide
P.O. Box 3124-R
Durham, North Carolina 27715
(919) 683-1570
Video, audio, and book materials are featured with many contributions by Asian, Native, Africana, and Latina women.

Longman Publishing Group
10 Bank Street
White Plains, New York 10602-1951
(800) 447-2226
Send for African/Arab studies catalogue of literature and textbooks.

Martin Luther King Center for Nonviolent Social Change, Inc.
449 Auburn Avenue, N.E.
Atlanta, Georgia 30312
(404) 524-1956
Houses archives on historical and cultural data relating to greater study of African American history.

Moonstone, Inc.
532 Baimbridge Street
Philadelphia, Pennsylvania 19147
(215) 574-9157
Coordinates Celebration of Black Writers each fall. Contact for information on Union of Writers of the African Peoples, which holds membership of writers of African descent across the globe.

Moorland-Spingarn Research Center
500 Howard Place
Howard University, N.W.
Washington, D.C. 20059
(202) 806-7239

Houses information on African, African American, and other multicultural texts. Gives helpful information about resources available throughout the District of Columbia's diverse community.

Multicultural Literature for Children and Adults
Wisconsin Department of Public Instruction
Publication Sales
Drawer 179
Milwaukee, Wisconsin 53293-0179
(800) 243-8782
Ask for their *Multicultural Literature of Children and Adults*. The guide is available for purchase and is a wonderful resource for potential classroom texts.

Multi-Media Education
19363 Livernois
Detroit, Michigan 48221
313-342-1261
(800) 342-1261
Ask for catalogues specific to multicultural literature.

Museum of the American Indian
3753 Broadway at 155th Street
New York, New York 10032
(212) 283-2420
Ask about program of visiting Native American artists and artisans.

Najda: Women Concerned About the Middle East
P.O. Box 7152
Berkeley, California 94707
(408) 732-5484
Ask for the *Arab World Note Book*.

National Afro-American Museum and Cultural Center
P.O. Box 578
Wilberforce, Ohio 45384
(513) 376-4944
Ask for Educational Development's Traveling Trunk, which brings exhibits to schools. Letters to the archivist will also receive careful responses and accompanying research.

National Arts Education Research Center
New York University
School of Education, Health, Nursing and Arts Professions
Room 21
New York, New York 10003
(212) 998-5060
Ask for "A Framework for Multicultural Arts Education."

National Association of Black School Educators
    2816 Georgia Avenue, N.W.
    Washington, D.C. 20001
    (202) 483-1549
    Publishes reports and presentations gathered from their annual conference on better educating African American students.

National Association for Equal Opportunity in Higher Education
    400 12th Street
    Washington, D.C. 20002
    (202) 543-9111
    Ask for a current list of available publications.

The National Black Arts Festival
    236 Forsythe Street, Suite 400
    Atlanta, Georgia 30303
    (404) 730-7315
    Write for audios of poetry performances during this annual event as well as information on theater, museum exhibits, artwork, and film series connected to this event.

National Clearinghouse on Literacy Information
    1118 22nd Street, N.W.
    Washington, D.C. 20037
    (202) 429-9292
    Ask for information about literacy materials. They carry free articles on teaching ESL and physically challenged minority students.

National Congress of Black Faculty
    P.O. Box 93457
    Cleveland, Ohio 44101-5457
    (216) 687-5490
    Provides a newsletter and national conferences as well as "Civil Rights Employment Discrimination and Legal Rights." Has information on hiring black faculty, as well as on promoting minority research and distribution of that work.

The National Council for Black Studies, Inc.
    The Ohio State University
    1030 Lincoln Tower
    1800 Cannon Drive
    Columbus, Ohio 43210
    (614) 292-1035

Will be happy to put callers in touch with council members who will talk about classroom concerns.

National Council of Teachers of English
1111 Kenyon Road
Urbana, Illinois 61801
(217) 475-9500
Ask for "Guidelines for a Gender-Balanced Curriculum in English" and "Non-White Minorities in English and Language Arts Materials."

National Museum of African Art
3176 A Street, N.E.
Washington, D.C. 20002
(202) 357-4600
Ask for the brochure on films, slides sets, and other available classroom materials.

National Reading Conference
11 East Hubbard, Suite 200
Chicago, Illinois 60611
(312) 329-2512
Sponsors a yearly conference of which diversity is a popular topic. The annual *National Reading Conference Yearbook* offers scholarly discussions about multiculturalism and can often be obtained at local libraries.

National Research Center on Literature Teaching and Learning
Education B-9
1400 Washington Avenue
University at Albany
Albany, New York 12222
(518) 442-5134
Request information about how to obtain center reports on multiculturalism.

National Women's History Project
7738 Bell Road
Windsor, California 95492-8518
(707) 838-6000
Offers a catalogue of books, videos, and educational materials on minority women in history.

New American Library
A Division of Penguin USA
Academic Marketing Department
375 Hudson Street
New York, New York 10014-3657
(212) 366-2000
Ask for Literature and Language catalogue.

The New Jersey Project: Integrating the Scholarship on Gender and Race
315 White Hall
William Paterson College
Wayne, New Jersey 07470
(201) 595-2000
Has published texts and articles on multicultural education and facilitated discussions of racism, classism, and sexism in the classroom.

New York Council for the Humanities
198 Broadway, 10th Floor
New York, New York 10038
(212) 233-1131
Request information about their yearly workshop on classroom diversity.

New York State African American Institute
State University of New York
State University Plaza
Albany, New York 12246
(518) 443-5798
Publishes journal of African Americans in New York history and life, as well as reports on health, education, and political participation of black New Yorkers.

Oneida Nation Museum
Box 365, 886 Double E Road
Oneida, Wisconsin 54155
(414) 869-2768
Carries many books on Iroquois sprituality and history. They give educational tours and provide a good inroad to other resources in the reservation's community.

PBS Video
1320 Braddock Place
Alexandria, Virginia 22314-1698
(800) 344-3337

Call for *Eyes on the Prize* and *Eyes on the Prize II* videocassette series on African Americans and the civil rights movement. Instructional guides to accompany this series are available.

P.E.C.: The Association to Preserve the Eatonville Community, Inc.
P.O. Box 2586
227 East Kennedy Boulevard
Eatonville, Florida 32751
(407) 647-3307
Established annual festival and newsletter to preserve memory of Zora Neale Hurston and her artistic peers of the Harlem Renaissance.

Program in African American Culture
National Museum of American History, Room 1015
Smithsonian Institution
14th Street and Constitution Avenue, N.W.
Washington, D.C. 20560-0001
(202) 357-4176
Upon request they will send their guide by Bearnice Johnson Reagon entitled *Black American Culture and Scholarship: Contemporary Issues.*

The Red Sea Press, Inc.
15 Industry Court
Trenton, New Jersey 08638
(609) 771-1666
Publishers and distributors of literature, textbooks, histories, cookbooks, visual materials, and more related to African, African American, and Caribbean culture. Publishes thorough catalogues frequently throughout the year.

Redwood Cultural Work
P.O. Box 10408
Oakland, California 94610
(510) 835-1445
Publishes multicultural books and tapes detailed in their catalogue.

Resolution, Inc./California Newsreel
149 Ninth Street
San Francisco, California 94103
(415) 621-6198
Distributes films on African and African American culture and race relations.

Rethinking Schools
Rethinking Schools, Ltd.
1001 East Keefe Avenue
Milwaukee, Wisconsin 53212
(414) 964-9646
Publishes a magazine three to four times a year which includes scholarship about a variety of multicultural topics.

Ruiz Belvis Cultural Center in Chicago
1632 North Milwaukee Avenue
Chicago, Illinois 60647
(312) 235-3988
Houses a large collection of Hispanic, Puerto Rican, and Caribbean collections available on site. Their staff also gives presentations, traveling art exhibits, and cultural lectures throughout the Chicago area public school system. Staff members are available by written request for performances and class discussions.

SCETV (South Carolina Educational Television) Marketing
Box 1100
Columbia, South Carolina 29211
(800) 553-7752
Write for catalogue entitled *Video Resources for the Black Studies Curriculum*, which features films for ninth-grade through college-aged students.

Schomburg Center for Research in Black Culture
The New York Public Library
515 Lenox Avenue
New York, New York 10037
(212) 491-2200
Offers resources connected to African American, Caribbean, and African cultures. Major collections of film and photographic media, manuscript archives, community documents, and periodicals are available for research.

Seneca Iroquois National Museum
P.O. Box 442
Salamanca, New York 14779
(716) 945-1738
Call for current exhibits, programs, and lectures.

Seneca Nation Library
Box 231
Salamanca, New York 14779
(716) 945-3157
Books with Iroquois myths and legends are available for loan.

Six Nations Museum
    P.O. Box 10
    Onchiota, New York 12968
    (518) 891-0769
    Offers reading materials in addition to on-site exhibits and lectures.

Skipping Stones: A Multicultural Children's Quarterly
    P.O. Box 3939
    Eugene, Oregon 97403
    (No phone number listed)

Social Science Education Consortium, Inc.
    855 Broadway
    Boulder, Colorado 80303
    (303) 492-8154
    Offers curriculum guides on Japanese law and culture.

Southern Poverty Law Center
    P.O. Box 548
    Montgomery, Alabama 36101
    (205) 264-0286
    Ask for the Teaching Tolerance department to obtain their
    publications on southern poverty.

Stanford Program on Literature and Cross Cultural Information
    Spice Little Field Court, Rm. 14
    300 Lusuen Street
    Stanford University
    Stanford, California 94305-5013
    (415) 723-1114
    Offers teaching materials, curriculum guides, and staff development
    literature promoting Asian studies.

The Studio Museum in Harlem
    144 West 125th Street
    New York, New York 10027
    (212) 864-4500
    Ask for the Education Department to obtain information about
    current exhibits, group tours, workshops, and publications.

The Turtle
    25 Rainbow Boulevard
    Niagara Falls, New York 14303
    (716) 284-2427

Has publications in their bookstore. Lectures on appropriate curriculi on Afro-American culture are available for their outreach program (for a fee) for classes of all ages. Resources emphasize the humanity of Indians.

Women Make Movies
225 Lafayette Street
New York, New York 10012
(212) 925-0606
Distributes catalogue of films by and about Asian, African, American, Latina, and Indian women.

Woodland Indian Cultural-Educational Centre
84 Mohawk Street, Box 1506
Brantford, Ontario N3T 5V6
(519) 759-2650
Will send an information packet about resources. They carry publications, host exhibits, and coordinate visitations of lecturers.

Write Source
Educational Publishing House
Box 460
Burlington, Wisconsin 53105
(414) 763-8258
Ask for catalogue with grade-level multicultural libraries.

About the Editors

Barbara McCaskill is an assistant professor of English at the University of Georgia. Her research specialization focuses on the literature and autobiographies of nineteenth-century and fin de siècle Black women writers. She is working on a book-length study of the personal narratives of formerly enslaved women, for which she received a 1992–93 Scholars-in-Residence fellowship from the Schomburg Center for Research in Black Culture of the New York Public Library. She teaches courses in African American, Caribbean, and multicultural literatures and literary theories.

Suzanne M. Miller is an assistant professor and coordinator of English education at the State University of New York at Albany. She is on the faculty of the National Research Center for Literature Teaching and Learning, where her ethnographic research focuses on how text discussion in socioculturally diverse groups shapes students' thinking. She teaches courses on language and literacy, the teaching of English, and multicultural literatures.

Contributors

Valerie Babb is presently an associate professor of English at Georgetown University. She completed her graduate studies at the State University of New York at Buffalo with a specialization in American literature. Her publications include a critical study of Ernest Gaines and articles on Alice Walker, Charles Chesnutt, and others.

Phillip C. Gonzales is codirector of the California Literature Project at California State University, Dominguez Hills (CSUDH), where he also coordinates the Emergency Elementary Teaching Credential Internship Program. Both responsibilities necessitate visits to classrooms where core literature is the content of English-language arts instruction. Teachers in the Literature Project and the CSUDH Credential Program are trained to avoid misusing ethnic literature in the manner described in his chapter.

Violet J. Harris currently teaches courses in children's literature at the University of Illinois at Urbana-Champaign. Her research interests include historic literature written about and by African Americans, literacy materials created for African American children before 1950, and the sociopolitical aspects of publishing literature by and about people of color. She is active in IRA, NRC, and NCTE; she also serves on the review boards of journals sponsored by these organizations. She recently was appointed to the Reading Commission of the National Council of Teachers of English.

Alpana Sharma Knippling is an assistant professor of postcolonial literatures at the University of Nebraska-Lincoln. Her interests range from issues of multiculturalism and pedagogy to the writing of Salman Rushdie and Bharati Mukherjee. She is currently engaged in researching for a book on Indian nationalist discourse and Indo-Anglian literature.

Gregory A. Morris is director of reading and literature for kindergarten through grade 12 for the Pittsburgh Public Schools. A member of the Department of Curriculum and Program Management, he is responsible for developing the curriculum, selecting the instructional materials, training the staff, and monitoring the instructional activities in the classrooms. Dr. Morris also works closely with program development efforts in early childhood and multicultural education.

Hasna Muhammad teaches writing at A. B. Davis Middle School in Mount Vernon, New York, and at the College of New Rochelle. She is currently a doctoral candidate in the English Education Department at Teachers College, Columbia University. Her dissertation is on the implementation of multicultural education in the Mount Vernon school district. Hasna's poetry has previously appeared in *Catalyst Magazine*. She is the author of two unpublished collections of poetry entitled, "notesfromahousewife", and "Dear Alice".

Alan C. Purves is director of the Center for Writing and Literacy, codirector of the National Research Center for Literature Teaching and Learning, and professor of education and humanities at the State University of New York at Albany. A specialist in English literature and literary theory with a secondary interest in composition and its assessment, his expertise lies in cross-cultural studies of the learning of literature and literary criticism and composition.

Kathleen Sims is a doctoral student in Composition Studies at the State University of New York at Albany. She is a former Ford Foundation Teaching Fellow. She currently works for the National Research Center on Literature Teaching and Learning researching multicultural literature. In her work she promotes diversity, critical feminist theories, and literacy.

Catharine R. Stimpson is university professor and former dean of the Graduate School at Rutgers University, New Brunswick. In 1990 she served as president of the Modern Language Association. Her most recent book is *Where the Meanings Are: Feminism and Cultural Spaces* (1988).

Suzanne K. Sutherland is director of English-language arts for grades K–12 in the Houston Independent School District. Her responsibilities include setting policy and programs for the district, directing the writing and publication of support materials for language arts, and designing and conducting staff development opportunities for teachers and administrators.

Ron Welburn's *Council Decisions* (1991) is his fifth collection of poems. His stories and poems have appeared in over eighty literary magazines and anthologies. He holds degrees from Lincoln University in Pennsylvania, the University of Arizona, and New York University. Currently he teaches American literatures at the University of Massachusetts at Amherst.

Junko Yokota is an assistant professor of Reading and Language Arts at the University of Northern Iowa. Prior to joining the faculty at the University of Northern Iowa, she was an elementary classroom teacher and elementary librarian for ten years. She is interested in issues related to culture, literature, and literacy.

Reggie Young is an assistant professor of English at Louisiana State University, where he teaches literature and creative writing. As a writer he has received an Illinois Poet Laureate Award for Significant Illinois Poets and a PEN Discovery Award. He is currently working on a series of essays on Black Chicago literature.

Index